SCIENCE, POLITICS AND THE PUBLIC GOOD

Margaret Gowing

Science, Politics and the Public Good

Essays in Honour of Margaret Gowing

Edited by
Nicolaas A. Rupke
Wolfson College, Oxford

**MACMILLAN
PRESS**

First published 1988

Published by
THE MACMILLAN PRESS LTD
Houndmills, Basingstoke, Hampshire RG21 2XS
and London
Companies and representatives
throughout the world

Printed in Hong Kong

British Library Cataloguing in Publication Data
Science, politics and the public good: essays
in honour of Margaret Gowing.
1. Science and state
I. Rupke, Nicolaas A.   II. Gowing, Margaret
500   Q125
ISBN 0–333–44159–1

Contents

List of Illustrations

List of Tables

Preface

At the end of the academic year 1985–86, Professor Margaret Mary Gowing (*b* 26 April 1921) retired from the Chair of the History of Science at Oxford. The purpose of this book of essays is to honour Margaret Gowing on the occasion of her retirement. As pointed out in the introductory 'Appreciation' (Chapter 1), and again in a concluding 'Postscript' (Chapter 13), Professor Gowing's *magna opera* on the history of British atomic energy helped to make the history of science an essential part of the mainstream of public history. The story of the atomic bomb and of atomic power dramatically demonstrates the close interconnections between scientific ideas, technological innovation, industrial enterprise, national government and international affairs. Professor Gowing has explored this 'old and intimate relationship' (as she called the connection between science and politics), not only in her books on 'Britain and atomic energy', but also in her Inaugural Lecture and her Wilkins, Bernal, Rede and Spencer Lectures (see the bibliography on pp. 241–6). Thus the title of our Festschrift, *Science, Politics and the Public Good*, aptly expresses the general theme of Professor Gowing's *œuvre*.

The contributors to this volume belong to Professor Gowing's wide circle of colleagues and friends, junior as well as senior. Each contributor addresses a particular aspect of the general theme of her work, and in each chapter a specific instance is discussed of the close relationship between science, politics and public welfare. Our examples are taken from the past 150 years, from a wide range of subject-matter, and from four different countries, namely the UK, Germany, the US and Russia. Chapters 2, 3 and 4 focus on the Victorian period when state endowment of scientific research first became an intensely political question in Britain. Chapters 5 and 6 discuss examples from the early decades of the twentieth century when the First World War and the emergence of the Nazi ideology cast a dark shadow over parts of scientific research. This shadow grew considerably more ominous when, by the end of the Second

World War, it was cast by the mushroom clouds over Hiroshima and Nagasaki; chapters 7 and 8 examine several of the military and civilian aspects of nuclear power in East and West. Chapters 9, 10 and 11 feature examples which give a more centre-stage role to the 'public good' of our title, namely health and radiation, health and party politics, and the economics of technological enterprise. Chapter 12 discusses the service which professional historians themselves can render, in the form of 'public history', to both government and private authorities.

One aspect of Professor Gowing's career which deserves additional mention is her work in the area of archives and public records. Margaret Gowing not only made extensive use of archives as part of her historical studies, but she also has been one of the architects of the modern, official records system. Her archival experience was first gained during many years in the Historical Section of the Cabinet Office (1945–59). Subsequently it was enriched when she worked as an historian and archivist at the UK Atomic Energy Authority (1959–66).

In 1952, when only thirty years of age, Margaret Gowing was appointed a member of the Committee on Departmental Records, under the chairmanship of Sir James Grigg. At this time there existed no general right of access to modern departmental records, and the arrangements governing these were still based on the hopelessly inadequate and outdated Public Records Acts of 1838 and 1877. In its *Report* (1954), the Grigg Committee recommended six radical changes: (1) a minister of the Crown (the Lord Chancellor) should be responsible for the Public Record Office; (2) he should be assisted by an Advisory Council on Public Records; (3) in each governmental department, Record Officers should be appointed; (4) the Public Record Office should have enhanced authority in its dealings with the departments; (5) a system of first and second reviews (at not less than five years, and at twenty-five years) should operate to select departmental records for preservation; (6) records surviving the second review should be transferred to the Public Record Office and in most instances be opened to the public after a fifty-year interval. The Grigg Report became the blueprint of the modern records system, set up by the Public Records Act of 1958, and by the Act of 1967 which reduced the fifty-year rule to thirty.

The UK Atomic Energy Authority, hived off from the Ministry of Supply in 1954, was not a Government department and thus not subject to the Act of 1958. Nevertheless, it opted to be scheduled under the new Act and at the same time decided to put in hand a history of the British atomic energy project. It advertised for an archivist–historian and appointed Margaret Gowing who began her new task by organising the Authority's archives on the principles of the Grigg Report. This work provided her with a unique experience of the Grigg system in operation, and the historical fruits of this work were *Britain and Atomic Energy* (1964) and *Independence and Deterrence* (2 vols, 1974).

When in 1973 Margaret Gowing came to Oxford, after a period as Reader in Contemporary History at the University of Kent (1966–72), she continued her innovatory work as an archivist. In collaboration with Professor Nicholas Kurti and with the support of the Royal Society, Professor Gowing established the Contemporary Scientific Archives Centre of which she was the Director until her retirement (1973–86). The CSAC rescues and processes the personal collections of papers of leading British scientists. Before the establishment of the Oxford Centre, no such system existed, and much valuable material had been irretrievably lost. As Lord Bullock relates (Chapter 1), during Professor Gowing's tenure as Director, the CSAC catalogued the papers of well over 110 twentieth-century British scientists and placed the sorted collections in appropriate archives. Recently, upon Professor Gowing's retirement, the Centre was moved from Oxford to Bath.

In the meantime, in 1978, when the Grigg system had been in operation for two decades, Professor Gowing and others argued for a review. The Advisory Council on Public Records recommended an enquiry, and Lord Hailsham appointed a committee 'to review the arrangements for giving effect to the provisions of the Public Records Act 1958 and 1967 which relate to the selection of records for permanent preservation and to subsequent access to them'. The new enquiry was chaired by Sir Duncan Wilson, and it had Margaret Gowing and Paul Osmond as members. In the course of two years, the Committee took evidence from 168 individuals and 142 organisations, and visited the US, France, West Germany, The Netherlands and Sweden. The Wilson Report, published in 1981, amplified and reaffirmed the recommendations of the Grigg Report, and concluded that these had not yet been fully implemented.

Professor Gowing's archival expertise was acknowledged in the form of invitations to serve on the Lord Chancellor's Advisory

Council on Public Records (1974–82) and on the BBC Archives
Advisory Committee (1976–9). Her major and lasting contributions
to both contemporary history and to the organisation of historical
records constitute a unique, double achievement.

   The editor thanks Lorna Arnold and Nicholas Kurti for information
about Margaret Gowing's archives work.

                                              NICOLAAS A. RUPKE
Wolfson College, Oxford

Notes on the Contributors

Lorna Arnold has been at the UK Atomic Energy Authority since 1959, where in 1967 she joined Margaret Gowing to assist in producing the two-volume study of Britain and atomic energy, *Independence and Deterrence* (1974). Her interests include health and safety, nuclear weapons policy and public records. She recently published a history of the British nuclear weapons tests 'down under', *A Very Special Relationship: British Atomic Weapon Trials in Australia* (1987).

Lord Bullock (Alan Louis Charles Bullock) is Founding Master of St Catherine's College, Oxford (1960–80), and has been a Fellow of the College since 1980. He served as Vice-Chancellor of the University from 1969 till 1973. His many contributions to twentieth-century history include *Hitler, A Study in Tyranny* (1952; rev. edn 1964) and *The Life and Times of Ernest Bevin* (Vol. I, 1960; Vol. II, 1967; Vol. III: *Ernest Bevin, Foreign Secretary*, 1983). He is editor of *The Oxford History of Modern Europe*.

Sir Alec (Alexander Kirkland) **Cairncross** was Head of the Government Economic Service (1964–69), Master of St Peter's College, Oxford (1969–78), and has been Chancellor of Glasgow University since 1972 and Supernumerary Fellow of St Antony's College, Oxford, since 1978. He has served in prominent capacities as an adviser on, among other things, the Channel Tunnel Project. His many publications range from a textbook, *Introduction to Economics* (1944), to such studies of the economic history of the postwar period as *Years of Recovery* (1985) and *The Price of War* (1986).

Dr Allan Chapman is an historian of science at Wadham College, Oxford. His main interest is the history of astronomy, and his publications include *Three North Country Astronomers: W. Crabtree, J. Horrocks and W. Gascoigne* (1982) and an edition (with introduction) of *The Preface to John Flamsteed's Historia Coelestis Britannica, 1725* (1982). At present he is engaged in a biography of George Airy.

Dr Willem D. Hackmann is Assistant Curator at the Museum of the History of Science, Oxford. His interests range widely, from

xiii

eighteenth-century scientific instruments to twentieth-century warfare technology. His publications include *Electricity from Glass* (1978) and *Seek and Strike* (1984), a history of underwater sonar. He is currently editing *The Oxford Companion to Science*.

Dr Richard G. Hewlett was Chief Historian at the US Atomic Energy Commission (1957–75), at the Energy Research and Development Administration (1975–77), and at the US Dept of Energy (1977–80). He then founded History Associates Inc., which carries out archival and historical work on contract to both government and private authorities. He is joint author (with O. E. Anderson) of *The New World, 1939–46* (1962), (with F. Duncan) of *Atomic Shield, 1947–52* (1969) and (again with F. Duncan) of *Nuclear Navy, 1939–62* (1975).

Dr David Holloway is Professor of Political Science, and Member-in-Residence at the Center for International Security and Arms Control, at Stanford University. He is the author of *The Soviet Union and the Arms Race* (1983), co-author (with Sidney Drell and Philip Farley) of *The Reagan Strategic Defense Initiative* (1984), and co-editor (with Jane Sharp) of *The Warsaw Pact: Alliance in Transition?* (1985).

Sir Michael Eliot Howard was a Fellow of All Souls College from 1968 and Chichele Professor of the History of War from 1977, both till 1980 when he became Regius Professor of Modern History and Fellow of Oriel College, Oxford. Two of his historical studies won prizes, *The Franco-Prussian War* (1961; Duff Cooper Memorial Prize, 1962) and *Grand Strategy*, vol. IV in the UK History of the 2nd World War, Military Series (1971; Wolfson Foundation History Award, 1972). Among his other books is *War in European History* (1976).

Jack B. Morrell is Reader in the History of Science at the University of Bradford. He has written extensively on the social history of British science during the first industrial revolution, and is co-author (with Arnold Thackray) of *Gentlemen of Science* (1981), a history of the early years of the BAAS. He is currently working on a book on John Phillips.

Sir Rudolf Ernst Peierls was Wykeham Professor of Physics and Fellow of New College, Oxford (1963–74), now Emeritus Fellow.

During the War he worked on the Atomic Energy Project in Birmingham (1940–43) and in the US (1943–46). His many publications, primarily on quantum physics, include *Quantum Theory of Solids* (1955), *The Laws of Nature* (1955) and *Surprises in Theoretical Physics* (1979). More recently he published his autobiography, *Bird of Passage* (1985).

Dr Nicolaas A. Rupke is a geologist and an historian of science at Wolfson College, Oxford. He has published widely on deep marine clastics and is the author of a scientific biography of William Buckland, *The Great Chain of History* (1983). He edited *Vivisection in Historical Perspective* (1987) and is currently writing a book on Richard Owen.

Dr Charles Webster has been University Reader in the History of Medicine and Director of the Wellcome Unit at Oxford since 1972. His extensive writings on early-modern science and medicine include *The Great Instauration* (1975). Recently his publications have related to health care in the twentieth century. His book *Problems of Health Care: the British National Health Service before 1957* is appearing in the peacetime Official History series.

Dr Paul Weindling is Research Officer at the Wellcome Unit for the History of Medicine, Oxford. He co-edited (with Pietro Corsi) *Information Sources for the History of Science and Medicine* (1983), edited *The Social History of Occupational Health* (1986) and has a monograph on German social Darwinism in press. He is currently writing a history of German eugenics, health and population politics.

1 Margaret Gowing: An Appreciation

Lord Bullock

I cannot think of any episode in my period as Vice-Chancellor of Oxford on which I look back with more satisfaction than the University's decision, after much debate, to establish a chair in the history of science. For a university in which science has been studied since the Middle Ages, which contributed to the foundation of the Royal Society and which has long been a major centre of historical studies, the decision had been long delayed. Fortunately, the board of electors[1] proceeded to make an appointment which proved successful beyond our hopes and more than compensated for the delay.

At the time, our choice occasioned some surprise. Margaret Gowing, who retired in 1986 after holding the chair for fourteen years, did not fit the traditional pattern of the subject. Her training had been at the London School of Economics and in the Cabinet Office Historical Section, where she had worked for fourteen years on the economic and social history of the Second World War. Her contribution had so impressed Sir Keith Hancock, the editor-in-chief, that when the master volume of the series, *The British War Economy*, was published in 1949, he insisted that Margaret Gowing's name should appear on the title-page as joint author with himself. In 1952–54, she was one of the most active members of the Grigg Committee set up to review the selection and preservation of government records, and in 1959 she became the first historian and archivist of the UK Atomic Energy Authority.

All this pointed to a strongly developed interest in the relationship between science, especially applied science, and the world of politics and economics. The publication of *Britain and Atomic Energy, 1939–45* in 1964 showed equally clearly that this interest extended to the most recent period of history and to the most controversial areas. Its reception demonstrated that, although without scientific training, she could convince nuclear scientists and engineers that she had grasped the real issues at stake. No less important, the fact that her book was published at all established that, in addition to a knowledge of twentieth-century government archives which few historians could rival, she was able to persuade politicians and senior

1

civil servants to trust her judgement in using them.

Her inaugural lecture *What's Science to History or History to Science?* made explicit Professor Gowing's wish to see the scope of the history of science altered and enlarged. In the past, she wrote, it 'has tended to be an esoteric profession, too often uncongenial to mainstream historians and scientists alike'. She argued that this was due to the combination of the history with the philosophy of science:

> The philosophical questions about science – about method, theories of knowledge, the universe and man's place in it etc. – will always be of great importance to science. But historians' excessive preoccupation with the philosophy of science has had three unfortunate results.
>
> First, the leading exponents of the history of science have restricted themselves to the physical sciences, and have largely excluded ... the biological sciences and geology.
>
> Second ... philosophically minded historians ... have given natural science its own separate lineage through the ages, separated from the mainstream historical context of each period, so that scientific ideas from Thales to Einstein are still staple history of science fare. Thus scientists are too often treated as a race apart, and the turmoil of history is lost.
>
> Thirdly, philosophy has concentrated attention on one facet of science, that is on so-called pure science ... And pure science is assumed to be done by pure scientists ... The myths and stereotypes present scientists as essentially rational, ethereal, rarefied and unworldly ... Whereas they are just human, like other mortals, with the same mixed motives, mixed politics and mixed relations with their colleagues and competitors.[2]

The University had already acted to remove the principal cause of Professor Gowing's concern by separating the history from the philosophy of science and placing each firmly under its faculty board – thereby improving cooperation between them. She herself announced that she would regard applied science and technology as well as the biological and earth sciences as within the chair's terms of reference, and welcomed the prospect of cooperation with the then newly-established Unit for the History of Medicine set up by the Wellcome Foundation (another episode in my period of office on which I look back with satisfaction).

For the other changes which she hoped to see she relied on

historians becoming persuaded that, just as scientific ideas are an essential part of the history of ideas, science and technology are an equally essential part of the history of politics and society. She had some sharp comments to make on the narrow-minded approach of political historians to the nineteenth century. She pointed out that of all centuries this was the one in which British politics and society were revolutionised by the impact of applied science; yet historians continued to study it with hardly a reference to the century-long debate on government science policy, state support for both scientific research, and scientific and technical education – questions that have lost none of their cutting edge today. She contrasted this neglect with the record of Oxford's Chichele Chair of economic history, all four holders of which (G. N. Clark, Keith Hancock, H. J. Habakkuk and Peter Mathias) had shown their awareness that economic history is inconceivable without the technological revolutions. The same was true of Renaissance and seventeenth-century historians who had come to recognise that their periods could not be studied without paying attention to the role of science.

Granted that nineteenth- and twentieth-century historians might undergo a similar conversion, what had the historian to offer to the scientist which might change the view recorded by Sir Peter Medawar as 'widely prevalent among the Young Turks of science, that interest in the history of science is a sign of failing powers'?

Professor Gowing's answer was: to bring historical evidence to bear in challenging the myths which had grown up about science, chief among them the belief that the progress of scientific ideas has been something autonomous, divorced from the turbulence of the social, political and economic life contemporary with it, and that this scientific paradise continued to exist right up to the Second World War, when it went up in the mushroom cloud of the first atom bomb. She wrote:

> This interpretation of the history of science is bunk. Of course the great creative and imaginative leaps in our understanding of nature will always be in the centre of history, but they must be understood in the context of their times, in the context of causes and consequences and applications. The development of modern science in the last 400 years has been, indissolubly, part of the development of modern society. Even in the 16th and 17th centuries the interests of the scientists and technologists were influenced by the economic and social pulls of the day.[3]

This was her constant theme throughout her fourteen years in the Oxford chair: the continuous interaction of science and technology, not only with each other but with politics and society; 'an old and intimate relationship' as she phrased it in her 1982 Herbert Spencer lecture. What could be more appropriate, she asked, as an essential part of the necessary preparation, for any undergraduate intending to embark on research in today's world, than an understanding of the historical relationship between science, as the art of the soluble, and politics, as the art of the possible? How she set about providing this in practice can be illustrated in several ways.

First of all, as a teacher. Taking advantage of her earlier interest in economic history, she explored the conditions of successful innovation arising out of scientific discovery in the nineteenth and twentieth centuries. She took examples from the chemical and electrical industries; from Babbage's calculating machine, an experiment that failed, and from the invention of telegraphy, a highly successful but under-rated invention. She balanced this with biological themes: 'Science and intellectual ferment: Darwin and evolution', and, still in the nineteenth century, the potential of biology. Charles Webster was a frequent collaborator, and other younger historians of science were brought in to speak on their special subjects.

Government policy and science was another constant topic, ranging from the neglect of scientific and technical education in nineteenth-century Britain (the subject of her Wilkins Lecture to the Royal Society in 1976), with its striking quotation from Lyon Playfair's address to the British Association in 1885: 'How is it that we find whole branches of manufactures where they depend on scientific knowledge, passing away from this country in which they originated, in order to engraft themselves abroad, although their decaying roots remain at home', to the history of nuclear physics and what happened to German science under the Nazis. Another collaborator was Alastair Buchan, professor of international relations at Oxford, with whom Margaret ran a series of seminars on science, technology and international politics.

Secondly, as organiser and archivist. The history of science, as of any other subject, depends on the preservation of the written (and spoken) word for the future; yet, as Margaret Gowing had learned from her own researches into the history of atomic energy, scientists and engineers frequently fail to prevent their papers and correspondence being dispersed or destroyed. It was at her urging that the Royal Commission on Historical Manuscripts and the Royal

Society joined hands to remedy the situation. Amongst other results, this led to the setting up in Oxford, under Professor Gowing's Directorship, of the Contemporary Scientific Archives Centre which, working on a shoestring, but with the benefit of her guidance, in thirteen years processed, catalogued and deposited in suitable archives well over 110 collections of papers of twentieth-century scientists. At the same time she encouraged the National Portrait Gallery, of which she was appointed a Trustee, to take more interest in securing portraits of British scientists and engineers.

Finally, as scholar and writer. Much of Margaret Gowing's influence derives from her willingness to help and further the researches of younger scholars and scientists; but her authority derives from her own published work. In 1974 she published two further volumes, each more than 500 pages long and wholly written from original sources, on *Independence and Deterrence: Britain and Atomic Energy, 1945–52*, the first on policy-making, the second on policy-execution. Her election as a Fellow of the British Academy, as well as the pleasing combination of honorary DLitts from Leeds and Leicester Universities with honorary DScs from Manchester and Bath, was a well-deserved recognition by her fellow historians of her masterly handling of one of the major themes of contemporary history. How far this reaches into international relations as well as domestic politics, nuclear science and engineering, is shown in her contribution to '*The Special Relationship': Anglo-American Relations since 1945* (edited by the late Hedley Bull and Roger Louis), a curtain-raiser to the final volume of her trilogy, *Interdependence Regained: Britain and Atomic Energy, 1952–58*, the completion of which will be among the first fruits of her retirement.

Margaret Gowing concluded her inaugural lecture by saying that 'science and history are divided not by deep chasms but by man-made frontiers'. She spoke of her hope that these could be overcome by a good spirit of collaboration, adding: 'If we do not achieve this collaboration by the time I leave this chair, I shall have failed to fulfil the purposes for which it was established'.[4]

This Festschrift is the clearest proof that, whatever the difficulties, she has overcome them and more than fulfilled the purposes for which the chair was founded and the hopes of those who appointed her to be its first holder. She has laid the foundations of the modern study of the history of science in her own university, made an influential contribution to its development far outside Oxford, and,

the most convincing of all testimonies, secured the esteem and
admiration of her colleagues, scientists and historians alike.

NOTES

1. Among the electors, who met under my chairmanship, was one of the
   contributors to this Festschrift, Sir Rudolf Peierls, as well as Professor
   Trevor-Roper (now Lord Dacre) and Sir Frederick (now Lord) Dainton.
2. Margaret Gowing, *'What's Science to History or History to Science?*
   (Oxford: Clarendon Press, 1975) pp. 18–19.
3. Quotation from an unpublished Oxford lecture by Margaret Gowing:
   'British science in decline?'
4. Note 2 above, p. 25.

2 Science and Government: John Phillips (1800–74) and the Early Ordnance Geological Survey of Britain

Jack Morrell

In 1835 the Ordnance Geological Survey was established, with Henry De La Beche as its Director. His enterprise was not the first national geological survey to be patronised by a government: in France and the USA surveys were started in 1825 and 1823 and employed geologists temporarily.[1] De La Beche's Survey was unusual at the time in that it not only endured but grew, even though government regarded it as temporary. It was also unusual in that, though not the first experiment by which geological surveying and research were pursued under the auspices of the Ordnance Survey, it survived, whereas most other attempts foundered. John MacCulloch's Scottish work, begun in 1814 and completed in 1836, was for government a painful example of jobbery and uncontrolled expenditure.[2] From the 1820s, Richard Griffith unofficially exploited his posts in the Irish Ordnance Survey and by 1835 had raised no alarm in government circles. From 1832, Joseph Portlock worked officially in the Irish Ordnance Survey on geology until in 1840 the project had become so expensive that government stopped it.[3] For England, fast becoming the workshop of the world, the economic argument in favour of geological surveying as part of the Ordnance Survey carried less weight than for Ireland. Even so, Thomas Colby, the Superintendent of the Ordnance Survey, encouraged a few surveyors to colour Ordnance maps geologically in the early 1830s. A fifth experiment was proposed, but not carried out, in 1831 when it was suggested to government that William Smith, the ageing Father of English Geology, should be appointed colourer of the Ordnance maps.[4]

Clearly De La Beche was an accomplished lobbier of government who from 1835 demonstrated his mastery of the sly *fait accompli*, of covertly changing the terms of an agreement, of hoisting his critics with their own petard, as means by which he built up a state-supported geological empire bit by bit: the Museum of Economic Geology was effectively established in 1837, the Mining Record

Office was opened in 1840, and the School of Mines established in
1851. His equally successful attempts to expand his staff were based
on the same incremental approach, which had the distinct virtue of
not alienating either Colby or the Treasury. Until the end of 1836,
De La Beche had as assistants only two experienced Ordnance
surveyors, Henry McLauchlan and Henry Still, who made topo-
graphic corrections to the outdated maps and helped geologically,
plus a hired miner who examined mines and excavated geologically
debatable ground. Subsequently, several geologists, such as William
Logan, Harvey Holl and William Sanders, worked with the
Geological Survey voluntarily but were never employed by it. Colby's
preference was to train existing Ordnance men for employment on
the Geological Survey, but De La Beche's first appointment was
that of John Phillips who was anything but a novice. Though the
standard accounts of the early Survey are generally accurate, they
are deficient about the four ways in which he was connected with
it.[5]

This essay is devoted to an analysis of Phillips' changing relations
with the Survey, starting in 1836 on a voluntary basis and culminating
in 1841 with a regular but annually renewable appointment as its
palaeontologist. Phillips' gradually increasing connection with the
Survey was not, as North asserted, merely a matter of time.[6] On
the contrary, it required careful negotiations which in 1841 involved
no less than the Prime Minister, Robert Peel. Though it would be
foolish to belittle the importance to the Survey of De La Beche,
some new light is thrown on its cultural politics in its early years if
one examines the contributions of Phillips, De La Beche's first
recruit to it.

De La Beche first approached Phillips to help the Geological Survey
in November 1836, not out of altruism but in order to serve certain
interests dear to De La Beche. One of these concerned the Devonian
controversy which had erupted in 1834. As Rudwick has shown,
this controversy was not just about fossil plants in the old rocks of
Devon: it soon provoked heated and protracted discussion of such
central issues as how to use fossils in determining the order of the
strata and it eventually spread to embrace the geology of the USA
and Russia.[7] By autumn 1836, the battle-lines were clearly drawn,
with Roderick Murchison, Charles Lyell and Adam Sedgwick lined
up against De La Beche. At the 1836 meeting in Bristol of the
British Association, his work on Devon, and by implication his

capacity to lead the fledgling Geological Survey, came under severe attack from Murchison and Sedgwick, the former exploiting the presence at the meeting of Thomas Spring-Rice, who as Chancellor of the Exchequer had authorised the Survey in 1835. De La Beche was caught off his guard by the unexpected and powerful onslaught made by Murchison and Sedgwick, and he began to fear for the future of the Survey and of himself. He was right to do so because Murchison and Sedgwick claimed that De La Beche was inadequate not only as a structural geologist in that he had been misled by the folding of the rocks but also as a palaeontologist apropos his dating of the troublesome Devon Culm. De La Beche feared that Murchison, an independent gentleman geologist, would use his undoubted influence to destroy the state-supported Geological Survey and thereby preserve his own intellectual dominance and geological territory. He suspected that Lyell, another gentleman geologist, would make sly cuts at the Survey whenever possible.[8] Moreover, he knew that Sedgwick, Professor of Geology at Cambridge, had put himself in a contradictory position: in 1832 and 1835 Sedgwick had assured government about De La Beche's geological competence, but in 1836 he had publicly questioned it. Presumably, De La Beche feared that government and especially Spring-Rice would regard specialist scientific advice, such as Sedgwick had given, as deceitful or incompetent. By late November 1836, De La Beche knew that Sedgwick had gone out of his way to protect the Survey, as well as to justify his own integrity as a scientific consultant to government. Sedgwick had told Spring-Rice that De La Beche had mapped Devon well according to the notions then in vogue and was therefore not to be blamed. He explained that Murchison and he were not attacking De La Beche's competence but were proposing a new classification of what everyone agreed was a very difficult area to understand. Sedgwick concluded by averring his continued support for the Survey.[9]

De La Beche was in an unstable position and defensive mood apropos the Survey when in November 1836 he asked Phillips to identify Cornish fossil specimens collected by it. His reasons were clear. At heart De La Beche was not a palaeontologist, yet the 1836 fracas at Bristol had shown him that stratigraphical geology was becoming more dependent on palaeontology and less dependent on mineral composition and on the observed order of superposition of rocks. He therefore needed help in the task of identifying strata from their fossil contents. Phillips was ideally qualified to do this.

He was an experienced field surveyor, mapper and geologist as well as a renowned palaeontologist who illustrated his works with his own drawings of fossils. In late 1836 he was preparing for publication two palaeontological works, one on fossils in general and the other on belemnites. He was recognised as the leading British expert on what was becoming known as the Jurassic system of strata, and in spring of 1836 he had added to his reputation by publishing a monograph on the mountain limestone of Yorkshire which was *de facto* if not *de jure* a treatise on the carboniferous system of rocks.[10] As an authority on the carboniferous limestone, Phillips was prospectively useful to De La Beche whose 1835 classification of strata put this limestone immediately above the Old Red Sandstone and the problematic greywacke rocks of Devon.[11] So Phillips could be helpful as the British authority on the geological system next but one and above the greywacke in the stratigraphical column. Moreover, De La Beche knew that small quantities of limestones occurred in various parts of the greywacke rocks. In the event of these turning out to be crucial in the Devonian controversy, De La Beche would have a recognised expert to call on, at best to secure victory, or as a *pis aller* to muddy the water.

There were in addition two attitudes which De La Beche and Phillips shared. First, each was critical of what might be called naïve Smithian palaeontology, which assumed that each stratum was labelled by the fossils it contained, and that these fossils were unique to it and usually few in number. For De La Beche, the varying local circumstances of deposition of fossils modified the fossil contents and mineral composition of a given rock stratum; so that in his view it was erroneous to assume that any stratum, especially if occurring over a considerable area, would contain throughout the same fossils. For De La Beche, fossil labelling of strata was inherently suspect, especially when the likes of Murchison were trying to make correlations of strata over long distances or to establish universal geological systems (such as the Silurian and Devonian) on the basis of merely local investigations. This was why in 1835 De La Beche had proclaimed that fossil content and mineral composition were subordinate to observed superposition in identifying strata.[12]

Phillips' views on these matters had not led him to a Bechean position of scepticism about the use of fossils. Instead, as the loyal nephew and pupil of William Smith, Phillips still believed in the importance of fossil-labelling, but only if it were done in a way which avoided the errors inherent in Smith's procedures. Whereas

Smith saw fossils as just distinguishing features of strata, Phillips viewed them as the remains of living creatures. In his interpretation of the Devon greywacke plants, given to De La Beche in spring 1835, Phillips had made it clear that fossils could characterise particular past environments and not particular past geological epochs.[13] Yet he wished them to perform the latter function and by summer 1835 had proposed in principle an answer to the problem. At the 1835 meeting of the British Association, Phillips denounced the practice of identifying rocks by a few allegedly characteristic fossil species; in a comment on the recently proclaimed Silurian and Cambrian systems of Murchison and Sedgwick, Phillips urged that strata should be identified by 'a combination of co-existing genera'.[14] This recommendation was in line with his views expressed in his long article on geology for the *Encyclopaedia Metropolitana*. There he revealed his expectation that further research would not sharpen but soften the contrasts between contiguous rocks and by implication between so-called systems adjacent to each other in the stratigraphical column.[15]

This general notion received particular illustration in spring 1836 in Phillips' monograph on the mountain limestone, in which he was at pains to distance himself from Smith and Murchison: he stressed that lines of division between geological systems were arbitrary and often of merely local validity; he acknowledged that the 'carboniferous system' was characterised not by the ubiquity but by the prevalence of coal, limestone and red sandstone; he claimed that the mountain limestone was not sharply separate from the sub-adjacent Old Red Sandstone but merged into it; he emphasised that varying local agencies, by causing a particular stratum to thin out in one direction, made stratigraphical correlations over a large distance a hazardous affair.[16] Phillips was so conscious of the significance of the distribution of certain fossils in various strata that he drew up a table showing, for each of the five strata in the carboniferous system, the total number of fossil species and how these species were distributed among nine zoological classes. From this table it seemed that the Millstone Grit formation contained a total of sixteen species and the Lower Scar Limestone 390, giving an obvious contrast between these two strata; but all sixteen species in the grit occurred more abundantly in this limestone, so that none of these species was specific to the grit.[17] Phillips was here taking preliminary steps towards some form of statistical palaeontology, based on the number and the distribution of species and of zoological classes, in order to escape from the limitations of fossil-labelling as practised by his uncle and Murchison.[18]

If De La Beche's and Phillips' attitudes to geology demonstrated what Phillips called in 1835 'a very unexpected coincidence of thought and feeling' in two men who then hardly knew each other; they were also united in their opposition to what they regarded as the speculative and premature theorising of Lyell.[19] There seems to have been mutual suspicion and sometimes antipathy between De La Beche and Lyell: certainly, from 1834 Lyell did not bother to conceal his personal dislike of De La Beche, while the latter deemed some of Lyell's theoretical positions to be simply ridiculous.[20] In a recent penetrating article on the early Survey, Secord has suggested that its Director's hostility to Lyell's preconceived opinions gave it coherence as a collective research enterprise.[21] Certainly Phillips, the first recruit to the Survey, fits this interpretation. In 1835, at the British Association, Phillips reinforced the criticisms De La Beche had already made of Lyell's percentage method for dealing with tertiary fossils: in Phillips' opinion, the method, though powerful, was subject to considerable error in practice.[22] This was precisely the view taken by Edward Charlesworth in his successful assault on Lyell's view that the Suffolk crag was one formation which belonged to the pliocene period. In his public attack, Charlesworth invoked Phillips as an authority for the crag being composed of two formations probably of miocene age. Phillips urged his friend Charlesworth to keep his self-command in the crag controversy.[23] For his part, Lyell saw Phillips as an accomplice of Charlesworth in that controversy, just as later he saw De La Beche and Phillips as united opponents of what he called his own 'gradual causes' approach to geological explanation. Socially, Lyell regarded Phillips as a gauche provincial unfamiliar with the niceties of the metropolitan conventions of the Geological Society of London.[24] Even so, Lyell saw Phillips as a formidable literary competitor; it is not fanciful to see Lyell's *Elements* as his response to the success of Phillips' *Guide*.[25]

De La Beche's faith in Phillips as an anti-Lyellian was not to be unfounded. In his works of the late 1830s, Phillips was uncharacteristically outspoken in criticising many of Lyell's views. For instance, apropos the London Basin, Lyell had argued for the gradual elevation of the Weald; Phillips dismissed this speculation as being an unsupportable and unopposable example of non-inductive geology. He continued his criticism of Lyell's percentage method for determining the relative ages of tertiary strata, arguing that causes of local diversity were strongest in the tertiary period and that Lyell had assumed that changes in living creatures were in exact proportion to the time that had passed.[26] Most tellingly he denounced Lyell's method as being neither an inductive inference nor a mathematical principle.[27] On the question of whether past geological causes were no more intense than present-day ones (as Lyell believed), Phillips claimed that such features as the Pennine fault, which involved dislocations about 3000 ft deep and 100 miles long, provided conclusive evidence for extensive but short-lived violent convulsions because there was no trace of the minutely confused and fragmentary strata which many small Lyellian earth movements would have produced.[28] Phillips was decidedly opposed to Lyell's theory that change of climate was caused by the change of position of land and sea: though not improbable, this theory was not sufficient to explain the effect. As for Lyell's steady-state theory about the earth's history,. Phillips argued strongly in favour of a progressive refrigeration theory which he thought might well become a general mathematical theory, like that of gravity and the wave theory of light, from which characteristic phenomena could be deduced.

All these particular criticisms of Lyell's views were based on Phillips' belief that geology was an inductive science, which had not yet attained a sound and general theory. Accordingly, he saw geological theory as 'the summit of a cone whose base continually enlarges to include every known fact appertaining to the subject.[29] In his view, Lyell was a pedlar of interesting but premature unsubstantiated hypotheses: there was no evidence for the uniform intensity over time of each geological agent, for the continual balancing of antagonistic causes, and for the production of equal effects in equal times. As an ecological palaeontologist *and* geologist concerned with faulting and flexing of strata, Phillips was aware that his own time was one of geological repose which could not legitimately be used as a measure of past geological violence. In Phillips' view, past natural agencies, acting with varying intensities in different combinations in varying conditions, could give extremely diverse effects. It was especially these varying conditions which for him made Lyell's uniformitarianism in its doctrinaire formulation as 'baseless as the fabric of a vision'. In Phillips' book, the geologist who claimed to have established the principles of geology was in fact a deviant from 'positive geology' and a cosmogonist like William

Whiston whose theory of the earth was nothing more than a reverie.[30] The fate of Lyell's hypotheses was therefore likely to be not permanent influence but temporary use.[31]

By the mid 1830s, Phillips was, of course, far more than a naïve Baconian inductive geologist; but his emphasis on geology as an inductive science and his opposition to Lyell's hypothetical approach fitted beautifully with the image of geology which De La Beche found it expedient to present to his Ordnance superiors such as Colby. Though De La Beche's *Researches in Theoretical Geology* (1834) had recently shown that he was more than a remorseless empiricist, the scientific persona he found it useful to present to Colby was that of the disinterested and unbiased observer of phenomena and collector of facts. In late 1836 and early 1837, De La Beche justified the work of the Survey to Colby on precisely those grounds. The Survey's prime purpose, he claimed, was to observe, to collect and to arrange geological facts, without attempting to establish or controvert theoretical opinions; and when the Survey did try to draw general conclusions from accumulated data, it did so cautiously and 'without bias in favour of any particular theory of the day'.[32]

In all these ways, Phillips was ideally qualified to help De La Beche's enterprise, but there were three drawbacks. Firstly, Phillips was a very busy man. Left an orphan at the age of eight, he pursued science out of pure love, but his relative poverty forced him into what he called 'scientific business'.[33] In late 1836, Phillips' emolument came from several sources: £200 a year from the British Association to which he acted as general factotum from his post as Assistant Secretary; £100 a year as Keeper of the York Museum run by the Yorkshire Philosophical Society; varying sums, often small, from his lectures as professor of geology at King's College, London, from his exhausting public lectures in northern towns, from his publications and from occasional consultancy work, such as that he undertook in the winter of 1836–37 for the Lancaster Mining Company.[34] This meant that De La Beche would have to offer substantial intellectual and financial rewards to Phillips in exchange for any extensive involvement in the Survey. Secondly, Phillips' leading London patron was Murchison, who in 1834 had taken the lead in securing an FRS for Phillips but was now arrayed against De La Beche on the Devonian question. Presumably, De La Beche realised that if Phillips were to work for the Survey he would have to walk a tightrope as he gradually transferred his allegiance from Murchison to

De La Beche; and that to increase Phillips' involvement in the Survey gradually and not suddenly would permit him to do this. Thirdly, De La Beche knew for certain that Phillips' palaeontological skill might be used to qualify or overturn De La Beche's own solutions to problems involving fossils. This had happened at the 1836 meeting of the British Association where, in response to Murchison and Sedgwick's interpretation of Devon, Phillips had argued that the Devon Culm strata were carboniferous and not pre-carboniferous as De La Beche still claimed.[35]

From November 1836 to March 1838, Phillips seems to have worked for the Survey voluntarily and without pay. In return for preferential access to the Survey's fossils and freedom to exploit them in any publication, he agreed to identify them and to permit these identifications to be used in Survey reports to the Ordnance. By May 1837, he was inspecting Cornish fossils for De La Beche, now a close associate, and at the same time giving substantial help to Murchison apropos the *Silurian System*.[36] Just at this time, De La Beche found himself needing more help from Phillips: in order to extinguish rumours about De La Beche's incompetence, government had agreed to publish his memoir on Devon and Cornwall at its expense and not his. From April 1837 to March 1838, De La Beche gradually lured Phillips into taking on more and more palaeontological work, by sending him first Survey specimens from Cornwall and then supplementing these with fossils from several private collections including some important Devon ones. At the same time, De La Beche lost no opportunity to denigrate the conduct of Murchison and Sedgwick as unfraternal and selfish. He stressed to Phillips that Murchison and Sedgwick were the only brethren of the hammer who had not helped the Survey when asked because they were obsessed with fame. In so doing he was playing on Phillips' belief that the leaders of English geology were characterised by 'invincible liberality of sentiment'.[37]

By February 1838, De La Beche, ready to go to press with his *Report* on Devon and Cornwall, was desperate for Phillips' account of the fossils of the area, but was in no position to compel compliance from his voluntary helper. By the time the *Report* went to press, Phillips had completed his identifications of the fossils from no more than three private local collections, those of William Harding, Samuel Pattison and Charles Peach.[38] Clearly De La Beche wanted quicker service from Phillips, who had just begun the busiest year's programme of freelance lecturing in his whole career with courses in London at the Royal Institution, the London Institution and King's College, and in the provinces at Bristol, Chester, Manchester, Sheffield and York. In order to show fellow geologists that the Survey was up-to-date in its approach and to convince government that his Survey was efficient, De La Beche wanted a palaeontological companion volume to his *1839 Report*. By spring 1838, Phillips had done enough good work on the fossils from Devon and Cornwall for De La Beche to be convinced that Phillips could provide just that. In general, De La Beche wished to patronise a new sort of palaeontology which would show that the days of the individual gentleman-geologist such as Murchison were numbered: in late 1837, he had welcomed Phillips' approach to the study of fossils as 'a thousand-fold richer than the mere bald and trifling notion of the identification of strata by their organic contents'.[39] Moreover, in late 1837 De La Beche had begun the Survey's work in South Wales, which the Treasury and Ordnance had authorised in January 1837. Here he soon received enthusiastic assistance in mapping from William Logan, a surveyor whose minute accuracy was then unparalleled in the United Kingdom; but Logan was no palaeontologist.[40]

In spring 1838, De La Beche transformed Phillips' voluntary and unpaid connection with the Survey into a contractual, paid, yet temporary *ad hoc* arrangement. After almost five months of negotiations, on 27 July 1838 the Treasury issued an order for Phillips to draw and describe the fossils of Cornwall, Devon and West Somerset for a fee of £250 plus expenses.[41] This second type of connection with the Survey occupied Phillips until early 1841 and it culminated in the publication in summer 1841 of his *Palaeozoic Fossils*, which was printed uniformly with De La Beche's *1839 Report*.[42] It seems that in early March 1838 both De La Beche and Phillips envisaged a fixed and permanent appointment for Phillips as palaeontologist to the Survey, but they settled for the *ad hoc* fee arrangement as easier to secure from government.[43] Each man was adopting the tactic of gaining a toe in the door. In 1835, De La Beche had persuaded government to transform an *ad hoc* fee arrangement for himself into a regular salaried position; and thus he saw no great difficulty in eventually doing the same for Phillips, for whom the *ad hoc* arrangement was a prelude to a fixed appointment with the Survey. It seems that it was Phillips who on

6 March 1838 suggested to De La Beche that government might give a special grant for the Devon and Cornwall fossil work, which Phillips estimated would take no more than a year. Financially Phillips proposed to be paid a fee of £250 plus expenses, an arrangement which De La Beche quickly put to the Treasury. By 12 March, he had obtained a gentleman's agreement from Francis Baring, Secretary to the Treasury. De La Beche then applied formally to the Treasury, supporting his application with testimonials from Sedgwick, Buckland and Whewell as President of the Geological Society about Phillips' prowess and suitability. He did so partly to disable any intriguer opposed to the arrangement and partly to justify it apropos Parliament.[44]

As soon as De La Beche had despatched the Treasury order of 28 July 1838 to Phillips, he began to lean hard on his assistant who knew that he would be paid only on completion of his task. De La Beche stressed to Phillips that cabinet work would not be enough: it would be necessary to inspect the sites from which specimens had been taken. Then he made a confidential offer to Phillips to join Charles Barry and himself on a royal commission appointed to discover the most suitable stone for the building of the new Houses of Parliament, of which Barry was the architect. The commission, De La Beche revealed, was partly his own brainchild: it had originated in a conversation between Barry and himself at the Museum of Economic Geology. Though De La Beche later complained to Colby that the Parliament stone commission was distracting him from his South Wales field-work and delaying publication of his *1839 Report*, he welcomed the opportunity of demonstrating to government the economic utility of the Survey, and of bringing Phillips into advantageous contact with what he called 'the higher powers'.[45] Phillips' response was decisive: though he was aware of the patronage that membership of the commission might generate, and that his time and expenses would be paid for, he simply could not squeeze in two months' more travelling. In addition, his old uncle, William Smith, was pained by the notion of Phillips' doing what he himself could do. Phillips soon decided that Smith was the man for the job: by the end of August, he had persuaded Barry and De La Beche to put Smith on the commission and be paid a fee of £150. Phillips was happy to help his uncle and at the same time to release himself from the 'plague of going to see stones and buildings'.[46]

He was wise to do so because in the next six months or so his pressing engagements prevented him from making much progress with the Devon fossil work. In early 1839, the appearance of two books, one by Murchison and the other by De La Beche, made that fossil work all the more important. In January, Murchison published his *Silurian System*, which elevated the Old Red Sandstone into a geological system, while referring occasionally to his views on Devon. His book was more than slightly indebted to Phillips, who had made a number of suggestions and corrections all of which Murchison had gladly adopted. Phillips also helped Murchison by providing illustrations of fossil crinoids, descriptions of bits of their stems, and an account of upper coal measures near Manchester; and by acting as Murchison's adviser and teacher on joints in rocks, a problem on which Murchison regarded Phillips as the English expert. Generally Murchison invoked Phillips as an expert on the oolite and carboniferous systems, Phillips' book on the latter being praised as the pioneering first monograph on the older fossiliferous rocks.[47] The following month, De La Beche produced his *1839 Report* on the geology of south-west England, in which he accepted Murchison and Sedgwick's interpretation of the structure of Devon, without giving more than the scantiest indication that they had first proposed it in 1836 at Bristol. On the vexed question of the age of the Devon Culm, he referred to it with deliberate vagueness as carbonaceous, instead of conceding to Murchison and Sedgwick by calling it carboniferous. Needless to say, Murchison was outraged by this mixture of plagiarism and obfuscation, deploring to the President of the Geological Society 'the ordnance jockeyship of riding home with false weights'.[48] As part of his obfuscation, De La Beche asserted that Phillips' work on the north Devon Culm, which Phillips had publicly dated as carboniferous, could be interpreted another way: it was rash to assume that these fossils were limited to the carboniferous epoch. On the related question of the lack of resemblance between the greywacke in north and south Devon, De La Beche offered two conjectures: first, that there was a difference in age, the south being younger; second, that they were of the same age, but the conditions of existence for animals varied between north and south. He then pointedly announced that Phillips would give the problem proper attention.[49]

This, of course, was what Phillips, too, wished to do, but his circumstances were unpropitious. In February 1839, Phillips was on the point of a nervous breakdown, a subsidence of mind, through over-work. After one of Phillips' lectures at the Royal Institution, London, Michael Faraday, an exemplar of unremitting work, agreed with Phillips that he should reduce his commitments for the sake of his health and of science. By 23 February, Phillips had at last taken action: he had indicated to the Principal of King's College his intended resignation from the geology chair, at the same time as he began to supervise at a distance the rebuilding of St Mary's Lodge, York, his newly acquired home.[50] Meanwhile, Murchison was fretting about whether he and Sedgwick should let Phillips see all their fossils: he feared parting with his palaeontological weapons and he suspected that De La Beche would induce Phillips to do field-work in Devonshire to supplement De La Beche's patent deficiencies. Simultaneously, Murchison acknowledged that Phillips' future work for the Survey 'would be well for the country'.[51]

His suspicion that De La Beche needed Phillips was well-founded. On 28 February 1939, with his *Report* published, De La Beche launched the negotiations which eventually culminated in Phillips' being elevated yet another rung on the Survey ladder, this time as a salaried Survey geologist. Initially, De La Beche offered tempting bait: as part of an expansion of the small Survey empire, Phillips was asked to be a sub-Director responsible for half of the English work, at a salary of £400 p.a. (£100 less than De La Beche) with £100 p.a. for expenses (the same as De La Beche). Phillips agreed to let his name be used in De La Beche's negotiations because the proposed remuneration would permit him to relinquish all lecturing and avoid its concomitant anxiety.[52]

Phillips had less than a month to mull over the possible consequences of accepting De La Beche's prospective offer before yet another fracas occurred between Murchison and De La Beche, this time in connection with the April 1839 paper by Murchison and Sedgwick on Devon and Cornwall, which contained a startling redefinition of the Devonian system compared with their views of 1836. In this paper, Murchison, the prime author, argued that the rocks of much of Devon were representatives of a previously unrecognised geological epoch (the Devonian) which occurred after the Silurian and before the Carboniferous periods. Murchison had re-named as the Devonian what in his 1839 book he had called the Old Red Sandstone system, even though Devon rocks and the Old Red Sandstone were different lithologically and, more paradoxically, had little in common apropos fossil contents (for example, the latter's fossil fish had not been found in the former). The other purpose of Murchison's paper was to expose De La Beche's alleged plagiarism: De La Beche's 1839 map, an integral part of his *Report*, was indebted to Murchison's and Sedgwick's 1836 account of Devon, but failed to acknowledge that debt. In Phillips' view De La Beche had laid himself open to such severe animadversions that his influence was likely to end soon.[53] In no time at all, Phillips discovered that he, too, had been attacked by Murchison for ungentlemanly plagiarism: in his little geological map of Britain, published in late 1838 by the Society for the Diffusion of Useful Knowledge, Phillips had coloured the Devon Culm as carboniferous but not as a productive coal field and had cited De La Beche as his authority. Phillips also found that he had 'promised' to correct this mis-acknowledgement and that De La Beche wondered whether this was so.[54] Though Phillips feared acrimonious controversy as personally disagreeable and a deviation from the true ethos of geology, he decided to assert his independence by publishing an explanation in the next issue of the *Philosophical Magazine*. Murchison expected Phillips to knuckle under and to withdraw his protest, but Murchison was mistaken: Phillips objected to the pledge which had been unexpectedly given for him and defended his own and De La Beche's scientific reputations. He made it clear that in early 1838 he *had* taken his colouring of Devon from De La Beche, but that it was unnecessary to give specific acknowledgement for the dating of the Culm as carboniferous because that was common knowledge.[55] These defiant remarks were printed immediately before a further statement by Murchison and Sedgwick, who expressed their deep regret about their unnecessarily sharp words about De La Beche's behaviour, but ignored Phillips' rejoinder because it was unanswerable. From then on Murchison, previously Phillips' chief London patron and his superior in the secretariat of the British Association, knew that Phillips would not kowtow to him. Both Murchison and Sedgwick appreciated that Phillips had put his foot in it by refusing to be silent or silenced. He had asserted his independence, demonstrated his moral allegiance to De La Beche, and might well repeat the performance.

Warmed by Phillips' public loyalty to the Survey, De La Beche began to exert what he called sincere and sometimes unpleasant pressure on Phillips to continue the Devon fossils work and not defer it. De La Beche feared that the Treasury might notice Phillips' inaction and become more obstructive in future, irrespective of which party happened to be in power. Moreover, in June, Robert

Austen had left Devon for Surrey, taking his fossils with him, so that he was no longer available to give help locally in Devon. For his part, Phillips pointed to some progress he had made in studying specimens and to practical difficulties, such as Austen's collection being split between three places. Phillips reaffirmed his dedication to producing 'a true history' of the Devon fossils, but confessed he was intolerably busy.[56]

In August 1839, Phillips threw off one burden, only to pick up another. Early in the month he told the Principal of King's that he would not be available to lecture during the forthcoming academic session. His reasons were clear: lecturing in London from a York base was inconvenient; he was exhausted by an excess of widely extended employments; he preferred the repose of the country to the bustle of the metropolis; and he wished to devote himself more to the advancement of science and less to its diffusion. By November 1839, his resignation was final and official.[57] In late August, his uncle, William Smith, died in Northampton in Phillips' presence, leaving him with the taxing responsibilities of clearing Smith's debts and of looking after Smith's insane wife. These were presumably responsible for Phillips applying to De La Beche for a financial advance for the Devon fossils work, a request De La Beche had to refuse as contrary to the Treasury minute authorising it.[58]

By 1840, Phillips had much reduced his free-lance lecturing and was able at last to spend two months (March and April) on field-work in Devon accompanied by his friend William Sanders. Fortified by this proof of Phillips' enthusiasm, De La Beche broached yet another proposition to him. Nothing having come of the February 1839 scheme for Phillips to be a full-time sub-Director of the English Survey, De La Beche fell back on a less ambitious idea, which involved Phillips working some time each year as palaeontologist to the Survey. This proposal, launched in March 1840 and fully authorised by government in February 1841, inaugurated the third type of connection Phillips had with the Survey, namely, as a salaried palaeontologist, full-time for part of the financial year, 1841–42, his tenure being officially limited to that year.[59] De La Beche certainly went out of his way to secure Phillips on this basis. He accommodated Phillips about the time of the year and the salary Phillips wanted. He thought hard about how to stop his proposal being referred back by the appropriate ministers which he feared would be a device for ignoring it. He dangled the visions of Phillips lecturing at the Museum of Economic Geology and of Phillips arranging the fossils in some large national museum. He arranged for Phillips' work on the Devonian fossils to be printed by order of the Treasury and secured helpful co-operation from the Stationery Office who published it. He tried unsuccessfully to secure for Phillips the award of the Geological Society's Wollaston medal, its most coveted award. He consulted Phillips' convenience in arranging for the lithographing of the plates to be done privately in York against HMSO rules and accepted the awkwardness of having the plates lithographed in York and worked off in London.[60] Finally, in December 1840, he used his skill as an experienced lobbier to get unwritten agreement from government about Phillips' being employed for one year as palaeontologist to the Survey. He knew that five minutes' talk with Francis Baring, the Chancellor of the Exchequer, was worth six months of scribbling memoranda, not least because the private secretaries made sad havoc with scientific matters in them. He took action in early December 1840, when ministers were in London and Parliament not sitting, having spotted that part of the previous years' Ordnance estimates were unexpended and therefore ripe for appropriation by the Geological Survey. Before Christmas he had secured the Chancellor's agreement. The following month he outlined his scheme to the Master General of Ordnance: as there would be by March a balance of £570 in hand, Phillips could be employed for eight months on field-work in Wales in the financial year 1841–42 at a salary of £300 p.a. plus expenses, which would continue and formalise for a year the previous *ad hoc* arrangement. Moreover, as De La Beche stressed, Phillips could be relied on: for his fee of £250, Phillips had just finished his important book on the Devon fossils. The Ordnance authorities agreed to De La Beche's proposal, Colby arguing that Phillips would be a faster and cheaper worker than anyone De La Beche could find locally in South Wales.[61]

Phillips had good reasons for accepting his third type of connection with the Survey. The death of his uncle, however sad, meant that he was totally free to go beyond his uncle's palaeontological approach. More importantly, the attractions of the Survey post were overwhelming for Phillips. He would work in the field for the warm part of the year, while retaining as his York base the refurbished St Mary's Lodge. He would be well paid for doing what he enjoyed, that is, studying fossils. He could anticipate more time for research and more opportunities for government-sponsored publication, while being able to relinquish most of the types of employment he had been forced to take in the past. He would be enabled to cut down his tiring lecturing engagements. In late December 1840, he severed his most enduring connection with York science when he resigned from the Keepership of the York Museum, which he had occupied for fifteen years. In addition, he obviously hoped that the one-year position would be a prelude to an appointment as permanent fossilist. With respect to income, the prospect of £300 for eight months' field-work plus expenses meant that he would be free from taking on various hack jobs to make ends meet. His own estimate in October 1840 of his total income in the period 1841–42 was £600. In January 1841, he augmented this to £700 when the British Association recognised his centrality to its machinery by raising his salary as Assistant Secretary from £200 to £300 per annum. He could look forward to being well paid for one year for contributing to what he regarded as an important national undertaking. That was why he not only accepted but welcomed De La Beche's insistence that the conclusions of his forthcoming Devon fossil book be kept secret: they agreed that government had the right to be the first announcer of the results of the work for which it had paid. In several ways, then, the one-year Survey post was ideal, as Phillips jubilantly told De La Beche:

> I cannot perceive in my country any other mode of occupation more consonant to my habits and feelings, more beneficial to my health, or more fertile of opportunities of performing useful labours in science, and so of founding or strengthening a claim to be remembered among the geologists of this age.[62]

This last wish was realised in July 1841, when Phillips' *Palaeozoic Fossils*, heavily subsidised by government, was published.[63] As Rudwick and Secord have rightly stressed, in this book Phillips offered a masterly vindication of Murchison's Devonian interpretation, but gave short shrift to the notion that there were well-defined geological systems such as the Devonian. As De La Beche was the other chief remaining sceptic about the existence of a Devonian system, Phillips' book gave face-saving and temporising protection to his boss, while agreeing in the main with Murchison's 1839 interpretation. This was in line with Phillips' announced purpose of avoiding controversy about the age and analogies of the rocks of north and south Devon. But Phillips did more than sit on the fence and try to maintain the geological peace: with mischievous modesty, he claimed that his work offered merely the 'natural results of a simple arrangement and contemplation of the phenomena'; in fact, he revealed a statistical palaeontology which was calculated to replace Murchison's preferred method of characterising geological systems by the fossils peculiar to them.[64]

Phillips was well aware that, to minimise the difficulties of labelling strata by their fossils, it was advisable to study a large number and full variety of fossils in strata thought to be analogous, preferably using strata not widely separate geographically. He therefore developed three modes of numerical estimation, each of which revealed the degree of similarity between two regions, such as north and south Devon: the first compared the total number of species in each region; the second compared the number of species in each zoological class in each region; and the third gave the number of identical, that is, overlapping, species present in each region. From these tables, it was clear that, though the Devon fossils were intermediate beween the Silurian and Carboniferous ones, there were no hard and fast differences between geological systems adjacent in the stratigraphical column. Phillips therefore coined a term, Palaeozoic, to cover all forms of life before the New Red Sandstone epoch; it subsumed Murchison's Silurian and Devonian systems, just as it expanded the meaning of the term Palaeozoic which Sedgwick had initially proposed to replace Murchison's neologism of Protozoic.[65] This sort of analysis was generalised by Phillips to embrace a triple division of all the strata into three great periods of organic life, the Palaeozoic, the Mesozoic and the Cainozoic.

Phillips' statistical palaeontology was the result of both debts incurred and frustrations endured. Positively, Phillips extended to animal fossils Adolphe Brongniart's statistical approach to fossil plants; and his obsession with long time spans, enshrined in his terminology of the Palaeozoic, Mesozoic and Cainozoic, roughly echoed that of Brongniart and three of the Frenchman's four distinct periods of plant life. In general, Phillips shared Brongniart's interest in ecological reconstruction of past climates, his belief in a cooling earth and his opposition to doctrinaire Lyellian uniformitarianism.[66] Negatively, Phillips was dissatisfied with Smith's and Murchison's palaeontology and with the free and easy way in which the latter created geological systems. These frustrations were apparent in his 1836 book on the carboniferous system, previously discussed, which had employed the second statistical method he used in 1841.[67] Moreover, Phillips used virtually the same zoological classes in 1841 as in 1836: in 1841 to show the degree of similarity between the lower Palaeozoic in Devon and Cornwall and the upper Palaeozoic; and in 1836 ditto for the Coal, Millstone Grit, Yoredale rocks and Lower Scar Limestone. The statistical tables of 1841 were generalised from the solitary table in the 1836 book. Such tables undermined the rigid division of strata into geological systems, a problem on which Phillips had long reflected. In an 1837 discussion of the Silurian system of Murchison, Phillips pointed out that it was based on no more than the study of Welsh border rocks and lacked the comparative and comprehensive element which the term system normally incorporated.[68] It was no more than a local and, therefore, limited generalisation. His other 1837 analysis was more explicit. For Phillips a system was a group of stratified rocks which had many characters in common. On this criterion he gave the status of a system to the oolitic and carboniferous without geographical limitation, but pointedly referred to the Silurian system, as it occurred on the border of Wales. Systems, in Phillips' view, had been erected on the basis of their characteristic fossils; but he knew that the number of these characteristic or '*monochromic*' fossils, as he called them, was continually diminishing and that their occurrence varied geographically. He had then concluded that in comparing distant regions only 'broader zoological features' ought to be employed. He knew, for instance, that the cretaceous systems of America and Europe had almost no characteristic fossils in common because of local physical differences. Here was the '*problem of contemporaneous differences*'.[69]

By 1840, Phillips had devised a solution to these related problems. He was by then convinced that the geographical range of any fossil species was limited and thus inadequate as an indicator of strata; that the geographical range of fossil genera was greater, but so was their geological range, so they, too, were inadequate as indicators of the geological age of strata; and that some strata, widely separated geographically but apparently contemporaneous, contained very few common fossils. Thus the use of so-called characteristic fossil species or of a few fossils of one genus was vitiated. But Smith's basic idea of fossil-labelling, if not Murchison's particular use of it, could be preserved if geologists used several species of characteristic groups to determine the 'combinations of organic life' which characterised each stratum.[70] In the tables in his *Palaeozoic Fossils*, Phillips offered a statistical embodiment of that insight. Similarly, the new meaning he had already given in 1840 to the occasionally used term 'Palaeozoic' reflected his long-established concern to identify systems of past life, not by characteristic species, but by what he called the preponderance of various zoological classes and families. In a further hit at Murchison, Phillips' category of 'lower Palaeozoic' competed directly with the term 'Protozoic', which Murchison had proposed to cover both the Silurian and Cambrian systems. This word proclaimed Murchison's belief that the Silurian and Cambrian were not only the oldest systems to contain fossils, but also that no life had existed before the Cambrian epoch. Phillips thought that 'Protozoic' was an inadequate term: it was ambiguous in relation to zoological protozoa; and it asserted more than was either necessary or known. He therefore adopted the acceptable term 'Palaeozoic', first used by Sedgwick as a synonym for Murchison's 'Protozoic'; but he extended it in 1840 to include the Old Red Sandstone and in 1841 to embrace the Carboniferous system and the Magnesian Limestone formation as well. Phillips thought the large and flexible meaning he attached to 'Palaeozoic' would not be vitiated by further research throughout Europe and time was to prove him right.[71]

Murchison's geological systems were named after areas where they were best represented, whereas Phillips' nomenclature avoided any reference to particular localities and referred only to periods of time elapsed. Murchison was outraged by this corrosive innovation by one of the two leaders of the Ordnance geological forces. By late 1841, Murchison had added a third 'ian' to his list of systems by coining the term 'Permian', so he was angry that Phillips' Palaeozoic classification gratified De La Beche by avoiding the word Devonian.[72] Not surprisingly, in his Presidential address to the Geological Society, delivered in February 1842, Murchison attacked Phillips' Palaeozoic nomenclature because it obliterated his own zealously promoted geological systems on which he had built his reputation. As he told Sedgwick, he gave Phillips his mind for cribbing the term Palaeozoic, for intolerable coxcombry in substituting lower Palaeozoic for Silurian, and for his intellectual colonialism in extending the term Palaeozoic. Murchison was so enraged that he broke off correspondence with Phillips for six months, peace being totally restored in 1843 when, in a deft quid pro quo between equals, Murchison accepted Phillips' wide definition of Palaeozoic in exchange for Phillips' public acceptance of the notion of a Devonian system.[73]

From early April to the end of December 1841, with a break for the British Association meeting at Plymouth, Phillips worked with the Survey in Pembrokeshire, confident that De La Beche would employ him for yet another year, finding errors in Murchison's map and section of the area, and exulting in the Survey's '*merry* company', which in June on Skomer Island provided the best day of his whole geological life. He was also buoyed up by the prospect of ultimately succeeding De La Beche.[74] For his part, De La Beche was so pleased with Phillips' performance, and with the work of Andrew Ramsay who had joined the Survey on 1 April 1841, that in October 1841 he began the lobbying which led the following month to the Prime Minister's agreement that for the financial year 1842–43 Phillips would be paid as part of the regular Survey expenditure for that year, and not as in 1841–42 from unexpended Ordnance funds of previous years. Phillips' fourth type of connection with the Survey put him in what might be called a tacitly permanent position, authorised by no less than Robert Peel, who became Prime Minister in September 1841 and who, in contrast with Melbourne, his predecessor, was well disposed towards science. De La Beche was so concerned to secure Phillips for the Survey that he approached Peel through two intermediaries: the first was William Vernon Harcourt, Phillips' chief York patron; the second was William Buckland, Reader in geology at Oxford and Peel's scientific adviser. Both were deputed to argue that all that was being asked for was a regularisation of the way Phillips would be paid, without any increase in his salary of £300 per annum for eight months' work. Buckland and Harcourt wrote to Peel within three days of each other, Buckland stressing that if Phillips were *de facto* to be dismissed from the Survey it would be a great public loss and a calamity to geology. By 8 November 1841, Peel had resolved that the Survey estimates for 1842–43 should not be curtailed, thus making the posts of Phillips and Ramsay tacitly permanent though formally renewable each year. Peel had taken the matter into his own hands, had given his personal imprimatur to the Survey, and had secured Phillips' future with it. De La Beche at last had a quasi-permanent fossilist on the Survey and promptly celebrated by securing Phillips' election to the Athenaeum in February 1842.[75]

There is something to be said for the view that, in contrast with the tradition of men of leisure devoted to geology for a lifetime but not a livelihood, the Geological Survey was a professional enterprise. Phillips himself regarded it as 'truly national labour' which rendered the work of Murchison inadequate; and he praised the standards of minuteness and accuracy attained by the Survey at the expense of the necessarily hurried way in which what he called 'gentlemen geologists' examined an area.[76] It is therefore tempting to assume that, *qua* a professional body, the Survey recruited its staff according to formal bureaucratic procedures. This was not so. As in France, personal approaches and negotiations, involving patrons and clients, were the order of the day.[77] De La Beche's indirect approach to no less than the Prime Minister in 1841 shows that he was not prepared to let his case stand merely on its merits; instead of going through the bureaucratic mills of the Ordnance and the Treasury, initially he side-stepped them and exploited the services of two men who had considerable personal pull with Peel. De La Beche realised that nothing came to him as an indisputable right, but only as a result of making interest in the right quarters at the appropriate time; hence he was occasionally importunate, the most unfortunate example being his unsuccessful manoeuvres late in 1842 to replace Richard Phillips by Lyon Playfair as chemist in the Museum of Economic Geology, a 'job' which Peel refused to countenance.

Compared with Airy, the Astronomer Royal, De La Beche rarely acted as a hatchet man for the Treasury: there seems to be no equivalent in De La Beche's career to Airy telling the Chancellor in 1842 that after mature consideration he deemed Babbage's calculating machine to be worthless and not worth spending government money on.[78] Instead De La Beche was a master of assembling his geological empire by edging forward bit by bit. In gaining and dispensing patronage, he usually avoided impulsive saltatory action. Nothing in the early history of the Survey shows this better than the way in which, during a period of six years, De La Beche employed Phillips on no fewer than four different bases in order to achieve the ultimate aim of enjoying his services as palaeontologist to it. This incremental mode of expanding the Survey enabled him to exploit the tactics of the thin end of the wedge and to transform his enterprise by appealing to established precedent. Under De La Beche, the Survey disturbed the dominance previously exerted by the gentlemanly clerisy within the Geological Society of London. The Survey brought into sharp focus questions relating to geological conduct, property, careers *and* knowledge. De La Beche was not merely a successful empire-builder who loved large national institutions *per se*: his Survey encouraged certain types of work, as the changing relations between Phillips and Murchison make clear. More generally, this case-study of the early Geological Survey instantiates the novel thesis that has been recently well argued by

Bourne, namely, that patronage permeated Victorian England and that it made an important contribution to both the tenacity and the flexibility of institutions.[79]

Acknowledgements

For valuable comments, I am indebted to Martin Rudwick and James Secord. For permission to cite or refer to manuscripts, I am grateful to: the Curator and Assistant Curator of the Geological Collections, University Museum, Oxford (Phillips Papers, cited as PP); the Keeper, Department of Geology, National Museum of Wales (De La Beche Papers, cited as DLB P); the Keeper of Manuscripts, Cambridge University Library (Sedgwick Papers, cited as Se P); the British Geological Survey (Institute of Geological Sciences Archives); the National Library of Ireland, Dublin (Monteagle Papers); the Library, Trinity College, Cambridge (Whewell Papers); the Library, American Philosophical Society, Philadelphia (Lyell Papers); the Yorkshire Philosophical Society; and the College Secretary, King's College, London (King's College Archives). The research on which this chapter is based has been greatly facilitated by a grant from the Royal Society of London, by a Visiting Fellowship at Brasenose College, Oxford, for the Michaelmas term 1985, and by the University of Bradford which granted me study leave for that term.

NOTES

1. For US geological surveys, see W. B. Hendrickson, 'Nineteenth-century state geological surveys: early government support of science', *Isis*, LII (1961) pp. 357–71; for France, V.A. Eyles, 'The first national geological survey', *Geological Magazine*, LXXXVII (1950) pp. 373–82.
2. On MacCulloch's financial malversation see: V.A. Eyles, 'John MacCulloch, FRS, and his geological map: an account of the first geological survey of Scotland', *Annals of Science*, II (1937) pp. 114–29; and 'Mineralogical Survey of Scotland. Account showing the several payments constituting the sums of £959/18/6d and £3,124/9/7d as expenses ... also of £3,000 expenses ... in the year 1828 and 1829 ...', *Parliamentary Papers*, XIV (1830–31) pp. 53–83. This return was made in February 1831 on behalf of the Treasury by Thomas Spring-Rice, Chancellor of the Exchequer 1835–39.
3. Authoritative accounts are: G.L. Herries Davies, *Sheets of Many*

Colours: The Mapping of Ireland's Rocks 1750–1890 (Dublin: Royal Dublin Society, 1983); Davies and R.C. Mollan (eds), *Richard Griffith 1784–1878* (Dublin: Royal Dublin Society, 1980); and J.H. Andrews, *A Paper Landscape: the Ordnance Survey in Nineteenth-century Ireland* (Oxford: Clarendon Press, 1975).

4. A. Geikie, *Life of Sir Roderick Murchison*, vol. II (London, 1875) pp. 180, 193–4.

5. The standard books are: J.S. Flett, *The First Hundred Years of the Geological Survey of Great Britain* (London: HM Stationery Office, 1937); E. Bailey, *Geological Survey of Great Britain* (London: Murby, 1952); A. Geikie, *Memoir of Sir A.C. Ramsay* (London: Macmillan, 1895); and P.J. McCartney, *Henry De La Beche: Observations on an Observer* (Cardiff: Friends of the National Museum of Wales, 1977).

6. F.J. North, 'Further chapters in the history of geology in South Wales; Sir H.T. Da La Beche and the Geological Survey', *Transactions of the Cardiff Naturalists' Society*, LXVII (1934) pp. 31–103 (46).

7. M.J.S. Rudwick, *The Great Devonian Controversy: The Shaping of Scientific Knowledge among Gentlemanly Specialists* (Chicago and London: University of Chicago Press, 1985).

8. For Lyell's non-venal careerist concerns, see J.B. Morrell, 'London institutions and Lyell's career: 1820–41', *British Journal for the History of Science*, IX (1976) pp. 132–46.

9. Sedgwick to Spring-Rice, 28 October 1836, Monteagle Papers 13382; Rudwick, *Devonian*, p. 176.

10. J. Phillips, *Illustrations of the Geology of Yorkshire; or, a Description of the Strata and Organic Remains of the Yorkshire Coast* (York: Wilson, 1829); Phillips, *Illustrations of the Geology of Yorkshire. Part II. The Mountain Limestone District* (London: Murray, 1836).

11. For De La Beche's 1835 classification of West European fossiliferous rocks, see his *How to Observe. Geology* (London: Knight, 1835) pp. 13–16.

12. De La Beche, *How to Observe*, pp. 16–19, 23–5, 220–1, 238–9, 306–7.

13. Phillips to De La Beche, 1 April 1835, DLB P; Rudwick, *Devonian*, pp. 121–3. For De La Beche's interest in reconstructing ancient environments, see J.A. Secord, 'The Geological Survey of Great Britain as a Research School, 1839–1855', *History of Science*, XXIV (1986) pp. 223–75 (241–51).

14. P.D. Hardy, *Proceedings of the Fifth Meeting of the British Association for the Advancement of Science, held in Dublin ... August 1835* (Dublin: Hardy, 1835), p. 108. For the Silurian and Cambrian systems, see the authoritative J.A. Secord, *Controversy in Victorian Geology: the Cambrian–Silurian Dispute* (Princeton: Princeton University Press, 1986).

15. Phillips, 'Geology', in *Encyclopaedia Metropolitana*, vol. VI (London: Fellows and Rivington, 1845), pp. 529–808 (533–4). This article was published separately in 1835.

16. Phillips, *Limestone*, pp. 11–12, 15, 18, 35, 58, 175–7, 194–5, and plate XXIV, the three sections and diagram 24. Subscribers' copies of this book were dated March 1836. Rudwick, *Devonian*, pp. 146–7, stresses

the originality of Phillips' work on lateral variation of strata.

17. Phillips, *Limestone*, p. 244.

18. Phillips, *A Guide to Geology*, 3rd edn (London: Longman, 1836) pp. 73–4, stressed that 'a judicious examination of a sufficient number of organic contents' was a desideratum.

19. Phillips to De La Beche, 1 April 1835, DLB P. They had first established contact by correspondence in 1830 when De La Beche tapped Phillips' knowledge of fossils: Phillips to De La Beche, 30 January and 13 March 1830, DLB P.

20. M.J.S. Rudwick, 'Caricature as a source for the history of science: De La Beche's anti-Lyellian sketches of 1831', *Isis*, LXVI (1975), pp. 534–60.

21. Secord, 'Geological Survey', pp. 244–5.

22. Phillips, 'Notice of a Newly Discovered Tertiary Deposit on the Coast of Yorkshire', *Philosophical Magazine*, VII (1835) p. 486.

23. L.G. Wilson, *Charles Lyell. The Years to 1841: the Revolution in Geology* (New Haven and London: Yale University Press, 1972) p. 469; E. Charlesworth, 'Observations on the Crag, and on the Fallacies involved in the Present System of Classification of Tertiary Deposits', *Philosophical Magazine* X (1837) pp. 1–9; Phillips to Charlesworth, 7 December 1835, British Library Add Ms 37951, f. 38.

24. K. M. Lyell (ed.), *Life, Letters and Journals of Sir Charles Lyell* (London: Murray, 1881) vol. I, pp. 450, 458; vol. II, p. 40; Wilson, *Lyell*, pp. 453–6.

25. By late 1836, Phillips' *Guide* had reached a third edition, 1st edn 1834, 2nd edn 1835. Lyell retaliated with *Elements of Geology* (London: Murray, July 1838).

26. Phillips, *A Treatise on Geology, forming the Article under that Head in the Seventh Edition of the Encyclopaedia Britannica* (Edinburgh: Black, 1837) pp. 169–70, 179–84.

27. Phillips, *Treatise on Geology*, vol. I (London: Longman and Taylor, 1837) pp. 249–52. This work was part of Lardner's *Cabinet Cyclopaedia*.

28. *Treatise* (Edinburgh) pp. 259–61, 270.

29. Phillips, *Treatise on Geology*, vol. II (London: Longman and Taylor, 1839) pp. 253, 264–6, 273–8, 240 (quote).

30. Phillips, 'Geology' in *The Penny Cyclopaedia of the Society for the Diffusion of Useful Knowledge*, vol. XI (1838) pp. 127–151 (132–41, 135 quote). With John Kenrick Phillips then constituted the York local committee of the SDUK.

31. *Treatise* (Edinburgh), pp. 252–3. Phillips' opposition to Lyell slots well into the interpretation of M.J. Bartholomew, 'The singularity of Lyell', *History of Science*, XVII (1979) pp. 276–93.

32. De La Beche to Colby, 26 December 1836 (quote), 25 April 1837, Ordnance Survey Letters relating to the Geological Survey, Institute of Geological Sciences, London, GSM 1/68.

33. Phillips to De La Beche, 26 January 1839, DLB P.

34. For a vignette of Phillips' career, see J. B. Morrell and A. W. Thackray, *Gentlemen of Science: Early Years of the British Association for the Advancement of Science* (Oxford: Clarendon Press, 1981) pp. 439–44.

35. Rudwick, *Devonian*, pp. 166–8.
36. De La Beche to Phillips, 6 November 1836, 21 and 31 May 1837; Murchison to Phillips, 3 April 1837, all PP.
37. De La Beche to Phillips, 3 June 1837, PP; Phillips, 'Geology' in *Encyclopaedia Metropolitana*, p. 534.
38. De La Beche, *Report on the Geology of Cornwall, Devon and West Somerset. Published by Order of the Lords Commissioners of Her Majesty's Treasury. Printed for Her Majesty's Stationery Office* (London: Longman, 1839) henceforth cited as *1839 Report*; De La Beche to Phillips, 29 October 1837, 13 November 1837, 12 December 1837, 5 and 19 February 1838, PP.
39. De La Beche to Phillips, 13 November 1837, PP quoting verbatim Phillips to De La Beche, 4 November 1837, DLB P.
40. On the voluntary help of Logan, who became first Director of the Geological Survey of Canada in 1842, see B.J. Harrington, *Life of Sir William Logan* (Montreal: Dawson, 1883) pp. 52–5, 59–71, 127–31.
41. De La Beche to Phillips, 26 and 30 July 1838, PP.
42. Phillips, *Figures and Descriptions of the Palaeozoic Fossils of Cornwall, Devon and West Somerset; Observed in the Ordnance Geological Survey of that District. Published by Order of the Lords Commissioners of Her Majesty's Treasury* (London: Longman, 1841) hence cited as *Palaeozoic Fossils*.
43. Phillips to De La Beche, 6 March 1838, DLB P.
44. De La Beche to Sedgwick, 12 March 1838, Se P, IC4; De La Beche draft to Treasury, 17 March 1838, PP; De La Beche to Phillips, 16 April 1838, PP.
45. De La Beche to Phillips, 5 August 1838, PP; De La Beche to Colby, 27 August 1838, from Edinburgh, Ordnance Letters, GSM 1/68. De La Beche was paid nothing for this commission work because he was already employed by government: Baring to Commissioners of Woods and Forests, 11 August 1838, Correspondence to the Director General, 1836–47, Institute of Geological Sciences, GSM 1/12.
46. Phillips to Ann Phillips, 9, 21 (quote) and 28 August 1838, PP.
47. Murchison, *The Silurian Sytem* (London: Murray, 1839) pp. XXVII, 4, 13, 15, 49–50, 86–9, 160–1, 244–7, 339, 580–1, 586, 648, 671–5, 703, 730. Phillips, *Guide*, 3rd edn., pp. 167–72 mischievously referred to field-work with Murchison in September 1836 near Ludlow in giving details of a calculation to correct the strike and dip of any joint-plane for any tilt of the strata. His geological intersector, designed for geologists (such as Murchison) who could not calculate, gave directly the corrected values of direction and dip of joint-planes. For Murchison's denigration of himself in 1836 in comparison with Phillips, see Geikie, *Murchison*, vol. I, pp. 232–3.
48. Murchison to Whewell, 7 February 1839, Whewell Papers, a.209[101]. For a telling account of this 1839 battle of the books, see Rudwick, *Devonian*, pp. 259–72.
49. De La Beche, *1839 Report*, pp. 136–8, 153–4.
50. Phillips to Ann Phillips, 22 and 23 February 1839, PP.
51. Murchison to Sedgwick, 22 February 1839, Se P, III D.9.

52. Phillips to Ann Phillips, 1 March 1839, PP.
53. Sedgwick and Murchison, 'Classification of the older stratified rocks of Devonshire and Cornwall', *Philosophical Magazine*, XIV (April 1839), pp. 241–260 (this article, dated 25 March 1839, is brilliantly analysed in Rudwick, *Devonian*, pp. 280–7); Phillips to Ann Phillips, 28 March 1839, PP.
54. For the SDUK map, see Rudwick, *Devonian*, pp. 257–9 and for its place in Phillips' mapping *oeuvre* see J.A. Douglas and J.M. Edmonds, 'John Phillips' geological maps of the British Isles', *Annals of Science* VI (1950) pp. 361–75; Sedgwick and Murchison, 'Classification', 257 (note); De La Beche to Phillips, 9 April 1839, PP.
55. Phillips, 'Remarks on a Note in Prof. Sedgwick and Mr Murchison's Communication in the last number', *Philosophical Magazine*, XIV (May 1839) pp. 353–4, dated 11 April 1839; Phillips to Sedgwick, 16 April 1839, Se P, IB 192; Murchison to Sedgwick, 16 April 1839, Se P, IIID. 26. Phillips' 'Remarks' are corroborated by De La Beche to Phillips, 7 April 1838, PP.
56. De La Beche to Phillips, 26 May 1839, 23 June 1839, PP; Phillips to De La Beche, 26 June 1839, DLB P.
57. Glennie to Phillips, 2 Aug 1839, Outgoing Letter Book 1834–43; King's College Council Minutes, vol. C, 1836–42, 8 November 1839; Phillips to Lonsdale, 6 August 1839, Incoming Letters, all King's College London Archives.
58. J. Phillips, *Memoirs of William Smith* (London: Murray, 1844) pp. 123–4; De La Beche to Phillips, 18 September 1839, PP.
59. De La Beche to Phillips, 25 March 1840, PP.
60. De La Beche to Phillips, 10 April, 3 May, 4 and 15 October, 22 November, 10, 23, 24 December 1840; J.R. MacCulloch of HMSO to Phillips, 1 December 1840, all PP.
61. De La Beche to R.H. Vivian, 27 January 1841; Colby to F.W. Mulcaster, 6 February 1841; R. Byham to Mulcaster, 17 February 1841; Colby to De La Beche, 23 February 1841, all in Ordnance Letters, GSM 1/68; De La Beche to Phillips, 23 December 1840, PP; Phillips to De La Beche, 19 February 1841, DLB P.
62. Phillips to De La Beche, 6, 20, 27 April, 16 June, 20 October 1840, 30 January 1841 (quote), DLB P; Phillips to Ann Phillips, 17 September, 20 October 1840, PP.
63. The cost of printing 754 copies was £234/17s/6d; by late 1843, 207 copies had been sold at 6/- each. If published commercially, *Palaeozoic Fossils* would have sold for about £1: 'Report of the Commissioners Appointed to Enquire into the Facts relating to the Ordnance Memoir of Ireland', *Parliamentary Papers*, XXX (1844) pp. 259–385 (266).
64. Rudwick, *Devonian*, pp. 371–5; Secord, *Controversy*, pp. 132–4, 140–2; Phillips, *Palaeozoic Fossils*, p. xi; Murchison, *Silurian Sytem*, pp. 13, 581–2.
65. *Palaeozoic Fossils*, pp. 160–7.
66. A. Brongniart, *Prodrome d'une Histoire des Végétaux Fossiles* (Paris and Strasbourg: Levrault, 1828) esp. the table on p. 219 which showed the number of species in each of six classes of plants for each of five

geological epochs, the last being the present; M.J.S. Rudwick, *The Meaning of Fossils*, 2nd edn (Chicago and London: Chicago University Press, 1976) pp. 146–9, 180–1. For Lyell's statistical palaeontology, revealed in vol. iii of his *Principles of Geology* in 1833, see Rudwick, 'Charles Lyell's dream of a statistical palaeontology', *Palaeontology*, XXI (1978) pp. 225–44. For Phillips' view of Adolphe Brongniart as the statistical pioneer, see Phillips 'Geology', *Encyclopaedia Metropolitana*, pp. 548–9; 'Organic Remains', *Penny Cyclopaedia*, XVI (1840) pp. 487–91 (487).

67. Compare the tables in *Mountain Limestone*, p. 244 and *Palaeozoic Fossils*, p. 166.

68. Phillips, *Treatise* (London) pp. 137–9.

69. Phillips, *Treatise* (Edinburgh) vol. I, pp. 37–9, 136–9 (138 quote), 156–7 (157 quote). The italics were Phillips'.

70. 'Organic Remains', *Penny Cyclopaedia*, p. 491.

71. Phillips, 'Palaeozoic', *Penny Cyclopaedia*, XVII (1840) pp. 153–4. Murchison's 'Protozoic', first suggested orally in spring 1838, appeared in print in 1839 in *Silurian System*, p. 11; Sedgwick's 'Palaeozoic' appeared in print in Sedgwick, 'A synopsis of the English series of stratified rocks inferior to the old red sandstone', *Proceedings of the Geological Society of London*, II (1838), pp. 675–85 (685).

72. Murchison to Lyell, 1 December 1841, Lyell Papers, American Philosophical Society Library, Philadelphia.

73. Murchison, *Proceedings of the Geological Society of London*, III (1842) pp. 637–87 (647–9); Murchison to Sedgwick, 26 February 1842, Se P, IID.36; Phillips to De La Beche, 14 December 1841, 27 May [1842], DLB P. On the *rapprochement* between Phillips and Murchison, see Rudwick, *Devonian*, pp. 371–5, 382, 385–6, 389, 392–3.

74. Phillips to Ann Phillips, 6, 8, 15 June (quote), 14 November 1841, PP.

75. De La Beche to Phillips, 25 October 1841, Harcourt Papers; Phillips to Harcourt, 26 October 1841 reproduced in E.W. Harcourt (ed.), *The Harcourt Papers*, vol. XIV (Oxford: Parker, n.d.) pp. 133–6; Phillips to De La Beche, 26 October 1841, DLB P; De La Beche to Buckland, 1 November 1841, British Library Add Mss, 40494, ff. 9–12; Buckland to Peel, 4 November 1841, BL 40494, f. 7; Harcourt to Peel, 6 November 1841, BL 40494, ff. 85–8; Peel to Buckland, 8 November 1841, BL 40494, f. 13; Phillips to De La Beche, 8 November 1841, DLB P; Phillips to Ann Phillips, 8 November 1841, PP; Peel to Harcourt, 10 November 1841, BL 40494, f. 89; Harcourt to Phillips, 12 November 1841, PP; Phillips to De La Beche, 15 and 23 February 1842, DLB P.

76. Phillips, *Treatise* (London), vol. II, p. 297; Phillips, talk on the Geological Survey, 6 March 1843, to evening meeting of Yorkshire Philosophical Society: YPS evening meetings minute book, 1839–48.

77. For a forceful account of the centrality in France of power, politics, vocation and authority, see D. Outram, *George Cuvier: Vocation, Science and Authority in Post-revolutionary France* (Manchester: Manchester University Press, 1984). For a hint that the concern with professionalisation is somewhat *passé*, see J.B. Morrell, 'Professionalisation', in G.N. Cantor, J.R.R. Christie, M.J.S. Hodge and R.C. Olby

(eds), *Companion to the History of Modern Science* (Beckenham: Croom Helm, 1988) forthcoming.

78. W. Airy (ed.), *Autobiography of Sir George Biddell Airy* (Cambridge: Cambridge University Press, 1896) p. 152.

79. J. Bourne, *Patronage and Society in Nineteenth-century England* (London: Arnold, 1986).

3 Science and the Public Good: George Biddell Airy (1801–92) and the Concept of a Scientific Civil Servant

Allan Chapman

Over the last three centuries, successive British governments have found it necessary to seek scientific and technical advice for the welfare of the nation. The first, and longest-standing, acknowledgement of this fact came in 1675, when Charles II founded the Royal Observatory, Greenwich, through which it was hoped that an astronomical solution to the longitude at sea might be found, to bring major advantages to the civil and military naval forces of England.[1] Scientific advice remained essentially military in character for the next 150 years, and while bodies such as the Royal Observatory, Board of Longitude and Ordnance Survey initiated independent 'philosophical' contributions, the formal advice which they rendered to the Crown still aimed at success in war.

By the early years of the nineteenth century, however, Britain's rapidly industrialising economy often found the legislature ill-prepared to deal with a wide range of technical subjects. Sporadic advice could still be obtained from eminent private gentlemen, such as Davy, Faraday or Buckland, though the pressure of business made this source of information inadequate. Faced with a range of technical problems which embraced coal gas regulation, railway gauges, telegraphy and cholera, Parliament was coming to need regular experts.

Statesmen like Robert Peel were aware of the value of science to government, though the sciences considered were seen only in their public, utilitarian contexts. Even sciences of great industrial potential, such as chemistry and engineering, or intellectually far-reaching ones like palaeontology, were left to private patronage. The greater part of science, ornamental to the nation as it might be, was considered no more suitable as a burden to the taxpayer than was art or music.

By the 1830s, however, a number of new departments had come into being. Captain Francis Beaufort had been made Government Hydrographer in 1829, Colonel Henry Sabine's recommendations for monitoring terrestrial magnetism received official backing, while

General Thomas Colby's Ordnance Survey Department was extended to include the Geological Survey, under Henry De La Beche, in 1835.[2] Most of these new scientific departments, however, were the brainchildren of retired senior military officers, and tended to retain aspects of armed forces' attitudes and protocols. Their directors, no matter how capable or hard-working, enjoyed the assured social rank, independent means and honourable perquisites of ex-Napoleonic fighting men, and saw themselves as adjuncts to government, rather than employees of it.

The Royal Observatory, on the other hand, was already an old institution, with established duties, and a Board of Visitors to keep its director in order. Unlike his colleagues in these new departments, moreover, George Biddell Airy, upon assuming office as Astronomer Royal in 1835, was neither financially independent, nor the senior member of an ancient profession, such as the Church or Armed Forces. His success could stand only on his achievements in the still somewhat nebulous profession of science, and having no pension or perquisites to fall back upon was more inclined to consider himself as a publicly accountable state employee. These circumstances, combined with his immense passion for the accumulation and dissemination of useful knowledge, made Airy into what might reasonably be considered the British government's first full-time scientific advisor.

Though the seventh man to hold the office of Astronomer Royal, Airy represented a new breed both of scientist and public servant. With the exception of Edmond Halley, who had entered office as a distinguished sixty-four year old, Airy was the first Astronomer Royal not to be in Holy Orders. Unlike most Cambridge dons without independent means, he fiercely resisted the pressures to become ordained, and demanded a profession which could support him without fulfilling religious duties.

For the previous 150 years, the government had maintained its Observatory on a shoestring basis, originally giving the Astronomer Royal a virtually nominal stipend – initially fixed at £100 per year – in expectation that these gentlemen, as former Oxbridge dons would either possess, or be eligible for, substantial ecclesiastical sinecures with which to subsidise their astronomical work. This had been the practice commenced by John Flamsteed in the 1680s, whose 'autumn fruits', received from his absentee Rectory of Burstow, combined with inherited wealth, had financed most of his forty-four year term at Greenwich. Not only were these salaries nominal, but adequate assistant staff was not provided by the government, and the first five Astronomers Royal muddled through with the assistance of pupils, friends and privately-hired hands.[3]

Considering these conditions, it is hardly surprising that these Astronomers did not regard themselves as 'Civil Servants', but private clerical gentlemen in nominal public office, whose observations and researches could be removed from the Observatory and privately bequeathed after death. Much of Airy's spare time over several years of his office, was spent in tracking down and obtaining duplicates of the manuscripts of his predecessors to establish the Observatory's historical archive.[4]

Like Herschel, Playfair and Babbage, Airy belonged to that first generation of British scientific men who refused automatic ordination, and demanded realistic professional returns from a scientific life.[5] Upon his appointment to the Directorship of the Cambridge University Observatory, in 1828, and then as Astronomer Royal in 1835, Airy extracted, for the first time, realistic salaries for these posts. As Astronomer Royal, he obtained a 25 per cent increase upon that of his predecessor, the Revd John Pond, to obtain £800 per annum with a separate £300 annual Civil List pension for his wife, along with a residence. In return for these substantial financial increases, Airy was willing to place the whole of his working life at the disposal of the state, and the vast technical and administrative minutiae which that involved.[6]

It was Airy's love of data collection which resulted in the enormous archive of his papers now on deposit at the Royal Greenwich Observatory, Herstmonceux. Airy's diligence produced a carefully organised personal and professional archive, which runs from his early Cambridge days, to the age of ninety, and could well rank as the most thoroughly recorded scientific life available. The manuscripts are arranged under 765 separate heads, while most of these heads contain many score of individual documents, including duplicates of most of his letters. In addition to the manuscripts, there are 518 printed publications, spanning a range from articles and reports to full length books. Only a part of this massive collection has been critically examined, or even read at all, though a mere glance at its many divisions reveals a rich source of information about the scientific and administrative history of Victorian England.[7]

Though Airy came to be involved in advising the government on a wide range of non-astronomical subjects, the Royal Observatory was, and remained, the centre of operations during his forty-six year official career, and a review of his functions as Astronomer Royal is an essential preliminary to understanding his work elsewhere. Fortunately, this part of his work is easily accessible in the published *Reports* which he submitted to the Observatory's governing Board of Visitors, at their inspection in June each year.

Airy's first priority, upon assuming office in June, 1835, was to rescue the Royal Observatory from the decline into which it had passed during the latter years of Pond.[8] As well as the important technical and administrative changes which this involved, Airy brought to the office a new sense of what the Observatory *should* do in the nation at large. In addition to fulfilling the original Royal Warrant functions of the Greenwich Observatory – the provision of astronomical data to the navy for the 'perfecting of navigation'[9] – he saw that the great expansion of science since 1675 should be spearheaded by his Royal foundation. He saw himself 'not as a mere Director of Greenwich Observatory, but ... as British Astronomer', with a pre-eminent and virtually supervisory mandate over all official science.[10] Though always careful to maintain the Observatory's practical function, agreeing with his superiors that theoretical researches should be left in private hands, he constantly sought ways in which to improve that role. Very early in his tenure, this led to the founding of non-astronomical departments of the Observatory; the monitoring of geomagnetic phenomena for its effects upon marine compasses, and the collection of meteorological observations to determine the possible correlation between weather patterns and the Registrar General's tables of epidemic mortalities.[11]

As the meridian astronomy in which Greenwich specialised lay at the foundation of all accurate timekeeping, Airy never ceased in his attempts to make standard time available first to the navy, then the merchant marine, and by the 1850s, the nation in general. In hindsight, it was probably in this timekeeping role that Airy and the Royal Observatory most clearly came to influence the lives of ordinary people in the nineteenth century.[12]

Time signals were originally made available to the shipping on the Thames by the mechanically operated time ball, erected by Pond in 1833, though with the invention of electric relay clocks, and the growth of the commercial telegraphic network by the 1850s, it was Airy's inspired innovation to transmit daily time signals to docks, Post Offices and railway stations, and eventually impose Greenwich Mean Time upon the various local time zones within the country.

The concept of a national time signal was far-reaching. It brought regularity to the planning of east–west-bound train timetables, meaning that Brunel's Penzance expresses ran from Paddington in accordance with a single time rating, rather than having to synchronise with Swindon, Bristol and Exeter local times. Even legal actions came to be fought concerning the official primacy of GMT before its statutory adoption in 1880.[13]

With the growth of submarine telegraphy, after the cross-Channel and Atlantic links in the 1850s, Airy exchanged time signals with the leading foreign observatories, whereby he determined their longitudes in relation to Greenwich.[14] This was to become internationally significant, as Greenwich imposed itself as the adopted zero longitude on world maps, and led more than anything else to the eventual recognition of the Royal Observatory as the arbiter of the International Date Line, in 1884.[15]

In reforming both instrumentation and staff skills, Airy developed another major international feature of the Royal Observatory; as principal custodian of standards in celestial cartography and measurement. In some ways, this lay implicit in the Royal Observatory's Warrant conditions, but with typical zeal, Airy expanded upon the idea. In many respects, Airy was less a pure scientist, and more an engineer, and by the time that he was thirty had come to enjoy an international eminence in the fields of optics and instrumentation. It was Airy's technical genius which made it possible for him to work so well with engineers and electricians, to turn Greenwich into the world's most advanced physical observatory. He redesigned the whole instrumentation along original lines, and also pioneered observer error analysis which he continued to refine through a range of 'galvanic' and photographic self-recording instruments, which placed relatively little stress upon the observer's personal skill.[16] Another aspect of Airy's concern with impersonally accurate data lay in his devising certain office practices at Greenwich, to render both the recording and retrieval of information as mechanical as possible. Even during his Directorship of the Cambridge University Observatory, he had introduced 'skeleton forms' into which the observer could enter details of an observation with the least confusion and, by 1836, they had become standard at Greenwich.[17] Over the years, moreover, he implemented an ingenious system for the filing of all Observatory documents. This depended on placing the papers in an 'extensive system of subdivided portfolios' in accordance with 'an invariable system of holes'. When strings were passed through specific holes, the correct papers could be immediately located.[18] He was willing to go to great lengths not to lose a single figure or detail, and sought a system which was as foolproof as human clerks could make it.

As a consequence of these practices, the Royal Observatory's positions for the heavenly bodies (and, in particular, the positions of the Moon, the motions of which he saw as lying at the heart of physical astronomy), formed an acknowledged standard of excellence. Thorough in all things, Airy realised that such excellence should be available to all who wanted it, in consequence of which, he became the first Astronomer Royal to tabulate, reduce and publish the Greenwich Observations on an annual basis. This was especially important during the first quarter century of his office, when most world observatories lagged behind Greenwich in such matters, and the fame of Greenwich standards can be seen in the fact that both Urbain Leverrier in Paris and John Couch Adams in Cambridge applied to Airy for positional data in their independent investigations for the unknown planet Neptune in 1845–46. In everything which Airy said or did, one traces the essential Baconian thread. Scientific knowledge, by its very nature, was to be made public and easy of access, and if the 'British Astronomer' could make it more so than the French, Germans or Americans, then such was the kudos of his foundation.[19]

Considering the energy which Airy invested into the purely astronomical side of his office, it is surprising to see how deeply involved he came to be in the non-astronomical claims which the state placed upon him. Only one of these non-astronomical claims, moreover, did he seem to resent, and that was a claim which was an already established Observatory function before he became Astronomer Royal: the testing and rating of government chronometers.[20] When one considers the limited technical resources on which the British government operated in the early nineteenth century, however, it is hardly surprising that the Royal Observatory should have been selected as the place where essential maritime objects be tested before commissioning into warships. In Airy's opinion, the growing number of chronometers on trial took men away from essential astronomical work, and because of its routine nature 'degraded [the Observatory] into a mere bureau of clerks'.[21] During the early years of his office, there were generally around one hundred chronometers on trial, the management of which, in 1841, was said to consume one third 'of our whole strength'. Though the Admiralty provided him with more staff, they repeatedly failed to relieve him of the burden, in spite of his regular reminders in the annual Reports, for in 1881, the year of his retirement, there were still 237 chronometers in his care.[22] Airy's handling of the unwanted chronometer burden is significant in so far as it indicates an awareness of his position as a senior Civil Servant. He would never *complain* to their Lordships, but constantly highlight the drain on resources which it occasioned, and thereby use it to gain concessions elsewhere.

What is surprising is the wide range of technical matters upon which the Crown came to consult Airy, and one can only assume that his willingness and versatility had much to do with it. His first non-astronomical involvement, the Weights and Measures Commission, came almost as soon as he was in office, in 1835. The disastrous fire which destroyed the Palace of Westminster in 1834 also destroyed the Parliamentary Standards of Weights and Measures which were traditionally housed there. Though duplicates were available, Airy came to be variously involved in the replacement of the Official Standards, partly through his reputation concerning matters of instrumentation, and partly through his friendship with Richard Sheepshanks, the leading expert on standards. Yet even after the new Standards had been made, and duplicates lodged at Greenwich, Airy's interest led to his involvement in many matters of weights, measures and currency, which was to extend across the rest of his career. With the public use of science forever before him, he next had bronze Standards of length set into the Observatory wall, so that citizens could test their rulers against an Official Standard.[23]

In total, Airy served upon, or gave advice to at least three dozen Commissions and Inquiries of a non-astronomical character during his forty-six years in public life.[24] Though at first sight they seem to cover an extraordinary range of subjects, he was generally involved through some aspect of mechanics or engineering. On other occasions, as in his involvement with the Coinage Commission of 1853, where he advised Gladstone on the possible decimal division of the pound sterling, his consultation derived from his acknowledged expertise in weights and measures.[25]

Airy's knowledge of the tides, his interest in the physics of waves and their effect upon structures made him an obvious consultant in the design of docks, tidal harbours,[26] breakwaters[27] and lighthouses.[28] It was partly because of his fame as an engineer, and partly because of his personal knowledge as a Greenwich resident, that he came to be involved in the Metropolitan Sewers Commission in 1848.[29] His standing as a physical scientist and instrument expert brought him into further consultation on the optical design of lighthouse beacons, the warranting of nautical telescopes,[30] the scientific training of naval officers[31] and the monitoring of the sale of coal gas.[32] His educational interests and wish to broaden existing curricula brought him into investigations of the ancient universities, religious tests for the new University of London,[33] and the public schools.[34]

Airy also came to be involved in several ways with the completion of Barry's new Westminster Palace, which replaced the one destroyed in the fire of 1834.[35] He was consulted about the Palace's smoky chimneys, though it was his status as a scientific horologist which involved him in the design of the 'Westminster Clock', soon to be known as 'Big Ben'. This crowning glory of the new Palace was destined to become the public time signal *par excellence*, the timepiece by which Parliament was to regulate its business, and politically significant in every sense. Involved since its inception in 1845, Airy demanded a seemingly impossible specification which would produce chronometer-accuracy from a movement the size of a railway engine. Though the subject of fierce controversies, when finally it came into service in 1859, its one second per day accuracy, monitored by electric signals from the Royal Observatory, made it a triumph.[36] Assiduous in all things, Airy even consulted a professional musician about the tone of the bells.

The use of iron as a shipbuilding material, and the effect of iron hulls upon ships' compasses was another problem which the Astronomer Royal was invited to investigate, and to which he was to make contributions of a fundamental nature. In 1838, Airy began trials on board a small iron vessel, the *Rainbow*, moored in the Thames, and determined from an exemplary set of experiments, that if artificial bar magnets were secured to the fabric of the ship in pre-calculated places, the effect of the iron hull upon the compass could be neutralised, enabling it to behave normally.[37] Airy's solution to this problem was classic, in so far as it was a cheap and practical one, in which a study in physics was transformed into a humane utility.[38] It was from these compass experiments that Airy came to establish the Magnetic Department of the Royal Observatory in 1838, to facilitate the systematic investigation of the wider parameters of geomagnetism. This was, of course, a subject being officially promoted in some respects under the auspices of Henry

Sabine, though the Astronomer Royal pursued the new line of investigation scientifically, practically and even historically, going to considerable lengths to obtain copies of Edmond Halley's magnetic charts of 1701 for comparison.[39]

While still at Cambridge, Airy had analysed mathematically the properties of machines and structures, and it was from these original studies that much of his fame as a consultant on matters of engineering derived.[40] The 1840s saw him involved in public consultations regarding railway bridges and, though Lord Auckland was able to extract him from the unwanted obligation, he was proposed in 1847, for the Presidency of the Commission into iron bridges.[41] It was unfortunate that in 1873 he was consulted on the erection of a bridge over the Tay Estuary, and in September 1878 visited the newly completed structure. In the public outcry which erupted following the collapse of the Tay Bridge a few weeks later, in December 1878, the seventy-eight--year-old Astronomer Royal was summoned as an expert witness before the investigating Commission, in the House of Lords. Much of the controversy hinged on the alleged inadequate allowance for wind pressure and the overall physics of the structure, and while this related to Airy's own field of expertise, he was not held personally culpable.[42]

The Astronomer Royal's expertise in matters of engineering involved him in many enquiries into railways. As Second Commissioner, he was a leading member of the Railway Gauge Commission in 1845–46, when he and his fellow members had to advise Parliament on the legally permitted gauges of new railways. It was the Commission which rang the death knell to Brunel's seven foot gauge system, though Airy still remained on good terms with both Brunel and Stephenson, who between them represented the broad and narrow gauges. This Commission was clearly both time-consuming and physically dangerous, for it not only required Airy to travel many hundreds of miles around England, but on one occasion, involved him in a potentially fatal accident, when an engine on which he was travelling came off the rails.[43]

Looking at Airy's career during the mid-1840s in particular, it is astonishing to find one man called upon to fulfil so many exacting tasks all at the same time. Though Airy was not the only scientific man being consulted by government at this time, he does seem to have been an automatic choice for membership to any enquiry involving the physical sciences, while his papers testify to the application which he devoted to the tasks with which he was burdened. In 1845–46 alone, he was providing meteorological data to the Registrar General, advising the Tidal Harbours Commission on the design of breakwaters at Plymouth and Cherbourg, suggesting improved sawing machines for Chatham Dockyard and undertaking preliminary enquiries leading to the construction of the new Westminster Clock. He was also involved in correcting compasses for Admiralty postal vessels, advising on the design of the Menai tubular bridge, and, of course, his work on the Railway Gauge Commission. None of these heavy demands were in the least concerned with astronomy, and it should also be remembered that at the Observatory, he was considering the introduction of a range of self-monitoring devices which in themselves amounted to a revolution in practical instrumentation. And when all of these additional demands had been met, he still faced the relentless task for which the state paid him: the collection, reduction and publication of the flawlessly accurate Greenwich Observations.[44]

THE NEPTUNE CRISIS

The years 1845–46 are crucial ones in which to view his additional responsibilities, for it was over this period that Airy came to commit what was, in hindsight, the greatest blunder of his career: the failure to discover Neptune. It is sad that one of the things for which Airy is best known today was his failure to initiate John Couch Adams' requested search for 'Planet X', based on the perturbations of Uranus. Airy was acquainted with and had supplied astronomical data to both Adams and Leverrier during the course of their investigative computations, yet ignored Adams' plea to look in a particular region of the sky. In consequence, Leverrier was able to 'steal' the priority of discovering Neptune, and the honour went to France. Yet to charge Airy with what was tantamount to a dereliction of his public duty, as several contemporary and subsequent writers have done, is to fail to appreciate Airy's far more pressing official commitments along with his concept of the role of the Royal Observatory.[45]

As we have already seen, Airy saw the Observatory as a place maintained out of public money for the compilation of accurate physical data for the navy and government. Initiating wild goose chases for hypothetical planets, especially when instigated by a man who had only just taken his undergraduate degree, as Adams had, was what Airy saw as the *real* dereliction of his duty. Airy would gladly supply his star catalogues and tables to whoever asked for them, though rendering such aid to sundry astronomers did not mean that he was willing to grant weeks of telescope and assistants' working time to the substantiation of their speculations. Over the years of his office, Airy received many letters soliciting aid for speculative schemes, and one should not judge too harshly if he seriously miscalculated on one of them. The Neptune affair nonetheless blew up into a major scientific incident with much of the condemnation directed against the Astronomer Royal. His old rival, Sir James South, brought allegations that Airy 'did not observe', though on 31 March 1847, he was 'triumphantly acquitted by the Admiralty'.[46] Airy further stated his position, and that of his Observatory, in the politically important *Report* to the Board of Visitors on 5 June 1847. In this *Report*, he stressed Greenwich's primary importance, as an observer of moon and stars for nautical purposes. The physical astronomy of the planets was not part of the Royal Observatory's brief, and while such a defence might sound unduly pedantic in the light of the importance of the discovery, Airy had a wholly valid case which the Admiralty acknowledged.[47]

In the wake of the 'Neptune scandal', it is all too easy to accuse the Astronomer Royal of lacking vision, yet in the long run it can be argued with equal force that it was his lack of scientific imagination, and determination to always keep his Royal Warrant before him, which made Airy such a valuable Civil Servant. In 1846, England may have lost a planet, but it had manifestly gained a highly efficient scientific department of state with a publicly accountable Director.

The Neptune affair is important in the present context for another reason. Airy first heard the announcement of the Berlin Observatory's discovery on 29 September 1846 while undergoing a form of convalescence at Gotha. The rigour of extraneous commitments during the period 1845–46 had taken their toll on the Astronomer Royal's health, and brought him to the edge of a nervous breakdown. Between August and October 1846, Airy and his family went on a recuperative holiday to Europe. 'We stayed for some time at Wiesbaden, as my nerves were shaken by the work on the Railway Gauge Commission, and I wanted the Wiesbaden waters'. It was in the midst of this well-earned official rest that he heard of Neptune's discovery, and dutifully returned to England to face the storm.[48]

THE ASTRONOMER ROYAL AND THE WIDER WORLD

Airy's public commitments discussed so far related primarily to English domestic matters, though both his position in the establishment and general omnivorous interests inevitably involved him in aspects of the Empire and its observatories. His relations with successive Directors of the Cape of Good Hope Observatory were good, and in 1870 he saw his own Chief Assistant, Edmund Stone, appointed to its Directorship.[49] The precise relation of the Astronomer Royal to the colonial observatories was not clear, and while it seems that the home government – at least in the 1840s – did not work on the assumption that Airy had a mandate over them, several colonial administrations seemed to believe that he had.[50] While it was natural that the Astronomer Royal should be invited to recommend staff and instruments to these institutions, it became a matter of some political sensitivity as to what control he could exercise over the policies and lines of research which they pursued. Always before him, Airy saw it as the duty of state observatories to collect useful data, and not to follow 'abstruse' lines of research such as astrophysics. On the other hand, it must have been difficult, especially for the younger generation of astronomers who were fascinated with the potential of the spectroscope and photographic plate, to keep to routine celestial cartography beneath the black and physically unexplored skies of the tropics.

Airy's conception of the essentially practical role of the colonial observatories, and of the Indian ones in particular, was borne out, at least in part, by their origins. Most had been founded either as meridian or trigonometrical survey stations, for cartographic or chronometer work, rather than as free research institutions in their own right. They were to fulfil specific uses, for colonial administration, the East India Company, or to act as useful supplements to the home scientific establishment.[51] With the great reduction in the oriental sea passage occasioned by the Suez Canal in 1870, and the extension of submarine telegraphs to India and Australia, the ubiquitous GMT signals could be transmitted around the empire, thereby reducing the timekeeping importance of many of these observatories.[52]

In the early 1840s, Airy was advising Major Wilcox of the Lucknow Observatory that the southerly location of India should be used to make measurements of the planets, for, in the tropics, they appear much higher in the sky than in England and could be seen with less atmospheric distortion.[53] By the late 1860s, however, he was adopting a more magisterial stance with Norman Pogson, British Astronomer at Madras, on the issue of official support and control of the Indian Observatories.

Starting from Pogson's complaint in his 1865 *Report* that the native staff at the Madras Observatory was 'perfectly useless', questions came to be asked in London about the necessity of supporting this and the Bombay Observatory for anything beyond routine geomagnetic work, when the Australian and Cape Observatories were better placed for southern hemisphere astronomy.[54] In October 1866, a Memorandum was drawn up by Lord Cranbourne of the India Office, with clear encouragement from the Astronomer Royal, recommending the rationalisation of scientific services in India. Pogson responded by justifying his office, his commitment to astronomy and the poor rewards which his years of diligent past service had earned for him.[55]

Whether Airy was deliberately attempting to extend his formal control over colonial scientific affairs, or simply suggesting a new economy is not clear, though it certainly did not pass unnoticed at home. Joseph Baxendell of Manchester, for instance, was sufficiently incensed to write personally to the Astronomer Royal asking by what authority he regarded Pogson as an underling and could direct the policies of the Indian Observatories.[56]

Though the Bombay and Madras Observatories continued to exist – the latter with great distinction[57] – their relations were placed on a more formal footing, and while Pogson played an important part in framing the *Code of Instructions* devised for his institution in 1869, he was required by Article 8 to be 'placed in official communication with the Astronomer Royal'. A prior ruling had already recommended a similar standing for the Bombay Astronomer in 1866, while Wilcox's institution at Lucknow had long since been closed down by King Oudh, in 1849,[58]

Airy's relationship with Pogson continued to be friendly in tone, though it is clear from their correspondence that while Pogson disliked being responsible to Greenwich, he stood in awe of the Astronomer Royal.[59] Airy was keenly aware of his role as Director of the patrimonal Observatory of the Empire, and knew how to use his position, and access to superiors such as Lord Cranbourne, to maintain his primacy.

Early in his career, in 1844, Airy had been keen to assert the Royal Observatory's Imperial Importance in the provision of standards and training for colonial boundary determinations. In the years 1843–44, a group of Greenwich-trained Royal Engineers Officers successfully completed, in accordance with the Treaty of Washington, a survey of the boundary between Eastern Canada and the United State of Maine. In his *Report* for 1844, Airy proudly reminded the Visitors of the Royal Observatory that these men, working in dense forests in the depths of winter, had started from two astronomically determined survey points seventy miles apart, and made contact to within 341 feet, which represented a longitudinal error of less than one quarter of a second of time. Airy reminded his official masters that such an accurate survey would not have been possible but for the services which the Royal Observatory placed at the disposal of the civil and military departments of state.[60]

In addition to his interests in horological telegraphy, Airy was consulted on telegraphic matters in the Empire and world at large. In 1856, he was engaged with matters relating to the projected Atlantic submarine telegraph, while the training which his staff received in managing the self-recording and time transmitting electrical instruments at the Royal Observatory could prepare them for subsequent careers in telegraphy.[61] Charles Todd, a former Assistant at Greenwich, was appointed to take charge of the telegraphic establishment at Adelaide, while Airy wrote several articles on the practical uses of electricity, including the submarine telegraph.[62]

As Astronomer Royal, Airy was often called upon to recommend persons to a range of Imperial scientific posts. In addition to his work with Imperial Observatories, he was also invited to propose candidates for chairs in the newly founded Australian and New Zealand Universities. In all forms of academic recommendations, moreover, he took the 'Liberal side', or the best man for the job irrespective of religious affiliation. In an age when the *Test Acts* still limited some academic appointments to Communing Anglicans, this was a radical step. His religious liberalism led him to support John Colenso, Bishop of Natal, who in 1863 was deprived of his see in the public outcry which broke following his criticism of the historical authenticity of the Pentateuch.[63]

While not part of his duties as a Civil Servant, one significant aspect of Airy's concern with the propagation of useful knowledge was his extensive body of publications directed at a general readership. Throughout his working life, Airy was a ceaseless informer of the British public on a wide range of subjects, writing to newspapers and popular journals, and contributing over thirty non-astronomical articles to the *Athenaeum* Magazine alone. Many of these pieces demonstrate the breadth of his learned competence, and the way in which the Astronomer Royal applied the principles of science to archaeology, Old Testament chronology and even the precise location of Julius Ceasar's landing place, from tidal evidence. Of his 518 listed publications, well over one hundred are non-astronomical in character, though all are rooted in a scientific approach to useful knowledge.[64] Almost characteristically for a senior Civil Servant, he maintained a lifelong passion for the Latin and Greek classics, and to the end of his life could recite them, along with the English poets, from memory, by the hour.[65] No other Astronomer Royal, before or since, either fulfilled so many diverse duties, or devoted so much time to keeping the public informed by writing and lecturing. Within this context of public office in which Airy saw himself, it is now important to examine his relations with his own staff, colleagues and official masters.

MASTERS, SERVANTS AND COLLEAGUES

Airy never lost sight of the fact that he had virtually recreated the Royal Observatory from scratch upon taking office. In 1835, Greenwich had been in decline, with a fractious staff headed by an 'old Master of the Navy' in the place of First Assistant.[66] Airy came to build up a team of assistants, discharging Taylor, the 'navy master', and replacing him with the Reverend Robert Main, thereby commencing the tradition of appointing a former Cambridge mathematics don to the First Assistant's place.[67]

Beneath Main came six other assistants, some of whom were of limited capacity; one, 'requires a good master to keep him in order', while another was 'without a particle of science ... and ... keeps a shop in the town', Airy informed the Admiralty.[68] Six, or sometimes seven, Warrant Assistants formed the full staff of the Observatory, though beneath them was an inferior staff of between six and a dozen 'supernumerary computers', employed on a semi-casual basis, at pay and conditions set personally by the Astronomer Royal to perform routine mathematical work. As he emphasised in many of his annual *Reports*, the 'Astronomer Royal is responsible to the government for everything that passes in the Observatory', from which he created a rigid chain of command over which he presided as an undisputed autocrat.[69] This strict differentiation of function was also enshrined in the Observatory's pay scales. In 1852, Airy's total official income was £1100, consisting of his salary of £800, plus the £300 per annum Civil List pension settled on his wife.[70] In 1856, his salary rose to £1000 a year, to produce a combined Exchequer emolument of £1,300.[71] At the same time, Robert Main received £470 per annum, his second assistant £240, (£200 plus a rent allowance of £40), down to the sixth and seventh assistants on £130 apiece.[72] 'The stipends and discipline of the computers is arranged entirely by me', Airy reminded the Board of Visitors in 1867, as the *ad hoc* monthly term of employment produced the best results with the least expenditure. Under good conditions, it was possible for a supernumerary to make £120 per year. Beneath them all was a small staff of three maintenance and watch men, with annual salaries of around £40.[73]

Influenced, no doubt, by the spirit of the Northcote Trevelyan Commission into the Civil Service in 1854, and the emphasis which it placed upon open competitive examinations, Airy began to introduce entrance examinations to test the 'competency' of prospective assistants and supernumeraries in the late 1850s. Supernumeraries were generally appointed as very young men and Airy wished to see schools in the district encourage and prepare capable boys to be examined for these posts.[74] It was often from the ranks of the proven supernumeraries that the lower Warrant Assistants were appointed. Hugh Breen, William Ellis, Edwin Dunkin and most of the early staff gained their posts as promoted supernumeraries. With the exception of the academically appointed First Assistant, they were not graduates, for J.T. Lynn, with his London BA degree became the first university man to be appointed to an ordinary Assistantship in 1856.[75]

Irrespective of these men's backgrounds, they must have been diligent observers and calculators to maintain Airy's favour, and while he did not commence the practice of mentioning them by name until his *Report* of 1846, he frequently gave official acknowledgement to their skill as a body. One also assumes that they must have been relatively happy in their positions, for in 1870 the six assistants beneath the First, had been there thirty-seven, thirty-two, twenty-eight, seventeen, fifteen and sixteen years respectively. The kudos of a position at the Royal Observatory also produced a succession of letters to Airy from men wishing to be considered *should* vacancies occur.[76]

With his obsessive concern about wasting public money, Airy kept the Observatory salaries at a level which E.W. Maunder called 'discreditably low',[77] so that in 1870 the Warrant Assistants (excluding the First) petitioned the Lords of Admiralty for a rise. The 'Memorial' which they drew up gives an excellent insight into the conditions in which they worked.[78] Airy, for his part, backed their claim, admitting that existing pay structures had been fixed years before, when the duties of the assistants had been 'humble', requiring attainments 'of the lowest class', whereas the new duties required a higher remuneration.[79]

The Assistants compared themselves with the Keepers of the British Museum in rank, though instead of receiving salaries on the scale £400 to £600 per annum as the Keepers did, they received remuneration equivalent to the 'lower classes of Civil Servants' at £200 to £340. Unlike the generality of Civil Servants who worked an official day of six hours, the Observatory staff could be called upon to make 'tedious night watches', which, in addition to their *five* hour day duties, could engage them for fifteen or eighteen hours on a stretch, including Sundays.[80] This was the 'regime of remorseless sweating', in accordance with which Airy was said to run the Observatory.[81] After enquiry into staff salaries in four other major observatories,[82] and much official prevarication, Airy received an Admiralty grant of £530 in 1871 with which to augment salaries.[83] The salaries issue is important in so far as it was a respectfully conducted grass-roots complaint, which was intended to bring home to their Lordships that one could not remunerate a body of government scientists on the rates of superior bank clerks.[84] One feels, however, that the message was not properly heeded, for even the revised scales left Airy's Assistants worse off than equivalently qualified men in the British Museum and Department of Works.

As the public face of British astronomy, Airy enjoyed a formidable reputation, serving as President of the Royal Society and Royal Astronomical Societies. He 'much pleased' Gladstone on the occasion of the latter's dining with the Astronomical Society Club in 1862,[85] while in 1860, Airy had led an international team of astronomers to observe the total eclipse of the Sun in Spain.[86] In England, he lived on terms of mutual respect with Herschel,[87] and – in spite of the Neptune affair – was greatly admired by J.C. Adams. It is true that Babbage never forgave Airy for condemning his calculating engine as a 'humbug' and waste of public money, though, by 1835, Babbage had few good words for anyone.[88] Airy also became a friend of the pioneer deep space astronomer, Lord Rosse, disagreed with Faraday about his lines of force, and admired William Thomson, Lord Kelvin's contribution to the physics of scientific instrumentation, along with the work of such eminent foreigners as Hansen, Struve, Encke and Leverrier.[89] Ironically, he seems to have had little contact with that 'next generation' government scientist, Lyon Playfair, with the exception of approaching him as a Parliamentary advocate during the salaries crisis of 1870–71.[90]

Playfair was, in fact, a very different type of both man and scientist to Airy. Though neither saw science as a subject of pure intellectual curiosity, Airy was content to use it as a medium through which to propagate useful knowledge, whereas Playfair was also aware of its potential as a social ladder upon which he might eventually ascend to political renown and a peerage.

Though Airy had his detractors, such as Sir James South and his critics of the Neptune affair, his personal credit and inexhaustible energy enabled him to override controversies within the scientific community.[91]

With other government scientists, however, one often detects both caution and condescension. His relations with Sabine of the Kew Observatory were formal and sometimes strained, and when the latter criticised certain practices at the Royal Observatory in the 1860s, Airy conducted a fierce and successful defence.[92] He enjoyed a most cordial relationship, however, with Thomas Colby, Director of the Ordnance Survey, and whilst operating on good terms with Captain Francis Beaufort, could still refer in an official document to Beaufort's Hydrographic Office as one of the 'inferior departments of the Admiralty'.[93]

It must also be remembered that several of Airy's staff ranked as colleagues, winning scientific recognition in their own right. Of the three successive First Assistants, Main became Oxford's Radcliffe Observer in 1861, Edmund Stone, Her Majesty's Observer at the Cape in 1870, while Christie succeeded his master to become eighth Astronomer Royal in 1881. His relations with these men were cordial, Airy addressing Main at Oxford as one of his 'friends'.[94] Even some of the non-university Assistants independently distinguished themselves, being elected as Fellows and Officers of the Royal Astronomical Society, while James Glaisher and Edwin Dunkin became full Fellows of the Royal Society. When Christie was made Astronomer Royal in 1881, his vacant First Assistantship was given to Dunkin, to provide the first significant instance of internal

promotion in the Observatory's history.[95] Unless their learned
society offices gave them supervisory powers above the Astronomer
Royal, such as *ex officio* seats on the Board of Visitors, then Airy
seems not to have greatly minded.[96]

One wonders, however, what strained relationship may well have
existed between Airy and the growing international reputation of
James Glaisher. As a Rotherhithe autodidact taken up by Airy as
a Junior Assistant, Glaisher became head of the Observatory's
Magnetic and Meteorological Department, and one of the founding
fathers of scientific meteorology. Glaisher's 120 publications, pioneer
weather maps and work on meteorology and public health won
him an unassailable scientific reputation, while his high-altitude
meteorological balloon ascents made him something of a public
celebrity. One senses a hint of resentment in the Astronomer Royal's
regular lament, by the 1870s, that meteorology would never become
a *real* science with a physical and predictive foundation, and remain
a collection of mere observations.[97] This was an odd complaint from
a man who, in 1838, had founded the Royal Observatory's
Meteorological Department. Airy and Glaisher not only held
differing views on the scientific status of meteorology, but also its
relation to astronomy. Following a flurry of interest in physical
'astro-meteorology' in the 1860s, Airy had firmly informed the Duke
of Manchester in 1862 that there was no scientifically observable
correlation between the lunar phase and the level of rainfall. In
1867, however, Glaisher published evidence favouring such a
correlation, based upon a statistical analysis of fifty-four years of
Greenwich weather observations.[98] When Glaisher retired after
forty-five years of government scientific service, Airy noted his
passing with a curt half-line statement in his 1875 *Report*. James
Glaisher was to enjoy a further twenty-eight years of life and
independent scientific activity, dying as the 'Nestor of Meteorologists'
in 1903, at the age of ninety-four.[99]

Though an autocrat in the scientific realm, much of Airy's success
depended on an absence of autocracy with the statesmen who
ultimately employed him. He was a forthright and honest man, with
a reputation for speaking his mind when asked, though he knew
how to bow with dignity before his masters. As a Civil Servant, he
appreciated the strengths and weaknesses of his position, and when
protocol occasionally prevented him from accepting a proffered
Order of Saint Stanislas, or the equivalent high military rank of the
French or Russian Imperial Astronomers, he could take the rub

without offence, knowing that he would derive benefits later.[100] Unlike Lyon Playfair, or even Lord Kelvin, he was an essentially modest man without aspirations in the wider world beyond official science, and while a lifelong staunch Liberal, was content to serve Parliament without being moved to obtain a seat in it.

These qualities which made Airy such a successful Civil Servant were, towards the end of his long reign, to reflect adversely upon him as a scientist. His utilitarianism, obsession with economy and being forever on official call, enabled him to work successfully with admirals and administrators, but not always with scientists. By the 1870s, the Royal Observatory was displaying weaknesses on its purely scientific side. Airy's concern with 'Warrant' meridian astronomy meant that the fledgeling science of astrophysics obtained no real footing. It had no 'deep sky' instrumentation, and even E.W. Maunder's appointment to a new photographic and spectro-scopic section in 1874 was not enough.[101] While Airy never doubted the intellectual importance of the new astrophysics, he insisted that '. . . the [Greenwich] Observatory is not a place for new physical investigations', which should be left in private hands, and not placed as a burden on the public purse until they 'have been reduced to laws susceptible of verification by daily observation'.[102] In the concluding section to his last *Report* in 1881, he re-affirmed his position, stating 'I yield to no one with the interest which I take in these new subjects', but pointed out that they were 'not parts of our original system', and should not be pursued at Greenwich.[103] Not until Airy had retired were their Lordships persuaded to widen the Observatory's research capacities.

One also perceives that the rigid, hierarchic structure of the Royal Observatory and vertical dictation of policy, diminished its appeal to young scientists not willing to conform to its regime. It is sad to note that Britain's leading astronomers of the Airy age were conspicuously *un*-attached to the Royal Observatory, in spite of the encomiums heaped upon its Director. Joseph Norman Lockyer, Britain's leading astrophysicist after 1870, was never a member of the Greenwich staff, though he did hold an official appointment as Director of the South Kensington Solar Observatory.[104] At the Royal Observatory by this time, however, one senses the stifling effect of a man who had once been an inspired innovator, but whose creativity had ossified into love of routine.

One cannot but wonder what were the attractions which kept Airy in office until the age of eighty? His income was low compared with that of a bishop or judge, and his real power modest. He was certainly not interested in honours, and turned down three knighthoods, before accepting on the fourth occasion in 1872. His general excuse for refusing knighthoods was the modesty of his estate, and in 1863 he turned down his third offer on the grounds that the fees would amount to £30.[105] Even academic honours seemed to mean little, for he almost caused embarrassment at Oxford in 1844, when he would have refused his Encaenia DCL degree upon being told that the ancillary charges would amount to six guineas. The Vice Chancellor saved the day by waiving the costs. He also turned down a nomination to the new Athenaeum Club in 1824.[106]

Though he received a variety of foreign honours in recognition of his work, they seemed to mean little to him. Only when he was made a Freeman of the City of London in 1875 did an appreciative chord strike within him. What he admired in this honour was not the acclaim of university or state, but the sober recognition of *practical* men of business, for his contributions to 'the cause of commerce and civilisation' which was, in Airy's estimation, 'the highest honour which it is possible to receive'.[107]

One is brought to the conclusion that Airy's greatest reward lay simply in fulfilling his public duty. To a man who derived deep satisfaction from the mere adding up of figures and whose hobby was the meticulous keeping of domestic accounts, one comes close to understanding what motivated the Astronomer Royal.[108] It was neither abstract intellectual curiosity, ambition, love of power or fame. It was order, and the organisation of useful facts, in consequence of which he found in the careful discharge of his duties a satisfaction and end in itself. When one remembers the spectrum of subjects over which Airy was involved during this crucial half-century of British history, one wonders what Her Majesty's government would have done without such a zealous and single-minded servant at its disposal.

Acknowledgements

I wish to thank the Librarian and Staff of the Royal Astronomical Society. My particular debt of gratitude, however, must go to Miss Janet Dudley, Librarian and Archivist, Royal Greenwich Observatory, Herstmonceux Castle, without whose encouragement and permitted access to the Airy Papers, this article would not have been possible.

NOTES

1. Eric G. Forbes, *Greenwich Observatory, 1; Origins and early history 1675–1975* (Taylor and Francis: London, 1975). John Flamsteed, *The 'Historia Coelestis Britannica' of John Flamsteed, 1725*, edited and introduced by Allan Chapman (London: National Maritime Museum Monograph No. 52, 1982).
2. Alfred Friendly, *Beaufort of the Admiralty* (Hutchinson: London, 1977). Jack Morrell, 'Science and Government (1800–74) John Phillips and the Early Ordnance Geological Survey of Britain', this volume, pp. 7–35.
3. H.P. Hollis, 'The Greenwich assistants during 250 years', *Observatory*, No. 619, December 1925, pp. 388–398.
4. George Biddell Airy, *Report to the Board of Visitors*, 1838, p. 2; 1842, p. 6; 1848, p. 2, 11; 1854, pp. 3–4; 1861, pp. 5–6; 1863, p. 5; 1869, p. 7; 1871, p. 5; 1876, p. 5. Hereafter cited as *Report*.
5. G.B. Airy, *Autobiography of Sir George Biddell Airy*, edited by Wilfred Airy (Cambridge University Press, 1896) pp. 79–80. Hereafter cited as *Autobiography*.
6. Lord Auckland to Airy, 8 October, 1832, Royal Greenwich Observatory 6, 1/151–2. Hereafter cited as RGO6. Airy to Duke of Sussex, 19 May 1834, RGO6, 1/145. Airy to Lord Auckland, 10 September 1834, RGO6, 1/153.
7. Though Airy did maintain a detailed personal archive, to which Wilfred Airy referred in the 'Personal Sketch' to his father's *Autobiography*, and from which Airy himself drew in the same work, many of its items are not to be found in the official Airy papers. One presumes that they remained in the possession of the family. Though Airy kept a diary, the 'Astronomer Royal's Journal', its entries are cryptic, RGO6, 24–27. At the time of writing, August 1986, the official Airy papers, along with those of the other Astronomers Royal, are in the library of the Royal Greenwich Observatory, Herstmonceux Castle, Sussex, and cited with the archive prefix, RGO6. As the Science Research Council has recently decided, however, to move the Royal Greenwich Observatory to Cambridge, and have made no provision for its unique 300-year-old archive, where they will be in five years' time is a subject of some speculation.
8. Airy to Lord Auckland, 15 June 1835, RGO6, 1/158. Airy, 'Statements respecting the assistants at the Royal Observatory', 1835, RGO6, 72/223.
9. Airy's Warrants remained similar to Flamsteed's in their essentials, from William IV, 11 August, 1835 RGO6, 1/193–4, and Victoria, RGO6, 1/195.

10. *Report*, 1842, p. 7.
11. *Reports*, 1839, p. 5; 1845, p. 12.
12. Derek Howse, *Greenwich Time* (Oxford University Press, 1980) pp. 81–113. J.M. Bennett, 'George Biddell Airy and Horology', *Annals of Science*, XXXVII (1980) pp. 269–85. Allan Chapman, 'Sir George Airy (1801–1892) and the concept of international standards in science, timekeeping and navigation', *Vistas in Astronomy*, XXVIII (1985) pp. 321–328.
13. Curtis v. March, 25 November 1858, *The English Reports*, CLVII, *Exchequer Division*, XIII (1916) p. 719. *Acts* 42 and 44, Victoria, c.9.
14. *Reports*, 1850, pp. 14–15; 1853, pp. 1–2; 1854, pp. 13–14; 1855, p. 11; 1863, Appendix III, p. 19; 1864, p. 18; 1867, pp. 20–21. Airy, 'On the telegraphic Longitude of Brussels', *Athenaeum*, No. 1368, 14 January 1854, pp. 54–5, RGO *APP* V, 173.
15. *International Conference held at Washington for the purpose of fixing a Prime Meridian and a Universal Day, October, 1884. Protocols of the Proceedings* (Washington: Gibson Brothers, 1884). See also in *Vistas in Astronomy*, XXVIII (1985) from the 1984 'Longitude Zero' Conference, held at Greenwich, to celebrate the hundredth anniversary of the International Greenwich Meridian.
16. Derek Howse, *Greenwich Observatory, 3; Buildings and Instruments*, (London: Taylor and Francis, 1975). See also *Autobiography*, pp. 373–403, for Airy's publications on instruments, and *Reports*, 1850, pp. 14–15; 1853, p. 10; 1854, p. 5; 1875, p. 25.
17. *Reports*, 1839, p. 5; 1841, p. 5. *Autobiography*, pp. 110, 116.
18. *Report*, 1868, p. 6. *Autobiography*, p. 131.
19. *Reports*, 1842, p. 7; 1844, p. 19; 1846, pp. 9–10; 1847, p. 10. Airy emphasised the excellence of Greenwich Observations in *Report*, 1875, pp. 24–5. Robert Grant, *History of Physical Astronomy* (London: Robert Baldwin, 1852) pp. 493–6.
20. *Report*, 1836, p. 4.
21. *Report*, 1837, p. 2.
22. *Reports*, 1841, p. 5; 1881, p. 17. For Standards Commission papers, see RGO6, 338–67.
23. *Report of Commissioners appointed to consider the steps to be taken for the Restoration of Standards of Weight and Measure, 21 Dec. 1841.* RGO *APP* (*Airy Printed Papers*) II, 76. Airy, 'Account of the construction of the new National Standard Length and its principal copies', *Philosophical Transactions* (1858), pp. 1–82, RGO *APP* VI, 201. The *Airy Printed Papers*, RGO *APP*, are bound into volumes I–XIV in the Royal Greenwich Observatory Library.
24. Figure obtained from Commissions cited in *Autobiography*.
25. Airy to William Gladstone, 26 March 1853, *Autobiography*, p. 217. Airy, 'On decimal coinage', *Athenaeum*, No. 1333, 14 May 1853, p. 588. RGO *APP* V, 166. Airy, 'Decimal Coinage', *Athenaeum*, No. 1350, 10 Sept. 1853, p. 1070, RGO *APP* V, 170. For papers relating to International Coinage Commission, see RGO 6, 446.
26. Tidal Harbours, RGO6, 499–518. Dee Navigation, RGO6, 519–22. *Autobiography*, p. 169.

27. *Autobiography*, pp. 176–7.
28. Lighthouses Commission, RGO6, 326. 21 February 1860. *Autobiography*, p. 240. RGO6, 326/152. *Report*, 1860, p. 21.
29. Sewers Commission, RGO6, 322–4. *Autobiography*, pp. 196, 231.
30. Warranting Admiralty telescopes from Elliots, RGO6, 436. *Reports*, 1860, p. 20; 1861, p. 19.
31. RGO6, 2/135–70. 7 December 1847, RGO6, 2/39. RGO6, 4/531–41. *Autobiography*, p. 185.
32. Sale of Gas, RGO6, 327–34. *Reports*, 1860, p. 21; 1861, p. 19. *Autobiography*, p. 237.
33. [Private] *Address to the Earl of Burlington*, 10 February 1838, RGO *APP* II, 52, pp. 1–10. *Autobiography*, p. 136. Oxford University Commission invitation, 12 March 1857, RGO6, 4/525.
34. *Autobiography*, p. 247. I have found no reference to Airy serving on a Public Schools Commission, though in RGO6, 492–8, he was involved with Charity, Blue Coat and other schools.
35. Correspondence with Mr Cowper, First Commissioner of Works, March–April, 1860. *Autobiography*, p. 240.
36. *Autobiography*, pp. 180, 187, 213, 217, 240, for Airy's correspondence with Denison, Dent and others regarding the clock.
37. Airy, *Results of experiments in the disturbance of the compass in Iron-built ships* (London: John Weale, 1840), pp. 4–16, RGO *APP* II, 64. *Report*, 1839, p. 4. *Autobiography*, pp. 135–6.
38. Airy, 'Discussion of the observed deviation of the compass in several ships, wood and iron built', *Phil. Trans.*, (1855) pp. 53–99, RGO *APP* V, 180. Airy, 'On the correction of compasses in iron ships', *Athenaeum*, No. 1423, 3 February 1855, p. 145. RGO *APP* V, 184.
39. *Report*, 1839, p. 4. Edmond Halley, *The three voyages of Edmond Halley in the 'Paramore'*, edited by N.J.W. Thrower (London: Hakluyt Society, 1981) p. 61.
40. Publications such as:- Airy, 'On the form of the teeth of wheels', 2 May 1825, *Trans. of the Cambridge Phil. Society,* (1825) pp. 1–10, RGO *APP* I, 6. 'On the strains in the interior of beams and tubular bridges', *Athenaeum*, No. 1824, 11 October 1862, p. 471, RGO APP, 270. 'On the numerical expression of ... the explosion of steam boilers & Co.', *Philosophical Magazine*, November 1863, pp. 329–36, RGO *APP* IX, 297.
41. Iron Bridges Commission, eight letters, June–August, 1847, RGO6 2/116–27. *Autobiography*, p. 185.
42. *Autobiography*, pp. 303, 324. A.J. Meadows, *Greenwich Observatory, 2; Recent History, 1835–1975*, (London, Taylor and Francis, 1975) p. 110.
43. *Report of the Gauge Commissions. And a letter to Sir Edward Ryan* (London, 1846) pp. 1–27, RGO *APP* III, 95. The Railway Gauge Commission papers constitute one of the largest non-astronomical sections of the Airy papers, in RGO6, 284–322.
44. Itemised, *Autobiography*, pp. 168–80.
45. Airy, 'Account of some circumstances historically connected with the

discovery of the planet exterior to Uranus', *Memoirs of the Royal Astronomical Society*, VII, No. 9 13 November 1846, pp. 121–52. RGO *APP* III, 100. *Report*, 1847, p. 10. The volume containing Airy's Neptune papers, 'RGO 694', has been missing for many years from the Royal Observatory archives. It was never listed in the recent RGO6 classification.

46. Sir James South's attack on Airy, 19 March 1847, RGO6, 2/250, produced a heavy correspondence until his Admiralty 'acquittal', 31 March 1847; RGO6, 2/267. *Autobiography*, p. 185.

47. *Report*, 1847, p. 10.

48. In the 'Astronomer Royal's Journal', 29 September 1846, he noted: 'While dining with M. Hansen, we received news of the discovery of the new planet beyond Uranus', RGO6, 24–7. See also, Airy's correspondence with Challis in Cambridge, Cambridge University Observatory, Boxfile 1846–47. *Autobiography*, p. 183.

49. *Report*, 1871, p. 19.

50. S.M. Razaullah Ansari, *Introduction of modern western astronomy in India during the eighteenth and nineteenth centuries* (New Delhi: Hamdard, 1985) pp. 44–5.

51. Lord Cranbourne, *To his Excellency the Right Honourable The Governor General of India in Council*, India Office, 31 October 1866, No. 91, RGO6, 149/1/32–3. 'Memorandum on the general question of retaining the Observatories of Bombay and Madras', 2 October 1866, RGO6, 149/1/27r–30v.

52. Airy, *British expeditions for the observation of the Transit of Venus 1874, December 8*, May 1874, pp. 13–15. Royal Astronomical Society copy bound into *Reports*, 1874–5. For telegraphic longitudes, see RGO6, 633–40.

53. Ansari, note 50, pp. 44–5.

54. Norman Pogson, *Report* of Madras Observatory, 22 June 1865, and ibid., 30 April 1866, RGO6, 149/1/39–41, 42–3. Lord Cranbourne, *To his Excellency*. 31 October 1866, No. 91, RGO6, 149/1/32–3.

55. Pogson to Airy, Madras, 22 December 1866, RGO6, 149/1/36–7. Airy to Pogson, 20 February 1867, RGO6, 149/1/48. Pogson to Airy, 28 March 1867, RGO6, 149/1/51.

56. Joseph Baxendell to Airy, Manchester, 6 February 1867, RGO6, 149/1/44. Airy to Baxendell, 7 February 1867, RGO6, 149/1/45. Baxendell to Airy, 8 February 1867, RGO6, 149/1/46. Joseph Baxendell's interest in this matter may well have derived from his being Pogson's brother in law, 'Obituary', Baxendell, *Manchester Guardian*, 15 December 1887.

57. C.R. Markham, *Memoirs of Indian Surveys*, second edn, (London, 1878) p. 340. Cited also in Ansari, op. cit., p. 28.

58. *Home Department Proceedings December 18th 1869, Preparation of a Code of Instructions for the conduct of work in the Madras Observatory.* RGO6, 150/2/11–17.

59. Pogson to Airy, Madras, 5 August 1870, RGO6, 150/2/22–3.

60. *Report*, 1844, pp. 19–20.

61. *Report*, 1854, p. 12.

62. Airy, 'The Atlantic cable problem', *Nautical Magazine*, May 1858, pp. 265–80, RGO *APP* VI, 207, 'On the mechanical conditions of the deposit of a submarine cable', *Philosophical Magazine*, July 1858, pp. 1–18, RGO *APP* VI, 211.
63. *Autobiography*, pp. 164–5. A careful search of the Airy papers has failed to locate these letters to Colenso, 24 July 1865, and to Selwyn, 6 May 1866. Like other items of his private correspondence, they may have been removed.
64. See *Airy Printed Papers*, RGO I–XIV, *Autobiography*, pp. 373–403.
65. Wilfred Airy, 'Personal sketch', *Autobiography*, pp. 10–11.
66. Airy to Admiral Richards, 14 March 1871, RGO6, 76/177v. Airy to Lord Auckland, 15 June 1835, RGO6, 1/158. Also, Airy, 'Statements respecting assistants . . .' 1835, RGO6, 72/223.
67. Airy to Francis Beaufort, 15 July 1841, RGO6, 72/134. Airy to Admiral Richards, 14 March 1871, RGO6, 76/177v. *Autobiography*, p. 109.
68. Airy to Beaufort, 15 July 1841, RGO6, 76/135.
69. *Report*, 1874, p. 19.
70. *Autobiography*, p. 107. I have been unable to trace the Peel–Airy correspondence in the RGO archives. Royal Warrant, 11 August 1835, RGO6, 1/193–4.
71. *Autobiography*, p. 107. See salaries list, 1856, RGO6. 4/93.
72. Ibid., RGO6, 4/93.
73. The salaries of the casually funded Computers is not easy to establish, and sums of £120 and £180 are mentioned for either individual or group payments, *Reports*, 1844, p. 18; 1847, p. 9.
74. *Reports*, 1857, p. 17; 1859, p. 16; 1860, p. 19; 1872, p. 20; 1873, p. 20; RGO6, 76/165.
75. *Report*, 1857, p. 15. Lynn was not designated 'BA' upon his appointment in 1856, but signed himself such in 1870, RGO6, 76/90.
76. Royal Observatory Assistants to First Lord of Admiralty, 19 April 1870, RGO6, 76/79–90, see p. 85.
77. E.W. Maunder, *The Royal Observatory, Greenwich* (London: Religious Tracts Society, 1900) p. 117.
78. Assistants, 19 April 1870, RGO 76/79–80. The original manuscript of this document was subsequently printed for the Board of Visitors, RGO6, 76/98, pp. 1–4. See below.
79. Airy to H.E. Childers (First Lord of Admiralty), 2–3 May 1870, RGO6, 76/91–7. For 'humble' assistants, see *Report*, 1872, p. 20.
80. *The Assistants of the Royal Observatory to the First Lord of the Admiralty*, 19 April 1870, RGO6, 76/98, pp. 1–4.
81. Maunder, op. cit., p. 117.
82. Airy consulted the Oxford, Cambridge, Paris and Pulkowa Observatory Directors, RGO6, 76/110–36.
83. The £530 seems to have been arranged as a provisional payment at a meeting on 3 March 1871, between Airy, Admiral Richards and W. Baxter, RGO6, 76/157.
84. RO Assistants' 'Memorial' to Airy, 30 Janaury 1871, RGO6, 76/141. *Autobiography*, p. 290.
85. *The Gladstone Diaries*, VI, 1861–68, ed. H.C.G. Matthew, (Oxford

University Press, 1978). See 14 November 1862.

86. *Autobiography*, pp. 241–2.

87. Günther Buttman, *The Shadow of the Telescope* (London: Lutterworth Press, 1870) pp. 122, 164, 167.

88. Maboth Moseley, *Irascible Genius; a life of Charles Babbage* (London: Hutchinson, 1964) p. 82.

89. *Autobiography*, pp. 319, 359, 364. L. Pearce Williams, *Michael Faraday* (London: Chapman and Hall, 1965), pp. 507–8.

90. Warren de la Rue to Airy, 1 February 1871, RGO6, 76/155. Wemyss Reid, *Memoirs and Correspondence of Lyon Playfair*, (London, 1899). No index reference to Airy or Royal Observatory.

91. Morton Grosser, *The Discovery of Neptune* (Oxford University Press, 1962).

92. RGO6, 695/1–3.

93. *Autobiography*, p. 124. Sir Charles Close, *The Early Years of the Ordnance Survey* (1926), (Newton Abbot: David & Charles, 1969), p. 97. Alfred Friendly, *Beaufort*, op. cit., pp. 297–8.

94. *Report*, 1871, p. 19. Airy to Robert Main, 28 May 1870, RGO6, 76/111.

95. William Christie, *Astronomer Royal's Report*, 1882, p. 16. 'Edwin Dunkin, Autobiographical Notes', Royal Astronomical Society, Add. Mss., 55.

96. Airy proposed Glaisher as a Juror for the Great Exhibition, 1851, see A.J. Meadows, *Greenwich Observatory*, 2, op. cit., p. 118.

97. *Report*, 1875, p. 25. This disappointment may also have derived from the inconclusive character of the 'Great Meteorological Reduction' of Greenwich weather records, 1847–73, RGO6, 698.

98. *Autobiography*, pp. 249–50. James Glaisher, 'The influence of the moon on the amount and frequency of rainfall as dependent on her age', *Proc. Met. Soc.*, 21 April 1869, pp. 347–50. Airy himself, however, had formerly held related views; 'On the relation of the direction of the wind to the age of the Moon . . .', *Phil. Trans.* (1851) pp. 411–12, RGO APP V, 148. See also, Jim Burton 'Robert Fitzroy and the early history of the Meteorological Office', *British Journal for the History of Science*, XIX (1986) pp. 147–76.

99. *DNB*, second supplement, 'Glaisher'.

100. Autobiography, pp. 190–3. 255–6.

101. Reports, 1874, pp. 18, 21; 1875, pp. 21, 26.

102. *Report*, 1875, p. 26.

103. *Report*, 1881, p. 26.

104. *Dictionary of Scientific Biography*, 'Lockyer'.

105. Airy refused Knighthoods in 1835, 1847, and 1863, before accepting in 1872. *Autobiography*, pp. 112, 187, 254, 296.

106. *Autobiography*, pp. 62, 165–6.

107. *Autobiography*, p. 311.

108. *Autobiography*, p. 2.

4 The Road to Albertopolis: Richard Owen (1804–92) and the Founding of the British Museum of Natural History

Nicolaas A. Rupke

INTRODUCTION

On Easter Monday 1881, the new Natural History Museum in South Kensington was officially opened to the public. As many as 16000 visitors crowded the spacious exhibition galleries during this first, historic day. At last, adequate space had been provided for the nation's immensely popular collections of natural history which, for nearly half a century, had suffered overcrowding, neglect and damage in the British Museum in Bloomsbury. The natural history collections had been on public display in the temple-like Bloomsbury building since 1831, having been moved there from the less commodious Montagu House. All too soon, however, a stream of new objects, antiquities, ethnographic items, plants, animals and fossils, from private collectors, from Near Eastern excavations, African expeditions, and colonial surveys had congested the Bloomsbury temple, even its basement, stairs and portico. Such an heterogeneous hoard might have been regarded as a perfectly congruous collection in the middle of the eighteenth century when the British Museum had originated from Hans Sloane's estate; but in the Victorian era, with its growing regard for specialised expertise, this mixture of natural objects and human artefacts made uneasy bedfellows.

The founding of the natural history museum in Kensington was not just the result, however, of overcrowding in Bloomsbury, nor merely a competitive imitation of rival natural history museums which adorned other capital cities (for example, Paris) or university towns (for example, Leyden, Oxford, Cambridge (Mass.)). Two distinct alternatives existed to the founding of a national museum of natural history, each of the two campaigned for in Parliament, defended in testimony to Parliamentary Committees, and urged on the Government in memorials signed by groups of scientists. The first and most obvious of the two alternatives was to keep everything together and simply expand the Bloomsbury Museum. The second was, not only to separate 'nature' from 'art', but in addition to break up the scientific collections into botany, zoology and mineralogy and place each of these in an independent, specialised metropolitan institution. A third possibility, namely, to leave natural history in Bloomsbury and remove the antiquities department to a different site, was mentioned, but never came close to being realised. The credit for founding a separate but unified national museum of natural history must go to Richard Owen (1804–92), who in 1856 was appointed to the new post of superintendent of natural history at the British Museum.

No sooner had Owen taken up his new post than he started a campaign for more space to accommodate the scientific collections. In the late 1850s and early 1860s he put forward a grand but detailed scheme for a national museum to represent a complete epitome of the three kingdoms of nature: plants, animals and minerals. This he did (1) in a 'Report and building plan' of 10 February 1859, sixty copies of which were privately printed for the use of the British Museum trustees; (2) in a lecture 'On the scope and appliances of a national museum of natural history', delivered at the Royal Institution on 26 April 1861, and printed in the *Athenaeum* (27 July, 3 and 10 August 1861); and (3) in a booklet *On the Extent and Aims of a National Museum of Natural History* (1862; the second edition, also of 1862, has changes on pages 83–6) which represented an enlarged version of his Royal Institution talk. Owen envisaged that his museum would contain a central 'index museum' in which indigenous, British collections and a limited array of type-specimens would be displayed, primarily for the benefit of the general public. In the various galleries, however, he wanted as complete a display as possible of genera and even of species, mainly to satisfy the needs of scientific visitors.

In order to dramatise the need for space, Owen argued in some detail for the desirability of a whale gallery in which the largest-known specimens of all whale genera and species would have to be displayed; small objects could be accommodated in any museum, 'but the hugest, strangest, rarest specimens of the highest class of animals can only be studied in the galleries of a national one'.[1] Owen also wanted to exhibit all known species of the largest land mammals, the elephants, arguing that in a national museum a naturalist should be able to study not only generic but also species differences. 'To pare down the cost of a National Establishment of

Zoology, by excluding the bulky specimens from the series, is to take away its peculiar and exclusive function as an instrument in the advancement of natural science.'[2] Because England was the main colonial power in the tropics, it had a special obligation to include in its national museum the large tropical mammals. Equally, the museum should contain the huge, palaeontological monsters of the past: mastodon, megatherium, dinornis and many others. In addition, Owen asked for laboratory space, a library and a lecture room, and he estimated that, *in toto*, a single-storey building covering ten acres was needed or a two-storey building of five acres. Owen tended to be non-committal about whether this additional space should be added onto the existing Bloomsbury building or not; but the very scale of his plan tended to favour the idea of a separate museum elsewhere in London: 'I love Bloomsbury much; but I love five acres more'.[3]

This chapter describes the controversy which Owen's grand plan engendered, both in Parliament and among his scientific colleagues. The issues that were raised and the allegiances of the people who were involved help identify the socio-political tradition which produced the grand cathedral of natural history in South Kensington. In recent years, historians have paid much attention to the institutionalisation of Victorian science, in studies of, for example, the Geological, Zoological and Royal Societies, the British Association, the Royal Institution, the emancipation of the sciences at Oxbridge, and of the 'Lit. & Phil.' movement. Curiously, the reform of the British Museum and the founding of the Museum of Natural History, architecturally the single largest and most monumental of all Victorian scientific institutions, has been entirely left out of these studies. This chapter aims to fill this gap by linking the controversy over Owen's museum scheme to the wider issues of the scientific movement of the 1860s. As such, it complements the recent historical contributions by A.E. Günther and W.T. Stearn to the centenary of the opening of the British Museum (Natural History).[4]

THE PARLIAMENTARY DEBATES

The state of the British Museum and Owen's scheme for a national museum of natural history aroused strong feelings in political circles, and throughout the 1860s the issues were repeatedly debated in Parliament. The most vehement exchanges occurred during the early part of the decade, in the period 1860–63. A variety of topics came in for debate, for example, gas lighting, evening opening, Sunday opening, public lectures, staff salaries and damage to specimens from dust and soot. On the main question, namely, of overcrowding and whether the natural history collections should be removed from the Bloomsbury building and relocated in South Kensington, the Commons was divided approximately along party lines (although at the time political parties were less well-circumscribed than they have since become, and there were several MPs who did not vote with the majority of their party).

Owen's strongest supporter was the then Chancellor of the Exchequer, W.E. Gladstone (1809–98). The most outspoken critic of Owen's plans was the MP William Henry Gregory (1817–92). Gregory had entered Parliament as a Conservative MP for Dublin (1842–47). After a period largely devoted to the turf, he re–entered Parliament as a Liberal–Conservative member for the Irish county Galway (1857–71). His politics became gradually more Liberal, and upon the death of Palmerston, in 1865, he formally joined the Liberal Party. His personal friendship with Disraeli was never replaced, however, by any close relationship with Gladstone whom in fact he disliked. Gregory's strong opposition to Owen was restricted to the early part of the 1860s, and his involvement in museum affairs was not primarily based on an interest in natural history, but derived from his love of art and archaeology. It should be emphasised that the affairs of the British Museum, the National Gallery and the South Kensington Museum (later re-named the Victoria and Albert Museum) were intimately connected and the subject of inquiries by various Royal Commissions and Select Committees. In 1867 Gregory was appointed a trustee of the National Gallery, on the recommendation of Disraeli. He himself owned a collection of pictures, the gems of which he presented to the National Gallery shortly before his death. Gregory was twice married; his second wife was the Irish writer and playwright Isabella Augusta, Lady Gregory.

At a meeting of the British Museum trustees, in January 1860, a resolution was passed by a majority of one vote, to remove the natural history collections from the congested Bloomsbury building. This slender majority was obtained by the attendance of several *ex officio* trustees (more about the trustees below), all members of the Liberal Government. In the Commons, Palmerston defended the trustees' resolution, arguing that, given the need for extra space, a new museum in a suburb would be very much cheaper than a museum extension in central London, in immediate contiguity to the British Museum: 'I agree with those who have said that this is entirely a question of expense.'[5]

Several MPs voiced objections to the trustees' resolution, and Gregory criticised the fact that 'out of the nine in favour of removal, six were Cabinet Ministers, whipped up for the occasion, seldom attending on other occasions'.[6] He moved for a Select Committee to look into the matter, and maintained that increased space could be found in and around the Bloomsbury building. Gregory's main argument in favour of keeping the natural history collections as an integral part of the British Museum was that they 'were the most popular portions of the Museum, the obvious reasons being that persons in a humble position of life were able to understand the objects contained in them, and did not require the special education which an assemblage of Egyptian, Assyrian, and Roman antiquities demanded for their appreciation'.[7] Other MPs, too, used this 'populist' argument: the Bloomsbury Museum was accessible to the mass of London's population; the natural history collections 'presented great attractions to the working classes; and, being there, those classes were gratified by the sight of other objects, by which their tastes were expanded and elevated'.[8] This public good would be defeated by the proposed removal to what was then a distant suburb.

In spite of the intervention by the Home Secretary, George Cornewall Lewis (1806–63), who reiterated the government's belief that removal was desirable and 'very much resolved itself into a question of expenditure',[9] the opposition carried the day and a Select Committee was appointed, presided over by Gregory, 'to inquire how far, and in what way, it may be desirable to find increased space for the Extension and Arrangement of the various Collections of the British Museum, and the best means of rendering them available for the Promotion of Science and Art'.[10] In its *Report*, the Committee advised against the removal of the natural history collections, citing as its principal reasons the accessibility of the British Museum to the general public and the extra expense involved in the construction of a new building and the formation of a new natural history library, the latter necessitated by the fact that the British Museum's national library would remain in Bloomsbury.

During the 1861 session of Parliament, Gregory enlarged upon the recommendations of his Committee's *Report* by attacking Owen's plan as 'crazy, rash, and extravagant' and again as 'foolish, crazy, and extravagant'. He believed that far less space was needed than five or ten acres and that a perfect exhibition of natural history specimens could be accommodated 'by giving up the whole of the second story of the British museum for the purpose'. Owen's scheme was not supported by his colleagues and it also 'would weary and disgust the public'. Gregory's attack was a reaction to Owen's lecture 'On a National Museum of Natural History', delivered at the Royal Institution not long before.[11] Especially the idea of a hall for the exhibition of whales came in for Gregory's ridicule:

> It was shown that the skins of whales could not be procured, and that, if they were procured, the stench would render it totally impossible for anyone but a professor to enter the place where they were kept. He could fancy a notice being posted, 'Shut at present on account of the stench'.[12]

Two Liberals, Austin Henry Layard (1817–94) and Richard Monckton Milnes (1809–85), defended the government's position that the departments of science and art should be separated and that the scientific collections should be removed and placed elsewhere. Gladstone flatly refused to accept the recommendations of the Gregory *Report* and instead jumped to the defence of 'the greatest living naturalist, whose splendid genius and high character ought to have exempted him from being the object of the terms indulged in by the hon. Member for Galway in speaking of Professor Owen's plans'.[13]

In the Spring of 1862 the Government then introduced a Bill to enable the trustees of the British Museum to remove the natural history portions of their collections to South Kensington. During the Commons debate which accompanied the Bill's second reading, the opposition managed to defeat the government, effectively turning the tables on Palmerston's team by appropriating the argument of economy. The stage was set early on in the exchanges by the leader of the opposition, Benjamin Disraeli (1804–81), who warned his fellow MPs of the 'progressive increase of expenditure on civil estimates' and emphasised the fact that the 'estimates of the actual year showed no surplus'.

This was immediately seized upon by Gregory, who repeated Disraeli's remark that the Liberals 'showed their liberality by the reckless manner in which they advocated every attack on the public purse'.[14] Virtually gone was the concern for the elevation of the working classes. The argument of economy was wrenched away from the grasp of the government by focusing attention on the extravagance of Owen's scheme. 'They had on the one side, and standing alone, Professor Owen and his ten-acre scheme, and on the other all the other scientific gentlemen, who were perfectly unanimous in condemning the plan of Professor Owen as being utterly useless and bewildering.' To inspect Owen's proposed galleries from beginning to end, a visitor 'would have to traverse no less a distance than five miles to accomplish it'.[15] And, Gregory warned the House, if the likes of Owen were granted what they asked for, one would have to excavate a second Serpentine as an aquarium, or construct a second Crystal Palace just to accommodate their collection of butterflies.

The same line of argument was followed by a Conservative MP for Oxfordshire, Joseph Warner Henley (1793–1884), who saw no end to the expense and warned his fellow Parliamentarians: 'Let the stone once be set rolling, and then all gentlemen of taste would have a kick at it, and it would be kicked from one to the other, and none of them probably would ever live to see an end of the expense'.[16] This concern about extravagant expenditure was echoed by yet other Conservative Disraeli–men, and even by such Liberals as Ralph Bernal Osborne (1808–82), who in spite of his dislike of the leader of the Opposition, urged the Government to stick to its 'promises of economy, and show that they wished to place the finances of the country in a wholesome state'.[17]

The Government's position was further weakened by one of its supporters, who argued that the issues were too big to be 'converted into mere questions of economy'. The voices of the Home Secretary and, across the floor, of Spencer Horatio Walpole (1806–98), Conservative MP for Cambridge, in support of the Bill, were to no avail. Even Palmerston's promise 'to exclude whales altogether from disporting themselves in Kensington Gardens'[18] proved of no use; the Bill was defeated by a large majority, and in Owen's estimate the building of a new museum was set back by about a decade.

The Government had lost this battle, but it had by no means lost the war, and the following year, in June 1863, it succeeded in winning the next skirmish. Although the Bill to remove portions of the British Museum collections to Kensington had been defeated, Palmerston now introduced a motion to buy the necessary land anyhow. The site of the Exhibition of 1862 in South Kensington, he argued, could accommodate not just the required addition to the

British Museum, but also a Patent Museum and a Portrait Gallery. This land was on offer from the Commissioners of the Exhibition of 1851, at very low cost, and thus the proposal was 'a very economical one'.[19] The argument of economy having been wrested back from the Opposition, Gregory was forced to return to his initial position, indignant at the fact that Palmerston disregarded both his *Report* of 1860 and the Government's massive defeat of the previous year:

> The noble Lord assumed that the art and science collections were to be separated; then that the Natural History Collection was to be removed to Kensington, and that the House of Commons was prepared to reverse the decision arrived at last year, that it would not adopt the gigantic plan, or sanction the gigantic expense attending Professor Owen's scheme ... Every one of the scientific men examined before the Committee of 1860 declared that the establishment of an enormous Natural History Museum, such as was proposed by Professor Owen, would not only be detrimental to the interests of science, but would rather injure than promote the instruction and recreation of the labouring classes.[20]

This time, however, Gladstone had a ready answer to deal with the class argument. He pointed out that a railway system for transporting the public from one point of the metropolis to another had proved to be practicable, easy and lucrative. He expected that in a couple of years a railway ring would be completed, a line of which was to pass close by the South Kensington site. The Government's motion was passed with a comfortable majority.

The Opposition's chance for revenge presented itself a few weeks later. In July 1863, the Government introduced a further motion, this time for the purchase of the International Exhibition Building of 1862 itself, which stood on the South Kensington site. Gladstone argued that this spacious edifice could be adapted to accommodate not only the natural history collections, but also the proposed Patent Museum and a National Portrait Gallery. Furthermore, although the building had been criticised as an unattractive brick structure, it could be improved by means of stucco ornamentation.

A long and furious series of exchanges followed the Chancellor's motion. Gregory derided the brick pile as structurally unsound, 'a ricketty building which would probably some day tumble down about its contents'.[21] The names of expert engineers and architects and their opinions about the Exhibition Building were hurled by the Opposition at the Government and vice versa. Gregory received powerful support from the Conservative Lord Elcho (1818–1914) who was interested in the question of national art galleries, and who read an extract which condemned the building as fit only for an international dog show or for a range of cavalry stables. 'Let us not have the shrine of art set up in the Temple of Ugliness.' Ruskin's opinion was cited, namely that stucco was a form of architectural dishonesty. 'To cover brick with cement, and to divide this cement with joints that it may look like stone is to tell a falsehood ... It is an imposition, a vulgarity, an impertinence, and a sin'.[22] Other members of the House joined in similar emotive attacks. The uproar was such that senior Conservatives, for example Disraeli and Stafford Henry Northcote (1818–87), intervened to calm down the House, but they were shouted down in scenes of confusion which *The Times* described as 'almost unexampled in Parliamentary experience'.[23]

In this greatest triumph over the Government, however, the opposition to Owen's scheme more or less exhausted itself. The political events of the mid-1860s removed much of the resistance to the idea of a separate national museum of natural history. Upon the death of Palmerston in 1865, Gregory changed his political allegiance and formally joined the Liberal party, although he remained opposed to the extension of the franchise and was party to the so-called Cave of Adullam which helped to defeat Lord John Russell's reform bill of 1866. Shortly after, the Tories returned to power under Lord Derby, and Disraeli having steered the Second Reform Bill through the Commons in 1867, succeeded Derby as prime minister in 1868.

Once in office, the Conservatives no longer opposed Owen's museum concept. In a variety of ways, the acquisition, study and display of natural history specimens from around the world, on the grand scale of the South Kensington plan, suited Disraeli's imperial policies. Throughout this period, many of Owen's papers dealt with mammalian fossils from Australia. During two further debates about the British Museum, in 1867 and 1868, Gregory, Disraeli and other former 'Bloomsbury unionists' joined the 'Kensington separatists'. One disillusioned MP accused Disraeli of having

lately been made a convert to a plan which would render the treasures of the Museum still less available – he alluded to the proposed removal of the most popular part of its contents, the

Natural History Collection, to a distant part of the town, out of the reach of the great body of visitors.[24]

Another member of the House turned against Gregory:

With regard to the natural history collection, the hon. Member for Galway was formerly eloquent on the site in Bloomsbury, and was one of the great champions for keeping the collections together. A change has now come over him, and he has turned his back on his former opinions, having apparently been initiated into some secret reason for separation.[25]

Owen, rather sardonically, ascribed the changed situation to 'the acceptance by Mr Gregory of the government of a tropical island'.[26] In fact, Gregory was not appointed governor of Ceylon until 1871. Although Disraeli dropped his opposition to the South Kensington scheme, he took no direct action to get the plan off the ground. It was not until Gladstone's first term as prime minister that the necessary means for the realisation of the new museum were granted by Parliament (without much further opposition or debate) and that, in 1873, the building began to rise out of a hole beside the Cromwell Road.

To some extent, the Parliamentary debates of the early 1860s reflected the opportunism of party politics. The use of the financial argument was part of the Tory attempt to question the success of Gladstone's economic policy of lower taxation, free trade and tariff reductions. Equally, the Conservative emphasis on the interests of the working classes can be seen as part of the preliminaries to the great reform debates of the mid-1860s in which the extension of the franchise to the lower classes figured prominently.

There was more to the British Museum debates, however, than a Tory attempt to frustrate the Liberal/Whig Government of the day. Owen's proposal was part of the larger issue of scientific emancipation and reform which, in the form of the planned natural history museum, forced the Parliamentarians to put a price on the scientific enterprise and allocate a social niche to the emerging class of professional scientists. The latter found a natural ally in the Liberal party, especially in its newer membership of middle-class merchants and industrialists. The Conservatives, by contrast, were more inclined to safeguard the ascendancy of the landed class and the aristocracy.

The Kensington site in particular, to which Owen's plan had been linked more or less from the start, had a strong ideological connotation of whiggishness. It represented part of the cultural heritage of Robert Peel's progressive, liberal Conservatism with its middle-class values of free trade, moderate reform, industrial enterprise, scientific research and education, much of which had been incorporated in Gladstone's Liberalism. Peel had been something of a father-figure to Prince Albert who had played a leading part in the inception and organisation of the Great Exhibition of 1851. With the profits of this hugely successful event, land had been bought in Kensington for a projected cultural complex centred on scientific and technological advancement, sometimes referred to as 'Albertopolis'. The Prince Consort cared little for aristocratic company and preferred the company of *literati*, scientists, educationalists, and so on. Culture superseded class, and the Kensington estate became the hub of a 'brave new world'.[27]

Owen himself belonged to the Peelite–Liberal camp. His early patrons had been liberal Anglicans, such as William Buckland; Peel had awarded Owen a civil list pension; Owen had been actively involved in the 1851 Exhibition, in a variety of capacities; he was a friend of the Prince Consort, invited to the Palace to instruct the Royal children (in the heat of the Parliamentary debates Owen's Kensington plan was at times referred to as a 'court job'); his friends included such Whigs as Macaulay and Russell; the Prince Consort and Macaulay had each called for Owen's promotion to the post of superintendent at the British Museum; Palmerston had accompanied Owen to examine the proposed Kensington site for the new museum; and Gladstone asked Owen for guidance, in person and through correspondence, in his efforts to provide a Kensington seat for the nation's natural history collections. Gladstone and Owen only disagreed in the matter of the proposed purchase of the 1862 Exhibition Building, which Owen regarded as unfit for the realisation of his scheme.[28]

Thus opposition to the removal of the natural history collections to 'Albertopolis' was more than a concern for the inconvenience of the location. It tended to express a Tory dislike of the middle-class entrepreneurial parvenu to whom scientific culture was a means of social advancement, and who had found a political niche in the Liberal party. Gregory had at times expressed his loathing of them: 'He did not wish to see all the institutions of the country fall into the grasp of that craving, meddling, flattering, toadying, self-seeking clique that had established itself at Kensington; that had been doing a good business there, and now wanted to extend its operations.'

And he read to the House a clipping which referred to the representatives of 'science and art' as 'parasites who have fastened themselves upon so many of the institutions which have already gathered about the great Kensington estate, or who are expectants of the new "kingdom come" to be established there'.[29]

REFORM OF MUSEUM MANAGEMENT

Conservative opposition to Owen's scheme was increased by the fact that the proposed move from Bloomsbury to Kensington went hand in hand with a demand for the reform of the British Museum's system of management by trustees, and for its replacement in the new, separate museum of natural history by a form of scientific self-rule in the person of a director. This demand demonstrated that the road to 'Albertopolis' led away from the control of traditional authority and patronage, away, too, from the prestige of title and fortune, to that of professional merit.

In the course of the half-century 1831–81, when the natural history collections were lodged in the Bloomsbury museum, no fewer than four Parliamentary inquiries (in the form of two select committees and two royal commissions) were held, which dealt either exclusively or in part with the condition and management of the British Museum. Each of these inquiries was initiated under a reformist, Whig/Liberal Government: the first in 1835–36 under Melbourne; the second in 1847–49 under Russell; the third in 1860 under Palmerston; and the fourth in 1870–74 under Gladstone.[30] In tandem with the Whig MPs, the scientists themselves emphatically and recurrently demanded reform of the management of the British Museum. This they did not only in testimony before the Parliamentary inquiries, but also in a series of five memorials addressed to the Government; the first in 1847; the two following ones in 1858; the fourth in 1866; and the last in 1879.[31]

The overall control of the British Museum was vested in a Board of Trustees, composed of forty-eight members. One trustee was directly appointed by the Crown. Twenty-three were *ex officio* trustees, who were prominent members of the Government, the Church and the Judiciary, but this category also included the Presidents of the Royal Society, the College of Physicians, the Society of Antiquaries and the Royal Academy. Nine trustees were representatives of families which had made major donations to the

British Museum, such as, for example, the Sloane, Cotton, Harley and Elgin families. Furthermore, fifteen members were elected trustees, chosen by the others. Nearly all family and elected trustees were aristocrats, among whom were several dukes, marquises and earls. Museum appointments came under the patronage of three official trustees, the so-called principal trustees, namely, the Archbishop of Canterbury, the Lord Chancellor and the Speaker of the House of Commons. In its *Report*, the Royal Commission of 1847–49, 'appointed to inquire into the constitution and government of the British Museum', concluded: 'Such a Board of Trustees, to any one who considers the individuals who compose it, with reference to their rank, intelligence, and ability, would give assurance rather than promise of the most unexceptionable, and, indeed, wisest administration in every department.'[32]

By 1847, not even a single, 'token naturalist' had been included among the elected trustees. This obviously rankled with the emerging class of specialists in botany, zoology, palaeontology and so on. As the *Quarterly Review* commented, in an article on 'The British Museum', a breeze was gathering: 'The Naturalists, who were to have been conciliated by the election of Dr. Buckland as trustee on the next vacancy, and who then would have been quiet and dumb as dormice, waxed exceedingly wroth when the honour was conferred on Mr. Macaulay, who canvassed for it.'[33] Indeed, in 1847, when Murchison was president of the BAAS, a memorial 'respecting the Management of the British Museum' was presented to the then Prime Minister, Lord John Russell. It complained that the interest of natural history was not adequately represented on the British Museum's Board of Trustees and it maintained 'that the qualifications of these gifted individuals do not necessarily include an interest in, or the ability to judge of, many of those measures which may best promote Natural History'. The memorial continued as follows:

> Fully acknowledging, that in their accomplishments and high characters the present Trustees offer the best sureties for the satisfactory execution of any duties connected with their own pursuits, we still think that, with the best disposition (and they have already done much good service) these distinguished men are unable adequately to direct the vast and rapidly increasing Natural History Departments of the Museum.[34]

The BAAS memorial suggested that a knowledge of natural history be recognised among the grounds for election to the trusteeship of the British Museum. Among the fifty-seven signatories were, apart from Murchison, the Presidents of the Linnaean, Geological and Entomological Societies, and such well-known names as Greenough, Buckland, Daubeny, Sedgwick, Lyell, Darwin, Hooker, Phillips and many more. Significantly, the President of the Royal Society, the Marquis of Northampton, was not among them. The following year, in 1848, Buckland was elected a British museum trustee. In the early 1850s, Philip de Malpas Grey-Egerton and Murchison himself were added, an aristocrat-palaeontologist and a gentleman-geologist respectively.

Owen, too, was among the scientists who signed the 1847 memorial. In his testimony before the Royal Commission of 1847–49, he complained that on the Board of Trustees the department of natural history was less adequately represented than that of literature and of antiquities; and that this had led to serious inadequacies, such as the lack of a proper conchological collection. Owen, who at the time still worked at the Royal College of Surgeons, advocated a type of intermediate body of experts, analogous to the Museum Committee of the Hunterian Museum which was composed of people 'who have taught anatomy and surgery, and have themselves been curators of anatomical museums'.[35] Furthermore, Owen described in considerable detail the administrative set-up of the Jardin des Plantes, in Paris, where each department was headed by a 'professor-administrator', directly responsible to the cabinet minister in charge of education. The *Quarterly Review* mocked Owen's testimony: 'Conchologists could not help becoming crustaceous when Britannia, who rules, or did rule, the waves, was short in shells and seaweeds.'[36]

A decade later, however, after he had moved from the Hunterian to the British Museum, Owen unequivocally suggested that a new and separate museum of natural history be managed by a director, without an intermediate body of trustees. In his presidential address to the BAAS of 1858, he drew attention to the successful administration of Kew Gardens, the Museum of Economic Geology, and the South Kensington Museum:

For this opens the question, whether in the event of acquiring, in whatever locality, the element essential to a National Museum of Natural History – space – any intermediate organization, unknown in the public establishments above cited, be really needed in the case of Natural History, in order to afford Parliament and the public the requisite guarantee of the good condition of the Collections, and the efficient discharge of the duties and functions of the National Museum of Natural History.[37]

That same year, a handful of scientists, headed by Huxley and including Darwin, again memorialised the Government in the person of the Chancellor of the Exchequer, requesting that any new scientific museum 'be placed under one head, directly responsible to one of Her Majesty's Ministers'.[38] This demand was reiterated in yet another memorial, in 1866, signed by twenty-five 'Darwinians':

> We are of opinion that it is of fundamental importance to the progress of the Natural Sciences in this country that the administration of the National Natural History Collections should be separated from that of the Library and Art Collections, and *placed under one Officer, who should be immediately responsible to one of the Queen's Ministers.*[39]

One of the signatories, P.L. Sclater, brought this memorial to the attention of the BAAS in 1870. He cited Kew Gardens and the Royal Observatory as model institutions, and criticised the fact 'that the actual government of our natural-history collections is at present vested in persons who have no special qualifications for the task'.[40]

In the meantime, one of Owen's parliamentary supporters, Richard Monckton Milnes, called in the House of Commons for changes in the system of government by trustees, citing the exemplary management of Kew Gardens and the Royal Observatory: 'I trust that the natural history collection will, when it is removed, be placed upon a similar footing, and that the system of trustees will, if continued at all, be confined within the present boundaries of the British Museum.'[41] Even Gregory, after his reluctant conversion to 'Kensington separatism', approvingly read to his fellow MPs from the 'Darwinian' memorial of 1866, and he deplored the fact that at the British Museum the superintendent of natural history should be subordinate to the principal librarian (Panizzi) 'who never scrupled to express the most thorough contempt for men of science'.[42]

The most comprehensive recommendations for administrative reform were made in the early 1870s by the Devonshire Commission on Scientific Instruction and Advancement of Science (1870–74). It concluded that the objections to the system of administration by trustees were, with respect to the natural history collections, well-founded and not 'attended by any compensating advantages'.[43] It recommended (1) that the move to Kensington be accompanied by a change in the administrative system; (2) that a director should be appointed by the Crown, immediately responsible to a minister of state, and in charge of the entire administration of the establishment; (3) that Owen be made the first director; and (4) that a Board of Visitors be constituted, nominated in part by the Crown and in part by the various metropolitan scientific societies. When, by the end of the decade, the Commission's recommendations still had not been implemented, the BAAS, in 1879, again addressed the Government, pressing its case for reform.[44] The Treasury continued to drag its feet over the issue, however, and answered:

> The general question whether public aid to science should, in a case like the present, not be allowed to be administered by a body with a certain real independence of its own is a very wide and a very important one; nor is the present the only case which raises it.[45]

In 1879, the Chancellor of the Exchequer was Stafford Northcote, serving in Disraeli's second Cabinet. The reluctance of the Conservatives to remove the natural history collections from under the aegis of the British Museum trustees was no wonder. The clamour for administrative reform was an integral part of the wider reform movement which had also manifested itself in other institutions, and, as Roy MacLeod has argued,[46] represented the gradual advance, not of any radical politics, but of the Peelite tradition of change combined with accommodation, effectively incorporated in Gladstone's Liberalism. During the reform decades of 1830–50, the shrill criticism voiced by Babbage, Brewster, Hamilton, and the *Edinburgh Review*, was assimilated piecemeal by Oxbridge's latitudinarian Anglican scientists, consolidated in the BAAS and in various metropolitan scientific societies. Although seemingly defeated when the Duke of Sussex was elected President of the Royal Society, the demand for reform was ultimately responded to when in the late 1840s the Royal Society changed its constitution and the aristocracy of birth began to give way to the aristocracy of talent.[47] This change occurred in 1847, and the BAAS memorial of that same year asking for adequate representation by scientists on the British Museum's Board of Trustees was a directly linked development.

HUXLEY'S ROAD-BLOCKS

The above makes it clear why traditional Tories did not help pave the way to let Owen take the natural history collections to Albertopolis. It is less obvious, however, why Owen's colleagues, scientists like himself, should have put up road-blocks to try and prevent him from carrying out his scheme for a national museum. Owen was indeed virtually alone in promoting the new museum of natural history. The rest of the scientific élite either did not support his scheme or actively campaigned to prevent it from being realised. Whether it were the somewhat older men such as Darwin and Lyell or the younger scientists such as Hooker Jnr and Huxley, or even British Museum trustees such as Murchison – they all were against Owen's Kensington vision. If it had not been for Owen's own authority and his friendships with leading Liberal politicians and *literati*, the grand cathedral of natural history would never have been built. Why should there have been this opposition to a scientific shrine in which subsequently the white marble statues of Darwin and Huxley seemed so appropriately placed?

In the 1820s and 1830s the idea had at times been put forward by, for example, young Lyell or by N.A. Vigors, to follow the continental example of placing natural objects and human artefacts in separate museums.[48] During the following two decades (the 1840s and 1850s), however, strong opposition had arisen to this idea, for the simple reason that removal of the scientific collections from the British Museum was perceived as denigrating to natural history and its practitioners. In his evidence before the Select Committee of 1835–36, Antonio Panizzi (1797–1879), the influential librarian of the British Museum who in 1856 was appointed principal librarian, had expressed his dislike of scientists, opposed the idea of scientific trustees, and advocated the removal of the natural history collections. As everyone acknowledged, the library formed the core of the Sloanian heritage. But why should natural history be severed from this stem of cultural legitimation? After all, during the first half-century or so of its existence (that is, the second half of the eighteenth century) the British Museum had consisted of manuscripts, printed books and natural history objects. In other words, natural history had right of primogeniture over the much younger department of antiquities. Why should the elder collection be evicted from the Bloomsbury estate?

Accordingly, the scientists tended to show an exaggerated and at times obsessive preoccupation with the national library and its importance to their research activities. In the 1847 memorial, they emphasised that 'we do not contemplate a separation of the Natural History collections from the other departments of the British Museum, as we well know that the cultivation of natural science cannot be efficiently carried on without reference to an extensive library'.[49] Owen was one of the people who signed this memorial, along with Darwin, Hooker, Lyell and others. They all, too, were among the 114 signatories to the first of the two 1858 memorials which was exclusively designed to oppose the idea of severance. They not only objected to the establishment of a new museum but also to the idea that the collections be broken up and dispersed among the specialised museums of the Royal School of Mines, the Linnaean Society, the Zoological Society or other potential, metropolitan depositories.[50] The latter idea had been put forward by, for example, the *Quarterly Review*, in 1850, as a denigrating way of getting rid of natural history:

> Assuredly the interests of wisdom would be promoted if the zoology, fossil and recent, were removed to the Regent's Park, where lecture-rooms might be properly established on Monkey's Green, and analogies and comparisons be assisted by juxtaposition with the living creatures – while scientific ladies would find charming bowers for subsequent colloquies; nor, as respects less ethereal spirits, would the ice-creams be far off. Again, Kew Gardens seem the very place for botany. There the perishable hortus-siccus might be illustrated by nature ever young, and renewed by Flora ever blowing and blooming. The fine Piccadilly Institution would thankfully receive the geological specimens, and any bone surplusage could be reduced by the Surgeons' College, as heretofore.[51]

The issue of piecemeal dispersal came before the Trustees in June 1858, when they considered the suggestion that the Banksian Herbarium be transferred from the British Museum to Kew Gardens, in the charge of the Hookers, Snr and Jnr. Before the sub-committee of natural history, Owen argued that perhaps Kew should receive the botanical collection from the British Museum, but that otherwise natural history, including mineralogy, should be kept together.[52] Darwin effectively expressed the same opinion, stressing the need to keep the natural history collections at the British Museum: some weighty arguments might be advanced in favour of Kew, but 'I think it would be the greatest evil which could possibly happen to natural science in this country, if the other collections were ever to be removed from the British Museum and library'.[53] Lyell registered unqualified opposition to the idea of severance: 'I heard with the greatest concern of the proposal of removing any part of the Botanical Collection from the British Museum to Kew', he wrote to Murchison.[54]

The first of the two 1858 memorials ended in a grand appeal to the Government not to yield to the argument that, because on the Continent objects of art and of nature are exhibited in separate establishments, the same separation should be copied in London. 'Let us, on the contrary, rejoice in the fact, that we have realised what no other kingdom can boast of, and that such vast and harmoniously related accumulation of knowledge is gathered together around a library, illustrating each department of this noble Museum.'[55] The *Quarterly Review*, however, in a discussion of the scientists' memorial, stated perceptively: 'we believe that all their arguments may be summed up into one which they have not expressed – the dread that the separation would diminish their importance'. The anonymous reviewer (John W. Jones, a librarian at the British Museum) pointed out that in fact a removal from the British Museum would liberate natural history, and in particular its superintendent, from the humiliating control of Antonio Panizzi, who as principal librarian was the head of the museum:

> Is this the proper position for a man like Professor Owen, who has spent his life in forcing nature to give up her secrets? Is it right that learning so extensive and so accurate should be confined to so narrow a sphere, and that the exercise of such rare powers of communicating information should thus be impeded? Let the natural history be elevated to its rightful dignity. Let it form an independent institution, with Professor Owen at its head, and let him have a temple of his own instead of being a lodger.[56]

This issue of the *Quarterly Review* appeared in July 1858, and Owen soon took up its suggestion. In September 1858, in his presidential address to the BAAS, he cautiously began to promote the idea of removal to a separate museum, and a few months later, in February 1859, he produced his first, detailed plan for a national collection of natural history.[57]

No sooner had Owen indicated that he was coming around to the idea of a separate museum, than Huxley started a campaign to thwart it, putting up road-blocks wherever possible to prevent the natural history collections from being transported to Albertopolis. As Adrian Desmond has explained, Huxley belonged to a fast-rising middle class of new-style biologists who nurtured a strong anti-clerical bias and who became the crusaders in the cause of Darwinian evolution. They manoeuvred to capture control of the key scientific posts in the metropolis, for example, in the Royal Society, the University of London, and so on.[58] The greatest obstacle to the attainment of this goal was Owen: he was regarded by many of his contemporaries as the greatest living naturalist, and his Peelite allegiance was entirely at odds with Huxley's aggressive and radical stratagem. To block Owen was, temporarily, a higher priority than to promote the cause of natural history, even if this required duplicitous tactics.

Huxley had signed the memorial of July 1858, which objected to the removal or dispersal of the natural history collections; but in November of the same year, shortly after Owen had come out in support of emancipation from the British Museum, Huxley composed a further memorial to the Chancellor of the Exchequer, supported by a small number of colleagues among them Darwin. In this memorial Huxley not only went along with what Darwin only four months earlier had described as 'the greatest evil', namely, removal from the British Museum, but in addition the memorialists argued that the natural history collections should be broken up and distributed among various metropolitan institutions. The main botanical collection, the Banksian Herbarium and the fossil plants, should be moved to Kew Gardens, in the charge of Huxley's close friends, the Hookers. For zoology there should be established a Popular Museum and a Scientific one, possibly in one and the same building; this museum would require an appropriate zoological library. Furthermore, Huxley *cum suis* recommended that the new Museum of Economic Zoology be further developed, and that the disposal of the mineral collection also be considered.[59] Although this was not spelt out, mineralogy would, if removed, most likely be deposited in the Museum of Economic Geology, where Huxley was professor and curator. The most obvious potential beneficiaries of this plan were Hooker and Huxley.

In spite of this double somersault away from the July 1858 memorial, Huxley self–righteously insisted in his testimony before the Gregory Committee of 1860 that 'I am at a loss to understand in what respect, or where, the inconsistency lies between the two documents.'[60] In reality, however, Huxley had changed his stance not only with respect to where the natural history collections should be located, but also in the matter of administrative reform (from trustees to a single director), lest Owen be elevated to the post of museum director: 'I am much inclined to believe, as matters now stand,' Huxley stated before the Gregory Committee, in support of the trustees system, 'that it is a very important circumstance to have a body of educated and liberal gentlemen, men of the world and of standing in society, interposed between men of science and men of letters on the one hand, and mere officials on the other'.[61]

Huxley also opposed Owen as to the space required for a proper museum display. Space was directly related to the issue of prestige. To Owen, a museum was first and foremost a place for scientific research and only in second place an institution for the entertainment and education of the visiting multitudes. That is what the prestigious Jardin des Plantes was, and during his tenure as Curator of the Hunterian Museum, Owen had nurtured the ambition of expanding the museum of the Royal College of Surgeons into a national museum, 'worthy of being the great national depository of the sciences with which it is connected'.[62] The *Lancet* readily supported Owen's ambitious South Kensington scheme.[63] Such a research institution needed comprehensive collections, even of the largest mammals, and therefore space:

> My idea of the scope and appliances of a National Museum of Natural History leads me to view it as the place where the naturalist would find the readiest means of comparing the most gigantic quadrupeds of Africa and Asia, not only in regard to the structure of their molar teeth, but as to the proportion of their height to breath, in the shape of the head, in the relative size of the ears (which differs extraordinarily in the two species in question), in the shape and proportion of the tusks, and in the degree in which those ivory weapons are developed in the male and female of each species.[64]

A national museum of natural history, Owen enthused, had to be

> an establishment not merely essential to the progress of that branch of knowledge, but, in a national point of view, constituting a material symbol of civilisation and appreciation of science, for the realisation of which the resources of the greatest commercial

and colonizing empire of the world give it peculiar advantages and facilities.[65]

Owen's parliamentary supporters, such as Monckton Milnes, echoed this vision in the Commons by calling for a serious, scientific museum, not 'a mere raree-show'; 'What we want to do is to rival that magnificent establishment, the Jardin des Plantes; an establishment which has satisfied the aspirations of all scientific men, but which it never occurred to any Frenchmen to unite with the Louvre.'[66] In an age of science, the nation needed a first-rate scientific museum, whether the public would visit it or not.

Owen's parliamentary adversaries, on the other hand, eagerly used the ammunition provided by Huxley (initially referred to as 'Professor Huxtable') who criticised Owen's elaborate scheme. The whale gallery, for example, would not interest the public, the whales would be difficult to obtain, the skins, even if procured, would produce an intolerable stench.

In fine, I should be extremely sorry to see the Government spending the prodigious sum of money which this building would cost, upon a plan that seems to have been so little matured, and which certainly would not be convenient, either for the man of science, or for the general public.

To alleviate the overcrowding of the British Museum, Huxley estimated that two (or two and a half) and not Owen's ten acres would suffice, even taking into account 'every specimen that is likely to be obtained in the next 50 years'.[67]

The issue of the purpose of a museum (whether for public instruction or for scientific research) and of museum organisation (what to exhibit and what to put in store) was a serious one, discussed by J.E. Gray and A.C.L. Günther, keepers of zoology at the British Museum, and later by W.H. Flower who in 1884 succeeded Owen as director of the new Natural History Museum.[68] During the crucial early 1860s, however, the issue of museum organisation and space was directly related to that of the purpose and prestige of natural history as a scientific subject and a profession. To argue that a limited display of selected specimens would best serve the interest of the working classes, as a number of MPs did who opposed Owen's scheme, was equivalent to downgrading natural history by implying that its primary purpose was no more than popular entertainment.[69] Owen's demand for space, on the other hand, was part of a strategy to elevate the social status of scientific work. Huxley's aiding and abetting of the parliamentary detractors of natural history can only be explained by his desire to block Owen. It is true that Huxley was a committed public lecturer, but so was Owen. Huxley's obstruction irritated the *British Medical Journal* which regretted the lack of appreciation of 'the expanded ideas of Mr. Owen':

> Professor Owen's name in public print seems to be invariably the forerunner of Professor Huxley's in the same. And thus we find in *The Times* a letter *per contra* from the latter gentleman, asserting that two acres – not ten, as Professor Owen says are sufficient for the purposes of a British Natural History Museum.[70]

History has not been kind to Owen. In 1885, little over a year after Owen's retirement from the British Museum (Natural History), Huxley unveiled Darwin's statue on the grand staircase of the central hall. In the *Life and Letters* of Hooker, the success of Owen's museum was ascribed to Hooker and Huxley.[71] Owen, on the other hand, is best known, not for his grand accomplishment in Kensington, but for his attack on 'Darwin and the origin of species', published in the *Edinburgh Review*. In his *Autobiography*, Darwin reminisced about his relationship with Owen as follows: 'After the publication of the Origin of Species he became my bitter enemy, not owing to any quarrel between us, but as far as I could judge out of jealousy at its success.'[72] The Owen–Darwin conflict has become one of the best-known instances of personal animosity in the history of science. Apart from Adrian Desmond,[73] historians have tended uncritically to perpetuate Darwin's (and Huxley's) account. This study does not deal with the question of Owen's personality or motivation. It does throw, however, a new and more even light on the Owen–Darwin controversy by showing that the Darwinian camp acted with the same jealous duplicity of which Owen is habitually accused. Moreover, Owen's attack on Darwin's crowning glory appeared in April 1860, nearly a year and a half after Huxley, Darwin and others had attempted to sabotage Owen's vision of what was to become his most monumental accomplishment.

CONCLUSION

The founding of the Natural History Museum in South Kensington must be credited to Owen's vision and Gladstone's political pertinacity. It was not merely an architectural expression of the popularity of natural history. The new museum, its dimensions and even its location, were the product of reformist ideals in the Peelite tradition, and represented a triumph mainly over right-wing opposition from Conservative politicians who resented the growing authority of science within the country's cultural institutions. It also represented a victory over left-wing obstruction, primarily from Huxley, Darwin and others whose socio-political allegiance was of a more radical, anti-clerical hue than Owen's, and who plotted to prevent the expansion of his institutional power base.

Acknowledgement

The author wishes to thank Drs William Bynum and Colin Matthews for scrutinising the penultimate version of this chapter.

NOTES

1. Richard Owen, *On the Extent and Aims of a National Museum of Natural History* (London: Saunders, 1862) pp. 22–3.
2. Ibid., pp. 29–30.
3. 'Report from the Select Committee on the British Museum', *Parliamentary Papers*, 1860 (540) XVI, p. 262.
4. A.E. Günther, *The Founders of Science at the British Museum, 1753–1900* (Suffolk: Halesworth Press, 1980). W.T. Stearn, *The Natural History Museum at South Kensington. A History of the British Museum (Natural History), 1753–1980* (London: Heinemann, 1981).
    At the time of the opening of the new museum, the events leading up to it were recounted by Owen in his presidential address to the biology section of the British Association, *Report BAAS, 1881*, pp. 651–61. This account was reprinted, *mutatis mutandis*, in R. Owen, *The Life of Richard Owen*, vol. II (London: Murray, 1894) pp. 28–58.
5. *Hansard's*, CVLIII (24 April 1860), col. 49.
6. Id., col. 41.
7. Id., col. 42.
8. Id., col. 48.
9. Id., col. 44.
10. 'Report from the Select Committee on the British Museum', *Parliamentary Papers*, 1860 (540), vol. XVI, p. ii.
11. *Athenaeum*, nos. 1761–3 (1861) 118–20, 153–5, 187–9.
12. *Hansard's*, CLXIV (22 July 1861) col. 1323–4.

13. Id., col. 1331.
14. Id., CLXVI (19 May 1862) col. 1913.
15. Id., col. 1908, 1910.
16. Id., col. 1932.
17. Id., col. 1930.
18. Id., col. 1931.
19. Id., CLXXI (15 June 1863) col. 907.
20. Id., col. 913.
21. Id., CLXXII (2 July 1863) col. 126.
22. Id., col. 99.
23. *Sir William Gregory, an Autobiography*. Edited by Lady Gregory (London: Murray, 1894) p. 225.
24. *Hansard's*, CLXXXIX (29 July 1867) col. 345.
25. Id., col. 350. See also (Elisabeth Eastlake and Harriet Grote), 'The British Museum', *Quarterly Review*, CXXIV (1868) pp. 147–79.
26. Owen, 'Address', *Report BAAS, 1881*, p. 656.
27. See, for example, Asa Briggs, *The Age of Improvement, 1783–1867* (London and New York: Longman, 1979) pp. 454–62.
28. Owen's contributions to the Great Exhibition of 1851 can be gauged from two of his publications: 'Raw materials from the animal kingdom', in *Lectures on the Results of the Great Exhibition of 1851* (London: Bogue, 1852) pp. 77–131; *Geology and Inhabitants of the Ancient World* (London: Crystal Palace Library, 1854).

    The Gladstone–Owen correspondence about the British Museum took place mainly during 1861–2; the letters concerning the Exhibition Building, Gladstone to Owen, 14 August 1862, and Owen to Gladstone, 18 August 1862, were transcribed by Owen in an 1879 autograph manuscript 'On the British Museum of Natural History', British Museum (Natural History), Owen Correspondence, vol. 59, pp. 210–14. The published version (note 4 above) omitted this exchange.
29. *Hansard's*, CLXXI (15 June 1863) col. 922–3.
30. (a) 'Reports from the Select Committee appointed to inquire into the Condition, Management and Affairs of the British Museum', *Parliamentary Papers*, 1835 (479) VII; 1836 (440) X.

    (b) 'Report of the Commissioners appointed to inquire into the Constitution and Government of the British Museum', id., 1850 (1170) XXIV.

    (c) 'Report from the Select Committee on the British Museum', id., 1860 (540) XVI.

    (d) 'Fourth Report of the Royal Commission appointed to make inquiry with regard to Scientific Instruction and the Advancement of Science', id., 1874 (c. 884) XXII.
31. (a) 'Memorial to the First Lord of the Treasury, presented on the 10th day of March, by Members of the British Association for the Advancement of Science, and of other Scientific Societies, respecting the Management of the British Museum, with the Names affixed', *Parliamentary Papers*, 1847 (268), vol. 34, pp. 253–6.

    (b) 'Memorial addressed to Her Majesty's Government by the Promoters and Cultivators of Science on the Subject of the proposed Severance from the British Museum of its Natural History Collections, together with the Signatures attached thereto' (presented 6 July 1858), id., 1857–8 (456), vol. 33, pp. 499–504.

(c) 'Memorial addressed to the Right Honourable the Chancellor of the Exchequer' (presented 19 November 1858), id., 1859 (126), vol. 14, pp. 64–7.

(d) 'Memorial presented to the Right Hon. the Chancellor of the Exchequer' (dated 14 May 1866), *Report BAAS 1879*, p. lxi.

(e) 'To the Right Hon. the First Lord of the Treasury' (dated 25 March 1879), id., pp. lx–lxi.

32. Note 30 (b) above, p. 7.

33. (Richard Ford), 'The British Museum', *Quarterly Review*, LXXXVIII (1850) p. 151.

34. Note 31 (a) above, p. 253.

35. Note 30 (b) above, p. 177.

36. *Quarterly Review*, LXXXVIII (1850), p. 148.

37. *Report BAAS 1858*, p. xcvii.

38. Note 31 (c) above, p. 66.

39. Note 31 (d) above, p. lxi.

40. P.L. Sclater, 'On certain principles to be observed in the establishment of a National Museum of Natural History', *Report BAAS 1870*, p. 124.

41. *Hansard's*, CLXVI (19 May 1862) col. 1914.

42. Id., CXCI (27 March 1868) col. 394.

43. Note 30 (d) above, pp. 9–10, 29.

44. Note 31 (e) above.

45. 'To the President and General Secretaries of the British Association for the Advancement of Science' (dated 22 July 1879), *Report BAAS 1879*, p. lxii.

46. Roy M. MacLeod, 'Whigs and savants: reflections on the reform movement in the Royal Society, 1830–48', in Ian Inkster and Jack Morrell (eds), *Metropolis and Province. Science in British Culture, 1780–1850* (London: Hutchinson, 1983) pp. 55–90.

47. Marie Boas Hall, *All Scientists Now. The Royal Society in the Nineteenth Century* (Cambridge University Press, 1984) pp. 63–91.

48. (Charles Lyell), 'Scientific Institutions', *Quarterly Review*, XXXIV (1826) 156. N.A. Vigors expressed his view before the Select Committee in 1836; note 30 (a) above, 1836 (440) X, pp. 115–17.

49. Note 31 (a) above, p. 354.

50. Note 31 (b) above, pp. 500–1.

51. *Quarterly Review*, LXXXVIII (1850) pp. 155–6.

52. 'Papers relating to the enlargement of the British Museum', *Parliamentary Papers*, 1859 (126), vol. XIV, pp. 55–6.

53. Darwin to Murchison, 19 June 1858, id., p. 61.

54. Lyell to Murchison, 21 June 1858, id., pp. 60–1.

55. Note 31 (b) above, p. 502.

56. (J.W. Jones), 'British Museum', *Quarterly Review*, CIV (1858) pp. 222–3.

57. Owen, 'Address', *Report BAAS 1858*, pp. xcv–xcvii. 'Report from the Superintendent of the Department of Natural History, 10 February

1859', *Parliamentary Papers*, 1859 (126), vol. XIV, pp. 72–5.
58. Adrian Desmond, *Archetypes and Ancestors. Palaeontology in Victorian London, 1850–1875* (London: Blond and Briggs, 1982).
59. Note 31 (c) above.
60. Note 30 (c) above, p. 301.
61. Id.
62. 'Hunterian Museum', *Parliamentary Papers*, 1851 (75), vol. XLIII, p. 395. Arthur Keith, 'Abstract of minutes of the Museum Committee. From 1800–1907' (Royal College of Surgeons, unpublished typescript, 1908) p. 72. See also N.A. Rupke, 'Richard Owen's Hunterian lectures on comparative anatomy and physiology, 1837–55', *Medical History*, XXIX (1985) pp. 237–58.
63. *Lancet*, 16 November 1861, p. 484.
64. *Athenaeum*, 27 July 1861, p. 119.
65. Owen, *Inaugural Address on the Opening of the New Philosophical Hall at Leeds, on Tuesday, the 16th of December, 1862* (Leeds, Philosophical and Literary Society, 1863) p. 16.
66. *Hansard's*, CLXVI (19 May 1862) col. 1915.
67. Note 30 (c) above, p. 303.
68. J.E. Gray, 'Address', *Report BAAS 1864*, pp. 75–80. A.C.L. Günther, 'Address', *Report BAAS 1880*, pp. 591–8. W.H. Flower, *Essays on Museums and other Subjects connected with Natural History* (London: Macmillan, 1898) pp. 1–53.
69. There were of course MPs, such as the 'advanced' Liberal, Ralph Bernal Osborne (1808–12), whose concern for working class education was more direct.
70. *British Medical Journal*, 24 May 1862 (I), p. 550.
71. Leonard Huxley, *Life and Letters of Sir Joseph Dalton Hooker*, vol. I (London: Murray, 1918) p. 380.
72. Gavin de Beer (ed.), *Charles Darwin and T.H. Huxley. Autobiographies* (Oxford University Press, 1983) p. 61.
73. *Archetypes and Ancestors*, passim.

5 Sonar, Wireless Telegraphy and the Royal Navy: Scientific Development in a Military Context, 1890–1939

Willem Hackmann

INDUSTRIAL AND INSTITUTIONAL RESEARCH

The development of sonar and wireless telegraphy (W/T) in the Royal Navy are prime examples of institutional research directed to specific short-term goals – research which the Americans call 'mission-oriented'. Sonar, or asdics as it was known by the Royal Navy until the early 1950s, has never caught the public imagination to the extent that radar has.[1] Both have a common origin in electronics, and their development was governed by an intricate web of factors: scientific, bureaucratic, tactical and political. In turn, these new technologies have had a profound impact on modern warfare. As this study will attempt to show, research in a military context is nearly always a mixture of research and development (R & D); the goal is not the elucidation of a basic principle, but an operational device. In this kind of activity, which is intensely complex, once it has been shown that the principle will work, non-technical factors begin to predominate. If it were an industrial invention, market considerations would take over, but in our present case it will be the military planners who will define the exact need.[2]

Most technological innovations in the eighteenth century were achieved by lone inventors, of whom James Watt is the popular stereotype. The rapid growth of science since the Industrial Revolution produced new technical markets: synthetic dyes, vulcanised rubber, electric power, the telegraph, electric light, and the telephone. These markets could only be sustained and expanded by new innovations. This led to the inception of industrial research by technical-based firms and of institutional research by Government agencies, including the Royal Navy.

The Germans pioneered the use of applied science on a notable scale, starting with their aniline dye industry in the 1870s, followed by their electrical industry. This made it increasingly difficult for English chemical and electrical firms to compete with their German rivals, and they began to follow suit, albeit slowly. The chemical firm of Read, Holliday of Huddersfield was possibly the first in this country to establish an industrial research laboratory by 1890, staffed almost entirely by German-trained chemists. Later that year, the United Alkali Company founded its research and analytical laboratory.[3]

Progress was slower in the physical sciences. In a sense, the oldest English laboratory in this area was the Royal Observatory at Greenwich, established by Charles II to improve navigation. Agitation in the late nineteenth century for a State physical laboratory by, among others, Kelvin, Oliver Lodge, and Rayleigh, resulted in the creation of the National Physical Laboratory in 1897.[4] Industrial physics laboratories were slower off the mark here than in Germany or America. Among the first of the American-organised industrial research facilities were Thomas Edison's laboratories, first at Menlo Park (1876) and then at West Orange, New Jersey (1887); the latter was the largest private research establishment in the world at that time. Edison epitomised the transition in America from the lone inventor–entrepreneur to organised industrial research, creating new products and markets. Other important American research laboratories established before the First World War were those of the American Telephone and Telegraph, Eastman Kodak, Du Pont and Westinghouse.[5]

The early record of the development of commercial research laboratories is very incomplete, especially in Britain. Many firms have destroyed their archives, and where information is available, it is often difficult to determine the exact nature of the establishment: was it a 'laboratory' or more simply a 'development department'?[6] They varied in scope from purely practical problem-solving, analysing and testing products, to inventing new products or processes. A very few concentrated on basic research, such as the American General Electric laboratory established in 1900,[7] and the now better-known Bell Telephone Laboratories of New Jersey, founded in 1925 and supported out of the income of the American Telephone and Telegraph Company.[8]

The Admiralty, like other Government agencies, has always been free to seek advice from civilian scientific advisors even if, as is the nature of conservative bureaucratic institutions, responses to scientific and technological changes were usually dilatory and, at the beginning, often negative. Thus, an exasperated Sir John Arbuthnot (later Lord) Fisher vented his feelings about the Admiralty's inability to grasp the importance of the submarine in future warfare in one of his characteristic memoranda, written shortly before the First World War: 'There is a strong animus against the submarine – of course there is! An ancient Admiralty Board Minute described the introduction of the steam engine as fatal to England's navy. Another Admiralty Board Minute vetoed iron ships, as iron sinks and wood floats.'[9] Allan Chapman has pointed out in this volume that the founding of the Royal Observatory in 1675 was the Government's first acknowledgement that benefit could be gained from scientific advice, especially in maritime affairs. Technical advice became increasingly more necessary with the dramatic growth in science, so that by the 1830s the then Astronomer Royal, Sir George Airy, served the Government on numerous Commissions and Enquiries on subjects as diverse as railway gauges, decimal currency and submarine telegraphy.

Other individual scientists, too, gave advice. Sir William Snow Harris developed a system of lightning conductors for Royal Navy warships, and in the early 1840s the Admiralty asked Michael Faraday's opinion about the electric telegraph. Within a few years, the semaphore stations were closed down in favour of the telegraph. The Admiralty also co-operated with the telegraph companies in the laying of submarine cables, and it did not take long for this system to become important tactically and strategically. The earliest recorded naval use of the telegraph was to report the capture of Bomarsund on 16 August 1854, in the Crimean War, the first war in which the telegraph was used extensively. This device was the harbinger of the communications revolution that was to come. By the end of the 1870s all the main British naval stations were connected by telegraph with the Admiralty; the telegraph had revolutionised warfare.[10]

Other inventions from the physical sciences, especially electrical, had a great impact on naval warfare in the last decades of the nineteenth century. The design of the electric dynamo had advanced sufficiently in the 1870s for powerful arc-light searchlights to be installed on ships. This made night action a viable possibility for the first time, and it could also protect ships at anchorage from attacks with one of the most potent of the new technological naval weapons – the Whitehead torpedo.[11]

The 'automobile' torpedo was even then a highly complex device, requiring the latest techniques in metallurgy for the manufacture of the pressure vessel for the compressed air engine, in precision engineering, and in electrics (based on telegraph technology). In 1871, the Admiralty bought the manufacturing rights for £15 000. Production of torpedoes began at the Royal Laboratories, Woolwich, the following year, transferring to the Royal Gun Factory in 1893. Whitehead had opened his factory at Weymouth shortly before, which survived until recently under the ownership of Vickers, Armstrong Ltd, but apart from during the First World War, nearly the entire production was sold abroad.

EARLY R & D AT THE TORPEDO SCHOOL

Until the First World War, the Royal Navy had little experience in R & D and in accommodating civilian scientists. The Torpedo School began teaching a certain amount of physics and electricity to naval officers from the 1870s, simply because the new torpedoes and other such devices contained electrical and mechanical components, and because this establishment had available a ready pool of expertise. Thus it was natural for the Torpedo School to become involved with the development of new electrical devices for the Navy. The School's ship, HMS *Vernon* at Portsmouth, designed, in conjunction with Portsmouth Dockyard, powerful ship-borne searchlights and, in the early 1890s, also started to investigate the feasibility of hydrophones (underwater microphones) for detecting submarines. The latter was based on contemporary work on telephony by Graham Bell and others.[12]

The US Lighthouse Board reported in 1889 on an underwater warning bell and hydrophone system designed by L.I. Blake of the University of Kansas. A similar system was invented a few years later independently by Elisha Gray and A.J. Mundy, which in 1901 was marketed as a navigational aid by the Submarine Signal Company, specially founded for the purpose.[13] The signals of these underwater bells, located under lightships, near lighthouses, shoals, wrecks and other hazards, were received by ships at ranges of about ten miles by hydrophones fitted in the bows. By 1912, this technology was well established in the US, Britain and Germany. The navies of these countries, too, were beginning to equip their ships with hydrophones for navigational use, and for underwater sound-signalling with submarines, but not yet for anti-submarine warfare.[14] However, by this time a serious competitor to underwater acoustic signalling and navigation had appeared – wireless telegraphy.

PRE-WAR RADIO R & D AT THE TORPEDO SCHOOL

Pioneering work on wireless telegraphy was also begun at the Torpedo School. The development of radio at sea is very largely the early history of radio itself.[15] When Marconi met Captain H.B. (later Admiral Sir Henry) Jackson in the early autumn of 1896, the latter had been involved independently in similar wireless experiments at the Torpedo School ship HMS *Defiance* at Devonport. Jackson, however, had not advanced as far as Marconi, and their professional association soon became a close friendship.

Jackson's interest in wireless grew from a new operational requirement brought about by the introduction of fast torpedo boats in the Royal Navy during the 1880s. These craft required an effective method of signalling with their parent ships, during both day and night, and unhindered by adverse weather conditions such as fog. In 1891 Jackson, then a young torpedo officer, suggested that the 'Hertzian' waves could perhaps be used for this purpose.[16] The Admiralty were dubious at first, but Jackson convinced them by practical demonstrations that the system was workable, and that the induction of the transmitter would not explode detonators, set fire to the ammunition magazines, electrocute, or affect magnetic compasses.[17] The decision was taken to develop wireless telegraphy, and the responsibility for its introduction into the Royal Navy passed from the Torpedo School to the Signal Committee of the Admiralty who, according to Admiral Sir Reginald Bacon, 'knew the colour of every flag and all about Morse code, but to whom electricity was a sealed science'. There was, of course, no reason why the Committee should have known in the past anything about electricity, and the technical development of wireless telegraphy remained with the Torpedo School until the reorganisation of 1917. Marconi, too, concentrated at this time on marine radio, and not on land-based systems, because of the interest shown by the Royal Navy.

The Portsmouth Torpedo School, HMS *Vernon*, became involved in wireless telegraphy in 1898, and eventually took over from HMS *Defiance* because of proximity to the Marconi stations at Alum Bay and Bournemouth. Furthermore, Jackson was temporarily appointed to *Vernon* in October 1899 to organise a Wireless Telegraphy Section and to establish a course of instruction for operators, after the success of wireless telegraphy in the summer manoeuvres, in which he commanded one of the three ships fitted with sets.[18] Lengthy negotiations about the amount of royalty payable to the Marconi

Company by the Admiralty were concluded in 1900. The Admiralty decided to accept the Company's terms because the Marconi sets were found to be superior to the 'service' sets developed at *Vernon*. Thirty-two Marconi sets were purchased, but service sets continued to be developed.

The first civilian scientist to be appointed to the Wireless Telegraphy Section of HMS *Vernon* was H.A. Madge in February 1904. He may well have had the distinction of being the first to have been employed directly on scientific and technical work for any of the three Services; in fact, of being the first 'Government scientist'.[19] A graduate of Trinity College, Cambridge, he gained his experience at Marconi before joining *Vernon*, when he was aged about 28. He left the Service in 1919 to become a missionary. Many of the early experiments were performed on an old frigate, HMS *Warrior*, the first iron-clad warship every built for the Royal Navy, taken off the Reserve and sent to Portsmouth for this purpose.

The W/T Section of the Torpedo School was kept very busy designing radio sets for shore stations, aircraft (including airships), ships, and submarines before the First World War. Research covered all aspects of radio design, and the emphasis was on developing practical sets, rather than on fundamental research. Notable break-throughs were made in the decades before the First World War. Sensitive headphones (based on the recent telephony technology) were incorporated in the receivers by 1905, signal ranges were increased dramatically, the transmitters became more directional and could be operated on different wavelengths to cut out interference, and power was increased by replacing the batteries and induction coil by an alternator with a transformer. Thermionic valves began to be studied in 1908, including the testing of valves produced commercially. An essential break-through during this period was the development of the continuous wave transmitter. The first transmitters were all of the damped wave type which suffered severe drawbacks. A possible solution was the 'quenched spark' transmitter, studied at *Vernon*, but this was abandoned in favour of the Poulson arc continuous wave transmitter developed by the Telefunken Company. *Vernon* began developing Poulson arc transmitters and continous wave receivers in 1913.[20] During this period *Vernon* not only remained abreast of the substantial advances being made in wireless technology in Great Britain, Germany and the US, but also adapted and improved this technology for the specific requirements of the Royal Navy.

By 1910 wireless telegraphy had become a serious competitor to underwater sound navigation and signalling. In the US, the Submarine Signal Company fought back by inducing Professor R.A. Fessenden, an electrical engineer and radio pioneer, to develop an underwater device capable of transmitting Morse code. His 'oscillator', a reciprocating electromagnetic induction motor moving a steel diaphragm 540 times per second, became available in 1913. Its continuous oscillations could be modulated into the sharp short dots and dashes of Morse by means of the ordinary telegraph key, and even experiments on underwater speech (that is, telephonic) transmission were partly successful. This device was also the first transducer: that is, one instrument being used both as a transmitter and receiver of underwater sound. It was, however, generally used as a transmitter with a conventional hydrophone receiver. In essence, this apparatus was the underwater analogue of wireless telegraphy, and came from the same technology. The British Consulate in Boston reported to the Admiralty the successful trials of Fessenden's apparatus, witnessed in the local harbour in June 1914. A set was immediately ordered for development at *Vernon*. Two versions were quickly designed and an extensive fitting programme was recommended, but owing to the exigencies of war this was effectively cut down to the fitting-out of submarines only, for underwater signalling.[21]

The second civilian scientist, Carl L. Glen-Bott, was appointed at *Vernon* in April 1908, to be in charge of civilian draughtsmen and specifications. He, too, came from Trinity College, Cambridge. The next senior civilian was Wilfred S. Peake, a graduate of London University, who joined as Design Assistant in 1911. His brother was a tutor at St. John's College, Cambridge, who had taught both Madge and Glen-Bott in the engineering laboratories at Cambridge. Peake first went to *Vernon* the previous year to demonstrate a new instrument, the Duddell thermo-ammeter for measuring high frequency currents, manufactured by the Cambridge Scientific Instrument Company. Partly as a result of this visit, he decided to apply in 1911 for the advertised post of 'Assistant to the Wireless Expert' at *Vernon*.[22]

The organisation of the W/T Section at *Vernon* was reviewed in 1913 by a committee under Jackson, by then a Vice-Admiral and Chief of the War Staff.[23] At this time practically all the actual experimental work was carried out by lieutenants (T), who were only there for a short time. This provided little continuity, and revealed the short-term nature of the work. One such lieutenant in 1913 was J.F. (later Admiral Sir James) Somerville, who joined for a brief period after having been Fleet Wireless Officer. In the Second World War this distinguished naval officer for a period led the British Admiralty Delegation in Washington, DC, one of the main channels for scientific and technical exchanges on naval matters.

The Jackson Committee recommended an increase in the civilian technical staff: a W/T expert to act as Supervisor of Research Work, a civilian electrical engineer to replace one of the torpedo lieutenants working on W/T, and an assistant for the specifications section. The idea that Professor C.L. Fortescue should be moved from the Royal Naval College at Greenwich to direct research was rejected in favour of appointing a well-qualified assistant to Madge. This was another Trinity College graduate, B.S. Gossling, who was working under J.J. Thomson on the refraction of radio waves, and whom Thomson highly recommended. He was appointed the day before the First World War broke out, and remained until May 1919, when he went to the GEC Research Laboratory at Brook Green, Hammersmith (later at Wembley). Glen-Bott's assistant on specifications was not appointed until 1916, and was chosen from 210 applicants.

ORGANISING SCIENCE FOR THE WAR AT SEA

The First World War had a dramatic impact on scientific research in the Royal Navy. The Admiralty, in line with most politicians and the general public, assumed that the war would be over in a few months. When it became apparent that this would not be the case, all avenues had to be explored to stop the German war machine, and especially the U-boat. On 22 September 1914, the Admiralty realised how unprepared the Navy was to combat the German submarine when the *U9* sank the three armoured cruisers *Hogue, Cressy* and *Aboukir*. The threat had become even more serious by 1917, during the unrestricted U-boat campaign against British mercantile supply lines. A key question to be resolved was how to organise science for the war effort.

As the months of war dragged on, with ever-mounting casualties, it became increasingly obvious to the scientific community that, in the words of H.G. Wells, the war had become essentially a 'struggle of invention'.[24] The fear was that the Germans, unlike the Allies, were making full use of their scientists. A sign of the Admiralty's growing anxiety was a circular letter sent round the Fleet in May 1915 offering prizes for ideas for effective U-boat counter-measures. Suggestions ranged from the use of kites, balloons and aircraft to technical devices such as magnetic detectors controlled from the shore, and hydrophones and electrically-controlled mines. The imagination was strong but the science weak, and the only real value of the exercise was to demonstrate that worthwhile ideas and techniques could not be initiated in this haphazard way.[25]

Criticisms from the wartime manufacturers about lack of scientific impact resulted in the setting up of the Advisory Council for Scientific and Industrial Research in July 1915, renamed the following year the Department of Scientific and Industrial Research (DSIR), which was not disbanded until the 1960s.[26] The Admiralty, too, was beginning to realise that, to be effective against the U-boat, both tactics and scientific counter-measures had to be reviewed more systematically. The Government set up two boards of civilian scientists in July 1915 to evaluate new ideas and initiate research; one was attached to the War Office, and the other, named the Board of Invention and Research (BIR) to the Admiralty. The BIR's history is somewhat chequered, not least because of the choice as its first Chairman of Lord Fisher, whose outspokenness did not help the Board's acceptance by the Royal Navy. Fisher's enemies dubbed it the 'Board of Intrigue and Revenge'. Another reason for the Board's unpopularity was its independence from naval control. However, its major success was that it showed once and for all the key role of science in modern warfare. For the first time, the Royal Navy had to cope with the influx of a large number of civilian scientists and technicians, and in a real sense the BIR heralded the beginning of the Royal Naval Scientific Service.

Initially, the BIR consisted of a Central Committee of three eminent scientists (Sir J.J. Thomson, Sir Charles Parsons and Dr (later Sir George) G. Beilby; a Consulting Panel of twelve scientific experts, including four chemists (Professor H.H. Baker, Sir William Crookes, Sir Percy Frankland and Professor W.J. Pope); four physicists (Sir Oliver Lodge, Sir Ernest Rutherford, Professor W.H. Bragg and R.J. Strutt, later Lord Rayleigh); three engineers, and one metallurgist. It also had a small secretarial staff drawn from the Admiralty.[27] The Board was divided into six sections:

I   Airships and general aeronautics
II   Submarines and wireless telegraphy

III   Naval construction
IV   Anti-aircraft equipment
V   Ordnance and ammunition
VI   Armament of aircraft, bombs and bombsights
Each section was served by a sub-committee consisting of three or four scientists and a naval officer serving as a staff secretary. That of Section II consisted of Rutherford, Bragg, W. Duddell (well-known at the W/T Department of *Vernon* for his pioneering radio work), R.T. Glazebrook, R. Threlfall and C.H. Merz, chaired by the Duke of Buccleuch. One of the secretaries was the physicist, Sir Richard Paget. In all, thirty-six scientists were appointed to the various committees, and those on the Consulting panel served on at least two of the sub-committees.[28] More than 37 500 suggestions were sent in by the general public during the BIR's twenty-nine months' existence; about 14 000 of these dealt with submarines, anti-submarine measures and wireless telegraphy. Of these, only a handful were worthy of serious study, an indication, perhaps, that this side of the BIR's work was more effective in restoring public confidence in the Government's handling of military scientific research than in producing valuable ideas. The BIR's own research projects, however, were certainly useful in the conduct of the war.

Section II assumed the greatest prominence, and received by far the largest Government grant: £625 for wireless telegraphy, £1000 for supersonics (sonar), and £17 048 for underwater acoustics. No stone was left unturned in the Section's desperate search for effective U-boat counter-measures, including dowsing, and the training of seagulls to recognise periscopes and sea-lions to locate submarines by their sound.[29] Other techniques investigated were detection by stray electric fields produced by the U-boats' electric motors, by induced anomalies in the earth's magnetic field and by possible thermal variations. Several of these were to be exploited successfully during the Second World War, when much more sophisticated technology was available, but in 1915 the most promising techniques involved underwater acoustics. This research was carried out in a number of experimental stations dotted around the country – some under BIR control, others under that of the Admiralty: see Table 5.1.

Wartime research on hydrophone detection of submarines was begun not by the BIR, but in the Royal Navy by Commander (later Captain) C.P. Ryan in late 1914, in the face of official indifference. Thanks to strong support from Admiral Sir David (later Admiral

Table 5.1 Main British W/T and anti-submarine research centres during the First World War

Place	Main work	Funded by
1 Parkeston Quay	Acoustics; magnetism; asdics; wireless; electrical	BIR; ASD (1918)
2 Dartmouth sub-station (of 1)	Asdics; training asdic operators	ASD
3 Wemyss Bay sub-station (of 1)	Hydrophone, etc.; training operators	ASD
4 Levenshulme sub-station (of 1)	Hydrophone, etc., also used by LASC	ASD
5 Mullion Airship Station	Hydrophones, towing kites	BIR
6 Felixstowe Air Station	Hydrophones	BIR (temp.)
7 Electrical Engineering Laboratory, Finsbury	Amplifiers; radio valves; very early asdics	BIR
8 Geological Survey Museum, Jermyn St, London	Cutting and testing quartz for asdics	BIR
9 Manchester University	Rutherford, Lamb, etc. on acoustics	BIR
10 Birmingham University	Lodge, etc. analysing underwater sound	BIR
11 GPO London	Underwater signalling	ASD
12 Submarine Signal Co.	Fessenden oscillator	ASD
13 Eastern Telegraph Co.	Hydrophones, magnetophones	ASD
14 British Thomson-Houston Co.	Diaphragms, magnetophones, hydrophones	ASD
15 Imperial College	Professor Callendar: electric & electromagnetic location	ASD

Place	Main work	Funded by
16 Western Electric Co.	Nash's fish hydrophone	ASD
17 Lancashire Anti-Submarine Committee (Manchester)	Hydrophones; sonic echo-ranging & signalling; training operators	ASD
18 Clyde Anti-Submarine Ctee (Glasgow Univ.; Shandon)	Sonic echo-ranging & signalling; operated the Shandon station	DER
19 Rugby Committee	Sonic echo-ranging & signalling; not very active committee	ASD
20 Hawkcraig	Ryan's hydrophones; HMS *Tarlair* Listening School	ASD
21 Elieness	Training towed hydrophones	ASD
22 Crystal Palace	Selection hydrophone operators	ASD
23 Cambridge Psychological Laboratory	Developing aural tests for selecting operators	ASD
24 HMS *Sarepta*, Portland	Listening School; testing towed hydrophones	ASD
25 HMS *Vernon*, Portsmouth	Torpedoes; wireless; electrical gear; instruments, hydrophones	DTM
26 Mining School, Portsmouth	Mines; depth charges, etc.	DTM
27 Signal School	Signals (W/T, Fessenden after 1917)	DTM
28 Wireless School, RN Barracks		DTM
29 Paravane Dept	Paravanes; towed bodies	DTM
30 Malta Experimental Station	Hydrophones & Mediterranean training centre	ASD
31 Gallipoli Hydrophone School	Training centre for Otranto Barrage	ASD

of the Fleet, 1st Earl) Beatty, he established the Admiralty Experimental Station at Hawkcraig in Scotland. Beatty and Fisher were ahead of most senior naval officers in appreciating the possibilities of science. Ryan, who had distinguished himself in the Torpedo course and had the reputation of having 'great turn for making mechanical instruments', retired from the Navy in 1911 to join the Marconi Company, but he rejoined at the outbreak of war. The creation of the Hawkcraig laboratory was solely due to this one man. His hydrophone submarine detectors, developed on a trial-and-error basis, became popular with the Admiralty. They were largely based on pre-war Submarine Signal Company technology and on the innovations of two civilian scientists working at the East London College.[30] Ryan's failure to see the need for basic research in underwater acoustics if substantial progress was to be possible resulted in serious clashes with the civilian scientists from the BIR with whom he had to co-operate.[31]

The first BIR scientists arrived at Hawkcraig in November 1915, but relations between them and Ryan soon became strained, primarily because of different attitudes towards research. The BIR scientists were outside Ryan's control, and they were not subject to naval rules and discipline. Eventually, the Admiralty supported BIR's proposals to establish their own laboratory at Parkeston Quay, Harwich, under Bragg as Resident Director. In the course of 1917, the scientific staff grew from six to more than thirty, and the number of mechanics from five to more than fifty. The laboratory was divided into two sections: Research and Executive. The former was concerned with scientific work and the latter dealt with the development and testing of prototypes. The most important of the sub-stations (or laboratories) was established at Dartmouth in June 1918 for work on the prototype sonar gear.[32]

Several attempts were made to reorganise naval science during the war. In December 1916, the Admiralty combined the Operations Intelligence Division and the Anti-Submarine Committee into the Anti-Submarine Division (ASD), under Lord Jellicoe, the First Sea Lord. The ASD dealt with all aspects of U-boat warfare: operational as well as scientific counter-measures. In September 1917, a report was compiled on the difficulties between the Admiralty and the BIR by Sir Sothern Holland, Sir Ross Skinner, and Jack (later Sir Alfred) Egerton of the Munitions Inventions Department.[33] Although sympathetic to the complaints of the civilian scientists against the Admiralty, the report was critical of both parties. The relations were found to be worst at middle management level. Attitudes of naval officers like Ryan and the Assistant Director of Torpedoes were crucial to the success of the BIR; the report suggested that the lack of co-operation at this level could well be caused by a clash of attitudes – the traditional insistence of the Navy's technical departments on pragmatic trial-and-error research and development, in contrast to the BIR's insistence on fundamental research. The Navy's approach could lead occasionally to rapid results, but they were not necessarily the best results and more often led to failure. A related problem was that commercial contractors would only undertake Admiralty projects which would be profitable in the short term. There existed no mechanism for the Admiralty to pay firms for long-term R & D work. On the other hand, the BIR had too many sub-committees to allow for an effective organisation, and the report's main recommendation was the replacement of the Board by a newly-created Department of Experiment and Research (DER) at the Admiralty.

The findings of the Holland–Skinner report were reinforced by a confidential Committee of Enquiry held on 24–26 September 1917, convened to pronounce on the alleged misconduct of two naval officers and a civilian who obtained funds from the ASD to investigate the detection of submarines by methods which both Hawkcraig and the BIR had already declared to be scientifically unsound. This Committee concluded that the ASD had inadequate resources for tackling experimental work and that a single research organisation should be established for the Royal Navy.[34]

At the same time, the W/T Department of HMS *Vernon* was also being reorganised. A small research laboratory (in Admiralty terms), sanctioned in June 1914, was finally fitted out early in 1915. Long-term problems and fundamental research not directly applicable to 'Service requirements', such as the source of radio atmospherics or the effects of the curvature of the earth on radio waves, were to be tackled by other laboratories, such as the NPL. Gossling was sent to the Cavendish Laboratory at Cambridge to work on thermionic valves. One of the most important wartime projects was wireless direction-finding, undertaken with the NPL and the Marconi Company. *Vernon* also continued to be responsible for underwater signalling.

In 1917, wireless telegraphy and underwater sound signalling R & D were transferred to the Signal School at the RN Barracks at Portsmouth, although *Vernon* continued some hydrophone work until 1925. Responsibility was now shared between the Director of the Signal Division (DSD), the Director of the Department of Torpedoes and Mines (DTM) (both created in 1917) and the Superintendent of Signal Schools. The Director of the Signal Division dealt with signalling policy (visual, wireless telegraphy, telephony and underwater sound), while the Director of Torpedoes and Mines was made responsible for R & D. The Superintendent, Signal Schools, advised both Directors on all questions of signalling. He supervised the planning of the installations (including design specifications, inspection, testing, and fitting), the experimental work, and the training of Signal and Telegraphist personnel.[35] To enhance liaison between all three, a Wireless Telegraphy Board was established in March 1918 and housed in the Signal Division of the Admiralty.

The plans for reorganising the civilian BIR were also finally worked out early in January 1918. Only the Central Committee and the Consulting Panel were kept, while the overall supervision of scientific research was transferred to the newly-created Department of Experiment and Research (DER) at the Admiralty. The first Director was the well-known electrical engineer, C.H. Merz, who in 1916 had recommended the 'grid' system of domestic electricity supply for the whole country. The BIR laboratories were transferred to the DER, Bragg was attached to the Anti-Submarine Division at the Admiralty, and his post of Director of Research at Parkeston Quay was taken over for the remainder of the war by Professor A.S. Eve. Not unexpectedly, Lord Fisher has left us with the most colourful summing-up of the Admiralty's treatment of the BIR:

> We were doomed to exasperation and failure by not being able to overcome the pigheadedness of Departmental Idiots. We had to deal with three First Lords, all cordial and appreciative, but they were all equally powerless because none of them would kick anyone out, so at last we had to kick ourselves out ... Never has the Admiralty Executive wholeheartedly supported the scientific and thoroughly practical proposals of the BIR research.[36]

Research at Parkeston Quay virtually ended on Armistice Day, 11 November 1918. Soon afterwards a Reconstruction Committee was formed to look into the most efficient ways of demobilising the ASD and its Experiments and Research Section.[37] The BIR was disbanded and, with it, the first large-scale co-operation between the Royal Navy and civilian scientists had come to an end, with many lessons learned that were to be invaluable for the development of naval science during the inter-war years.

Wireless telegraphy had been of immense importance in the war. The development of the hydrophone as a tactical device less so. Although used in great numbers, especially after the formation of the ASD in 1916, only four definite kills were made as a result of hydrophone contact.[38] During the war, submarines became faster, quieter, and more difficult to detect by hydrophones. Furthermore, these passive devices were only effective when the ships carrying them either proceeded very slowly or stopped altogether, thereby becoming ideal targets.

ASDICS

The most promising technique to overcome these problems was ultrasonic active echo-ranging (sonar), initiated by the French physicist Paul Langevin and the Russian electrical engineer Constantin Chilowsky in 1915. Their uneasy partnership did not last long and Langevin continued alone, with naval assistance, at the Toulon base. The apparatus was based on existing wireless telegraphy technology. Initial experiments with an electrostatic spark transmitter and carbon (microphone) receiver were not particularly successful.[39] In 1917 Langevin developed his piezoelectric transducer, consisting of thin slices of quartz sandwiched between steel plates. The breakthrough came when an improved eight-valve high-frequency amplifier became available, developed by the Radiotélégraphie Militaire. At last the weak signals of the quartz transducer produced by the echoes were not swamped by amplifier self-noise.

In England, too, experiments on locating submarines by means of echo-detection took place at a number of establishments. These fell into three categories, according to the frequency and type of sound wave employed: namely, sonic, ultrasonic and explosion. G.H. Nash of the Western Electric Company experimented with the Fessenden oscillator to transmit the sound beam and a directional hydrophone to receive the echo. Nash did not foresee the important developments that would take place in electronic amplification, currently under development at the Signal School and elsewhere. His system was based on wartime hydrophone technology, for which no amplifier was necessary. Furthermore, the broad low-frequency (sonic) sound beam emitted by the Fessenden apparatus gave poor directivity, so that when Nash withdrew from Admiralty service in

December 1918, his project was abandoned. The Signal School was developing an ultrasonic electromagnetic transmitter (cancelled when they were visited by Langevin in September 1917), and a considerable amount of work on echo-detection was done at the Shandon (Gareloch) laboratory of the Lancashire Anti-Submarine Committee, and on underwater sound-ranging for locating underwater explosions by BIR scientists.

Shortly after Langevin's experiments were reported to the BIR some time around May 1916, the Board put together its own asdics research team headed by the Canadian physicist, R.W. Boyle. Boyle's first experiments were performed in the laboratories of William Duddell and S.G. Brown, with Duddell's high-frequency Poulson arc transmitter and a Brown magnetophone (telephone). The NPL also became involved in the sonar work, and close technical liaison was maintained with Langevin's group at Toulon. By March 1918, the British team had obtained echoes from a submarine at a range of 500 yards (457 m), using a separate quartz transmitter and receiver, and the French amplifier. A prototype set with quartz transducer, housed in a canvas dome, was fitted for trials in the experimental ship, the trawler *Ebro II*, shortly before the Armistice, and the first 'asdic officers' were being trained. If the war had lasted another six months, sonar would have become operational. The French Navy, too, were almost ready to embark on a ship-fitting programme, and important technical advances had also been made in the United States.[40]

TOWARDS A CENTRALISED NAVAL SCIENTIFIC SERVICE IN PEACETIME

After the Armistice, there was an immediate cut-back on military spending, including research, but the Admiralty had learned one important lesson from its uneasy association with the BIR scientists: properly organised research – not necessarily by university-trained civilian scientists – could materially advance the Navy's offensive and defensive capabilities. The more far-sighted senior naval officers suspected that modern warfare would become increasingly dependent on science, a view expressed by the Controller of Supply Services when presenting his report to the Cabinet for the Navy Estimates of 1919–20.[41] There was much discussion on how to avoid the wartime problem of inadequate co-ordination and lack of provision for systematic reviews of work in progress, caused by hurried expansion. The main suggestion to emerge was to create a central research establishment for the Navy, and several grandiose schemes were proposed. The first casualty was the DER, replaced in December 1919 by the Department of Scientific Research and Experiment (SRE), under the Third Sea Lord. The functions of the new Department were to review scientific research undertaken by the various technical departments of the Navy (although responsibility for these investigations was generally shared between the Director of Scientific Research and the Heads of these departments); to advise the Admiralty on research taking place in industrial and university laboratories; to act as a channel to place research and development contracts with outside agencies; and to co-ordinate the reporting of naval research.

At the end of the war, those SRE scientists who, despite insecurity about salary scales and conditions, decided to remain in Admiralty employment were transferred to the Shandon laboratory taken over from the Lancashire Anti-Submarine Committee. At Parkeston Quay, the staff had been allocated research projects on almost a daily basis, but at Shandon research groups were instituted, based on the practice at the NPL. Arguments continued about the best site for a central naval laboratory, and eventually in 1921 Shandon was closed and a new laboratory, the Admiralty Research Laboratory (ARL) was opened adjacent to the NPL in Teddington.

It is not altogether easy to distinguish between the research undertaken by the ARL and the other naval establishments. In many respects, the ARL was the Admiralty's version of the NPL. The ARL was more concerned with fundamental research, while the other laboratories tackled R & D problems related to their own sphere of interest: mine design, torpedoes, and depth charges at *Vernon*, wireless telegraphy at the Signal School and, after 1927, sonar at the Anti-Submarine School at HMS *Osprey*. The ARL also acted as a 'problem solver' for the other R & D laboratories and had some long-term R & D projects of its own – on naval fire control, course-plotters, and echo-sounders, to name but three.[42]

A small committee was set up in 1919 under the chairmanship of Rear-Admiral Sir William Nicholson to review the organisation and staffing levels at the W/T Department of the Signal School. The Department consisted of six divisions: technical, experimental, development, application, testing and clerical.[43] The Nicholson Committee voiced the growing awareness that wireless telegraphy and asdics would play an important role in future naval strategy, and stressed the urgency of developing these devices. To make this possible, research would have to be expanded drastically in the Navy. It was felt that it was essential for secret systems or appliances having military applications to be developed 'in a Government establishment by Government employees', since experience had shown that security could not be maintained if R & D were undertaken by outside manufacturers. Certainly, the Admiralty went to extraordinary lengths to keep its sonar work secret, even to the extent of referring to the quartz making up the transducers as 'asdevite'. As late as 1938, submarine commanders were warned not to use their sonar sets near foreign warships. This R & D policy cut the technical departments off to some extent from what was happening in industry, and may explain why they were generally less innovative than their counterparts in the German and US Navies, who were making more use of industrial know-how. The Royal Navy, too, was to become increasingly dependent on commercial manufacturers in the final years before the Second World War, but it was only during the war that these firms became heavily involved in military R & D.

After the usual haggling with the Treasury, the Nicholson Committee was successful in increasing R & D at the Signal School. The status of W/T and sonar development was also improved at the Admiralty in April 1920, when the Signal Division was made a separate department. Previously it had been a Division under the Deputy Chief of Naval Staff, and combined the duties of the Signal Division of the Naval Staff and the W/T Section of the Department of Torpedoes and Mines. The Signal School became the direct responsibility of the Director of the Signal Department. F.E. (later Sir Frank) Smith, who had been at the W/T Section, was promoted to Director of Scientific Research (DSR) at the Department of Scientific Research and Experiment (SRE).[44]

One of his first tasks was to negotiate with the Admiralty and the Treasury on the conditions of service and the number of scientific staff to be employed at the various naval establishments. Many questions had to be resolved before a centralised naval scientific service could be established. For instance, should the civilian scientists be treated the same as university staff, as those working in Government laboratories such as the NPL, or in industry, or should they become civil servants? What equivalent naval ranks should be accorded to the various grades of scientific staff? The

Admiralty very briefly considered putting their civilian scientists into uniform, but decided that this would produce more problems than it solved.

On 5 September 1923, the Treasury sanctioned the formation of a scientific pool into which the scientific staff of all establishments would be absorbed.[45] At last, a common salary structure for civilian scientists was established throughout the Navy, similar to the one at the NPL. A common technical pool was not established until 1928. The DSR wanted a single scientific and technical pool for all personnel, but the Treasury insisted that the engineering staff should be treated the same way as naval architects and dockyard superintendents, that is as established civil servants. The scientists were treated more flexibly, which allowed them to return to university or industrial employment without financial loss. This argument was not resolved until the formation of the Royal Naval Scientific Service in 1946, when both scientists and technicians were at last fully integrated into a single structure.

SONAR, W/T, AND RADAR R & D IN THE INTERWAR YEARS

Work on sonar was continued in 1919, first at Shandon, then from the following year until 1927 at the Signal School, and finally until 1940 at the Anti-Submarine School, HMS *Osprey*, at Portland, near Weymouth. These establishments concentrated on sonar hardware, while the ARL at Teddington complemented this work by studying the more basic and theoretical aspects of piezoelectricity and magnetostriction, transducer design and the factors affecting the transmission, reflection and cavitation of underwater sound. The sources and behaviour of other underwater noises were also studied. As has already been mentioned, there was no clear-cut division between the types of research undertaken at the ARL and at the other establishments; for instance, at the ARL a high-frequency motor alternator was developed to power the sonar sets.

In sonar's move to *Osprey* in 1927, wireless telegraphy and sonar R & D finally parted company. This was one of the consequences of attempts, begun a few years earlier, to rationalise the Navy's scattered anti-submarine resources. Historically, sonar and wireless telegraphy shared a common origin, but this link was no longer considered necessary when wireless technology was widely diffused and freely available. In the early years, there were only a few wireless experts who could help with sonar and it was, therefore, sensible to have both systems developed in the same naval establishment. An important aspect of the move to *Osprey* was that for the first time anti-submarine training and R & D were unified at a single establishment.[46] The naval officers who specialised in anti-submarine warfare could now more easily pass on to the scientists their tactical experience of sonar gained in training exercises, and in this way influence its development.

In spite of the much publicised efforts to ban the submarine from naval warfare in the early twenties, the Admiralty pressed on with anti-submarine measures. Slowly, basic knowledge of underwater acoustics and the physics of the sea was pieced together, but this research was always subordinate to the development of sonar for the Fleet. This limited objective was successful in that, by the start of the Second World War, the Royal Navy possessed an operational underwater echo-ranging weapon system for destroying submarines. To achieve this, three components were developed by the Admiralty scientists: the transducer for detecting the prey; the streamlined dome in which the transducer was housed, to allow it to do so at speed; and the range recorder to provide a visual trace of the entire hunt. The accurate information of the submarine's course, speed and direction obtained by this system could then be used to place the depth charges (and, in the second World War, the ahead-thrown projectiles) in the best pattern to produce a kill.

The quartz transducer, begun in 1918, formed the mainstay of the sonar system up to the end of the Second World War. Although most of its design features remained constant throughout this period, it went through a long and tortuous development before it could be produced in quantity. The Naval Staff specified a maximum sonar range of 5000 yards (4.5 km) which was achieved by a 15-inch (28 cm) steel-quartz-steel sandwich transducer, resonating in the region of 20 kHz with an acoustic output of 50 watts.

The key years in the development of the streamlined sonar dome were 1927 to 1934. Again, not all the design criteria were scientific ones. For example, the dimensions were dictated by the amount of space beneath the hull when the vessel stood on chocks in dry dock, and by the size of the hole the Admiralty's naval contractors allowed to be cut in the keel. The first domes parallelled the hydrophone covers developed during the First World War; the eventual stream-lined shape was a compromise between acoustic transparency and strength. *Ebro II* was the first ship fitted with a dome; she was also the first to sit on it and totally crush it. During the late twenties, intrepid scientists were isolated in observation domes fitted under the hull. Linked to the ship's system by only a set of headphones, they observed the effects of noise, cavitation, and sea pressure, at speeds of up to 30 knots.

The range recorder was based on the 'Fultograph' apparatus, which electrochemically reproduced photographs transmitted by land line or by wireless telegraphy, begun at the ARL in 1928. At first intended purely as a research tool for studying echoes and reverberation, it soon became the kernel of the recorder for the non-secret Admiralty ultrasonic magnetostriction echo-sounder.[47] The scientists at HMS *Osprey* immediately recognised the tactical value of this device and developed it for echo-ranging in great secrecy. It was first fitted with sonar sets in destroyers in 1932.

By 1939, no fewer than twenty-two different types of sonar set had been developed and fitted in various classes of warship, ranging from drifters, destroyers, and submarines (for attack) to cruisers, aircraft-carriers, and battleships (mainly for self-protection). A pool of production sets had also been assembled, and the scientific and technical staff were being rapidly expanded to cope with the coming war.

In the last five years before the Second World War, great activity in wireless communication took place at the Signal School. Ship installations had grown complex: a battleship had eight transmitters, half of them of high power, and nine receivers, as well as a medium-frequency direction-finding set; a destroyer had four transmitters, two each of medium and low power, and eight receivers of various types. All these sets still operated on Morse code.[48] Extensive research on ship-borne radio-direction-finding, started at the Signal School in the early 1930s, pushed Britain ahead at the start of the war.[49] The most important project, however, was radar. The detection and ranging of aircraft and ships by radio waves had been suggested by far-seeing radio scientists from several countries before development began in the 1930s.[50] At the Signal School, L.S.B. Alder proposed such a system in 1928. A few years later, W.A.S. Batement and P.E. Pollard of SEE (Signals Experimental Establishment), Woolwich, recognised the possibility of long-range detection of ships by radio waves for coastal batteries. They were informed that there was no War Office requirement for such equipment, but were allowed to work on it in their spare time. Serious R & D work only began in the various British military establishments after Watson-Watt, then the Superintendent of the Radio Department of the NPL, demonstrated early in 1935 that radar actually worked, and the Air Ministry, followed by the Admiralty, could see clear operational advantages in such a system. The Admiralty remained cautious for some time because of the danger of giving away Fleet positions by the use of radar. A small beginning was made at the Signal School in late 1935, and wartime expansion began in 1938. At this time, the Signal School joined with G.E.C. in developing 50cm radar for gunnery-ranging. High-resolution 10cm radar for detecting submarines went into production in 1941.

CONCLUSION

The initial impetus for research in wireless telegraphy was the need for better communications, continuing the process started with the electric telegraph and underwater acoustics, which had begun as a navigational aid. During this period, the major advances in wireless telegraphy were made commercially, and were taken up and modified for naval use by Admiralty scientists. Sonar, and later radar, were developed almost entirely in a military environment.

The route from scientific idea to invention, prototype and finished product is highly complex. We have seen that naval R & D effectively began at the Torpedo School, HMS *Vernon*, in the early 1870s, but it was largely unplanned. The Admiralty had to take R & D seriously for the first time when the First World War was going badly, and the influx of a large number of civilian scientists had to be coped with. Successive reorganisations of the Royal Navy's R & D in the interwar years, in an attempt to integrate the naval and civilian scientific elements and formulate clear policies, eventually resulted in the founding of a comprehensive, centralised naval scientific service immediately after the Second World War. A remarkably similar development took place in the US Navy.[51]

The development of wireless telegraphy, sonar, and later radar, was governed by a number of interlocking factors, of which the contemporary level of scientific (or technical) knowledge was but one. Other factors were operational requirements (as laid down, for instance, by the Naval Staff), and political, bureaucratic, and even purely pragmatic ones. Thus, after the First World War, the US Navy and the Royal Navy developed mechanically-rotated echo-ranging 'searchlight' sonar for hunting submarines. The German Navy, on the other hand, concentrated on sophisticated hydrophone arrays fitted to their capital ships, so that they could detect torpedoes at long range and evade them. They were not allowed to possess submarines until 1935. It was in response to a different tactical requirement that the German sonar R & D programme moved in another direction from that of the Americans and the British. Again, at the start of the Second World War, Britain possessed an integrated sonar weapon system against submarines, and a radar air defence system against invading aircraft. America could have achieved the same but, unlike Britain, their R & D projects in the 1930s had not been directed towards clearly formulated operational objectives.

Technologically, the Second World War consisted of a series of technical thrusts and counter-thrusts. On the whole, the Allies had a more flexible and rapid response to new or dramatically improved weapons than did the Germans. A key factor was the immense scientific and technical manpower available to them for their numerous R & D projects. Industry, too, became absorbed in the development of military hardware; for political and economic reasons this industrial-military edifice is still with us today. From this complex military technology originates another key innovation, operational research – a term probably invented by A.P. Rowe after the 1938 Air Exercises to determine the optimum way of using the Chain Home radar system.[52] Operational research has become of immense importance: the scientist no longer supplies only the tools, but has been brought into the tactics of war.[53]

NOTES

1. There is a considerable amount of confusion about the origins of the word 'asdics'. The Oxford University Press was prompted on 11 December 1939 to ask the Admiralty about its etymology after Churchill referred to it in the House of Commons. They were told that it was the acronym of *A*llied *S*ubmarine *D*etection Committee, 'a body which was formed during the war of 1914–18, and which organised much research and experiment for the detection of submarines' (in Public Record Office (PRO): ADM 1/9880). However, this Committee has not been identified from the records and none has been found bearing this name. A likely candidate could be the three-day Allied scientific conference on submarine detection devices held in Washington

on 14–16 June 1917, which may have resulted in the setting up of an Allied committee, but there is no evidence for this (see 'The beginning of the New London Experimental Station as recorded in the personal notes of Lt.Col. R.A. Millikan'; and Cdr C.S. McDowell, 'American anti-submarine work during the war', deposited at the Library of NUSC, New London, and copies with the author at Oxford). The Millikan paper is also in NRL: Harvey Hayes Papers, box 10, folder 309. See also National Archives, Washington, DC: RG 45 box 267G, Naval Records Collection of the Office Naval Records, file 1911–27, LA-Reports (Anti-submarine, etc.); and PRO-ADM 137–1436, 'Report by Professor Sir Ernest Rutherford, FRS, and Cdr Cyprian Bridge, RN, on Visit to the United States of America in company with the French Scientific Mission, May 19th to July 9th 1917', BIR,28208/17). The first reference to this term is in the 'Weekly report of experimental work at Parkeston Quay', dated 6 July 1918, and two days later it was reported that at the Anti-Submarine Division's E & R Weekly meetings: 'It was decided to call the Supersonic Apparatus by the name of Asdic Apparatus' (see PRO:ADM 137/2719). No indication is given for the sudden appearance of this term. Wood (note 31), p. 39, has suggested that it stood for the initials of the Admiralty department which initiated this research: *A*nti-*S*ubmarine *D*ivision-*ics*, and the same explanation is given in the 1924 Report of the Torpedo Division of the Naval Staff (see PRO: ADM 186/244). In the US, too, this term was used in 1918 (see Naval Research Laboratory, Washington, DC): Harvey Hayes Papers, box 5, folder 66B, but in the inter-war period 'supersonics' was usually used. F.V. Hunt, the Director of the wartime Harvard Underwater Sound Laboratory, coined 'sonar' in 1942, an acronym of *S*ound *N*avigation *a*nd *R*anging, and the phonetic analogue of 'radar' (*R*adio *D*etection *a*nd *R*anging) was attributed to two US naval officers, E.F. Furth and S.P. Tucker, who coined it in 1940. In wartime England, the system was known as 'radiolocation' or 'RDF' (*R*adio *D*irection *F*inding), but the term radar was adopted officially in 1943. Sonar replaced asdic (or asdics) in the Royal Navy in the early 1950s. For a further discussion, see W.D. Hackmann, *Seek and Strike. Sonar, Anti-Submarine Warfare and the Royal Navy 1914–1954* (London: HMSO, 1984).

2. John Jewkes, David Sawers, and Richard Stillerman, *The Sources of Invention*, 2nd edn (New York: Norton, 1969) pp. 28–9; Thomas P. Hughes, 'The Development Phase of Technological Change', *Technology and Culture*, XVII (1976) pp. 423–4.

3. D.S.L. Cardwell, *The Organisation of Science in England*, revised edn (London: Heinemann, 1972) pp. 169–77.

4. H.W. Melville, *The Department of Scientific and Industrial Research* (London: Allen & Unwin, 1962) pp. 101–10; E. Pyatt, *The National Physical Laboratory* (Bristol: Hilger, 1983).

5. D.K. Allison, *New Eye for the Navy: The Origin of Radar at the Naval Research Laboratory* (Washington, DC: Naval Research Laboratory, NRL Report 8466, 1981) pp. 6–9; M. Josephson, *Edison: A Biography* (New York: McGraw-Hill, 1959) pp. 84–104; H.R. Bartlett, 'The Development of Industrial Research in America', in National Resources

Planning Board, *Research – A National Resource*, 3 vols. (Washington, DC: GPP, 1938–41) vol. II, pp. 19–77.
6. Cardwell, op. cit. (note 3), pp. 175–6.
7. Kendall Birr, *Pioneering in Industrial Research* (Washington, DC: Public Affairs Press, 1957); George Wise, 'A New Role for Professional Scientists in Industry: Industrial Research at General Electric', *Technology and Culture*, XXI (1980) pp.408–29.
8. M.D. Fagan (ed.), *A History of Engineering and Science in the Bell System*, 2 vols (Bell Telephone Laboratories, 1975, 1978); vol. III (1982) edited by G.E. Schindler, Jr.
9. Public Record Office (PRO): CAB 21/7, Submarine menace – Lord Fisher.
10. Arthur Hezlet, *The Electron and Sea Power* (London: Peter Davies, 1975) pp. 2–10.
11. G.J. Kirby, 'A History of the Torpedo', *Journal of the Royal Naval Scientific Service*, XXVII (1972) pp. 30–55, 78–105 (restricted journal).
12. PRO:ADM 189/2, Torpedo School Sound Signalling Section for 1882, p. 148.
13. J.B. Millet, 'Submarine Signalling by means of Sound', *Engineering*, LXXIX (1905) pp. 651–3; same title but more detail in *Journal of the Society of Arts*, LIV (1906) pp. 642–51; 'Recent Developments in Submarine Signalling', *Transactions of the Society of Naval Architects and Marine Engineers*, XXII (1914) pp. 107–32; for a biased company history, see H.W. Fay, *Submarine Signal Log* (Portsmouth, RI: Raytheon Company's Signal Division, 1962), and O.J. Scott, *The Creative ordeal. The Story of Raytheon* (New York: Atheneum, 1974). Gray coined 'hydrophone' in this context, a word previously used to decribe a waterbag attached to a stethoscope to intensify the sound of the heartbeat.
14. Hackmann, op. cit. (note 1), pp. 9–10; PRO:ADM 189/29 and 189/31, Torpedo School Submarine Sound Signalling Section for 1909, pp. 75–7 and for 1911, p. 107.
15. R.F. Pocock and G.R.M. Garrett, *The Origins of Maritime Radio* (London: Science Museum, 1972) p. 2.
16. PRO:ADM 116/570, Letter from Captain Jackson to Vice-Admiral Sir J.A. Fisher, dated 28 November 1900.
17. PRO:ADM 116/523, Letter from Captain F.T. Hamilton to Commander-in-Chief, Devonport, dated 2 November 1898.
18. O.L. Ratsey, 'As We Were: Fifty Years of ASWE History 1896–1946', typescript (Admiralty Surface Weapons Establishment, Portsdown, 1974) pp. 6–7. Available Naval Historical Library, Empress State Building, London. ASWE has gathered together a number of archives on the early history of W/T.
19. Ibid., pp. 19–20.
20. Ibid., pp. 52–4; Hezlet, op. cit. (note 11), pp. 59–82.
21. Ratsey, op. cit. (note 18), p. 71; Hackmann, op. cit. (note 1), pp. 6, 74 for reference.
22. Ratsey, op. cit. (note 18), pp. 39, 47, 59–60.

23. PRO:ADM 1/8409/17, Admiralty Committee on Wireless Telegraphy, 2 August 1913.
24. H.G. Wells, *The Times*, 11 June 1915.
25. PRO:ADM 137/2133, Battle Cruiser Force War Records, vol. V.
26. R.M. MacLeod and E.K. Andrews, 'The Origins of the D.S.I.R.: Reflections on Ideas and Men 1915–16', *Public Administration*, XLVIII (1970) pp. 23–48; 'The Committee of Civil Research: Scientific Advice for Economic Development', *Minerva*, VII (1969) pp. 680–705.
27. Hackmann, op. cit. (note 1), pp. 17–21. The seven secretaries drawn from the Admiralty staff were: Cdr Bridge, RN; Fl/Lt/Cdr Lord Edward Grosvenor, RN; Eng/Lt/Cdr C. Hawks, RN; T.H. Hoste; Lt J. James, RNVR; Sir Richard A.S. Paget; J.F. Phillips. Bridge was the BIR liaison officer in France.
28. DER, *Report on the Detection of Submarines by Acoustic Methods* (Office of DER, Admiralty, E.R. 01001, December 1918;, pp. 3–8, 56–7.
29. BIR, *Minutes of General Meetings, Central Committee and Panels*, 1915–1917; minutes for 10 May 1917; *Reports* and *Memoranda of the Meetings of the Sub-Committee of Section II*, 1915–1917, see 'Memorandum of Preliminary Meeting of Sub-Committeee, Section II, for 23 May and 7 August 1917'. These two bound volumes of the printed minutes of the BIR are deposited at the Naval Historical Library. PRO:ADM 218/104, Hydrophones and Acoustic Research. Various papers and miscellaneous letters (Bragg and Rutherford); E.J. Allen, 'Report upon Experiments on the Hearing Powers of Sea-Lions under Water, and on the Possibility of Training these Animals as Submarine Trackers', BIR 30051/17, with appendices by Paget, J. Woodward, A.B. Wood, and F.L. Pleadwell, Surgeon, USN. For similar American work with sea-gulls, see NRL (Washington): Harvey Hayes Papers, box 1, file 2–4.
30. PRO: ADM 212/1, Direction Finder for Sound in Water 1915–16.
31. A.B. Wood, 'Memorial Issue', *Journal of the Royal Naval Scientific Service*, XX (1965), pp. 185–284 (in the journal sequence, or 1–100 in this special memorial issue). The separate sections dealing with 1915–45 were first published separately in the same journal, which is restricted but has declassified articles. For the clashes with Ryan, see p. 23, and also PRO:ADM 212/157.
32. Hackmann, 'Underwater Acoustics and the Royal Navy, 1893–1930', *Annals of Science*, XXXVI (1979) pp. 255–78.
33. Hackmann, op. cit. (note 1), pp. 28–37; E. Egerton, *Sir Alfred Egerton, FRS, 1886–1959. A Memoir with Papers* (London: privately printed, 1963) pp. 21–2; PRO:ADM 212/158, Sir R. Sothern Holland, Sir H. Ross Skinner, and J. Egerton, 'Report on the Present Organisation of the Board of Invention and Research', Admiralty, 21 September 1917, and reactions to this report in ADM 116/1430; see also ADM 116/1806, private correspondence of Sir Eric Geddes 1917–19. See also the earlier report by BIR, 'Relations of the BIR with other Departments of the Admiralty', Memorandum dated 22 February 1917 to the First Lord (Balfour), BIR 4907–17.

34. PRO:ADM 116/3451, 'Detection of Submerged Submarines 1917–24'; J.K. Gusewelle, 'The Board of Invention and Research: A Case Study in the Relations between Academic Science and the Royal Navy in Great Britain during the First World War' (PhD thesis, University of California, Irvine, 1971), pp. 10–23 and elsewhere, is not only too severe in his judgement of the Royal Navy's antipathy to scientific research but also confuses hydrophones and sonar research.
35. Ratsey, op. cit. (note 18), pp. 64–5, 80.
36. St. Andrews University Library: MSS 4644, Memorandum by Fisher, 'How the Great War was Carried on', 3 January 1918, cited by R.M. MacLeod and E.K. Andrews, 'Scientific Advice in the War at Sea, 1915–17: the Board of Invention and Research', *Journal of Contemporary History*, VI (1971) p. 34, footnote 51.
37. PRO:ADM 137/2715, Mobilisation Proposals ASD and its E & R Section, 16 November 1918; ASD Memoranda 29 November, 9 December, 11 December 1918; DER Memorandum 25 November 1918; ADM 212/165, ARL Domestic File. Demobilisation 1918–1919; Admiralty, 'The Anti-Submarine Division of the Naval Staff, December 1916–December 1918', *The Technical History of the Navy*, TH7 (Admiralty, June 1919) pp. 35–9, of which a copy is in the Naval Historical Library.
38. Hezlet, op. cit. (note 10), p. 151. For the full account of these sinkings, see R.M. Grant, *U-Boats Destroyed* (London: Putnam, 1964) pp. 89–90.
39. Hackmann, op. cit. (note 32), pp. 272–6; French patent 502,913 (1920).
40. National Archives, Washington, DC: RG 189 'Report on an Inter-Allied Conference on the Detection of Submarines by the Method of Supersonics', Paris, 19–20 October 1918 (Paris Report no. 161 and 161A), and other reports in same file; Hackmann, op. cit. (note 1), pp. 88–9 for further references.
41. PRO:ADM 181/101, Navy Estimates 1919–20 and miscellaneous papers. Extract from report on Vote 6.
42. Wood, op. cit. (note 31), pp. 55–78.
43. Hackmann, op. cit. (note 1), pp. 106–7; Ratsey, op. cit. (note 18), ppp. 85–8; PRO:ADM 116/1845, Signal Organisation, Policy and Staffing Matters 1918–22.
44. He was promoted in February 1920, a month before the creation of the Signal Department.
45. PRO:ADM 212/175, Scientific Staff (complements, grading, etc.) ARL, 1928–35.
46. F.M. Mason, 'The History of Anti-Submarine Development' (including that of HMS *Osprey*), Portland, April 1938 (manuscript).
47. PRO:ADM 186/465, *Osprey* Quarterly Report no. 8, June 1929, section II. See British patents 329,403 (1930); 370,051 (1932); 448,331 (1936); 448,407 (1936); see also ADM 1/13801.
48. Hezlet, op. cit. (note 10), p. 183.
49. Ratsey, op. cit. (note 18), pp. 129–34.
50. S.S. Swords, *Technical History of the Beginnings of Radar* (London: Peter Peregrinus, 1986) pp. 42–81, 174–257; Ratsey, op. cit. (note 18),

pp. 141–65; Allison, op. cit. (note 5), pp. 137–52; but technically Swords gives the best summary.

51. Hackmann, 'Sonar Research and Naval Warfare 1914–1954: A Case Study of a Twentieth-Century Establishment Science', *Historical Studies in the Physical Sciences*, XVI (1986) pp. 83–110, which is a summary of Hackmann, op. cit. (note 1), but concentrates on the American connection with the Royal Navy's sonar R & D.

52. Air Ministry, *The Origins and Development of Operational Research in the Royal Air Force* (London: HMSO, 1963); Sword, op. cit. (note 50), pp. 253–4.

53. D.W. Waters, 'Seamen, Scientists, Historians, and Strategy. Presidential Address, 1978', *British Journal for the History of Science*, XIII (1980) pp. 189–210; his review of my book (note 1), 'ASW: The First 40 Years', *Naval Review*, LXXIV (1986) pp. 128–34.

6 The Rockefeller Foundation and German Biomedical Sciences, 1920–40: from Educational Philanthropy to International Science Policy

Paul Weindling

The Rockefeller Foundation has been one of the most powerful forces shaping twentieth-century science and medicine.[1] It has enriched the world with magnificently equipped institutes, provided fellowships and shaped national science and health policies.[2] The Foundation has been influenced by social trends that have been fundamental to the twentieth century: these forces include professionalisation and modern notions of management, the rising prestige of science, with the claim that it could provide socio-economic progress, and the United States' assumption of a global trusteeship of democratic and civilised values. Whereas during the nineteenth century Germany was regarded as leading the world in scientific and medical education, this role has been increasingly assumed by the United States. The course of the Rockefeller's relations with Germany is instructive, not merely as a case-study of the role of international agencies in a national context, but as giving insight into the emergence of overall policies and the organization of the Foundation.

Rockefeller patronage marks a shift from the wealthy individual patron to bureaucratic and corporate management of science policy by scientifically-trained experts. Initially, the Rockefellers set up diverse agencies, each to secure a philanthropic aim. The Foundation was only one of several powerful Rockefeller philanthropic enterprises. In 1901, the planning of the Rockefeller Institute for Medical Research began; in 1903 the General Education Board was established; between 1909 and 1915 the Rockefeller Sanitary Commission for the Eradication of Hookworm launched a model public health campaign; from 1919 to 1934, the Bureau of Social Hygiene was concerned with questions of public morality, hygiene and policing systems. After the Foundation was established in 1913, there followed in 1918 the Laura Spelman Rockefeller Memorial Fund, which was initially for family welfare work, and the

International Education Board in 1923. The Foundation achieved a pre-eminent position among these. Between 1913 and 1930, it underwent a process of rationalisation and expansion in the management of its programmes. This led to a unitary corporate structure and to the emergence of science as a major priority. In the process of the expansion of the Foundation, scientists ousted the philanthropists and educationalists.[3]

The extent, methods and motives of Rockefeller global patronage of the sciences, require historical evaluation to assess whether the programmes were effective in their own terms.[4] There is a more general issue of the origins and effects of the Foundation's rationale of attaining human betterment. Some historians believe that genuine Christian fervour motivated Rockefeller philanthropy.[5] Others see the Rockefeller Foundation as serving the needs of capitalism and of professionalising groups like doctors and scientists.[6]

A case-study of the Rockefeller Foundation's activities in Germany provides insight into general issues of the Foundation's policy. It shows how in the Foundation scientific aims displaced those of philanthropy during the mid-1920s. The Rockefeller's philanthropic empire was greatly influenced by a model of science education that originated in Germany, so making attitudes to German science and medicine especially revealing of the Foundation's overall policies. Not only did Germany receive four million dollars by 1940, but patronage of German science confronted the Foundation with fundamental issues. At the heart of the problem lay the Foundation's internal problems over the formulation of a science policy. As priorities shifted from education and public health to the funding of basic sciences, the Foundation's officers wished to support German research. But the special problems of German science required fundamental decisions as to the scope of policies and its definition of what constituted right and proper standards in science.

Why the Foundation should have been so committed to the support of medical and scientific research was bound up with the outstanding reputation of German higher education. In the 1890s, Americans were flocking to Austria and Germany for what was regarded as the best possible training in medicine. Frederick T. Gates, John D. Rockefeller Jnr's Baptist mentor in the divine mission of making and giving money, became convinced that medical research and science education would provide long-term solutions to poverty and disease. The German system of medical education, involving a thorough training in the basic natural sciences, was held to be the best way of raising professional standards so as to eradicate disease. The Rockefeller's General and International Education Boards set about instituting the German model in the USA and throughout the world. Certain institutions like Johns Hopkins University were selected as unique training centres for the professional élite. The Foundation established full-time professors of medicine, so emulating the appointments by the Austrian and German states. In 1912, Abraham Flexner published his Carnegie report on *Medical Education in Germany*, which underlined the immense advantages of the German university-based system of medical training. Flexner entered Rockefeller service for the General Education Board, where he gained a large degree of acceptance for his view.[7] Yet at the same time US foundations and scientists were moving towards a new organisational form for advancing science. In 1906, the Rockefeller Institute for Medical Research was opened, establishing a new model for a privately financed pure research institution. German scientists and officials sensed that they were losing their world lead in many disciplines. In 1913, they emulated the US model of industrial patronage with the Kaiser Wilhelm Gesellschaft. This provided industrial finance for institutes that were purely for research. These initiatives suggest that new institutional forms for the organization of research were emerging in both Germany and the USA.

The officials in the various philanthropic enterprises were embarrassed by public criticism of Rockefeller business methods. They consequently favoured the value-neutral and achievement-oriented sphere of science, and avoided interventive policies. The accusation of 'tainted money' meant that during 1911–13 Congress opposed a charter for the Foundation, which was eventually established in May 1913. When in 1914 during a strike at the Rockefeller-controlled Colorado Fuel and Iron Company six striking miners were shot, the Foundation's caution increased. Initially, John D. Rockefeller Jnr was both President and Chairman, but in 1917 an independent President, George Vincent, was appointed. He was adamant that the Foundation must neither influence public opinion on social questions, nor the policies of the institutions receiving funds. Vincent initially selected public health and medical education as major priorities. In 1919, a Division of Medical Education was established under Richard Pearce. Vincent's low-profile approach and attempt to avoid political or ideological issues, posed many difficulties. Vincent, like Flexner, Gates and Rockefeller Snr, was a self-made man with a faith in education. Every time a new set of problems relating to relief of poverty or education would occur to them, they established a new organisation, functionally suited to the task. The next generation of officers, like Pearce and his assistant, Alan Gregg, were professional scientists. They pressed for coherent policies in the type of science that should be funded, but above all for a unitary administrative structure based on rational scientific principles. Their combination of scientific and administrative expertise established the hegemony of science over education, preventive medicine and relief of poverty. The Paris Office shows in microcosm the development from a welfare programme – the relief of TB – to a grant-administering body. During the mid-1920s, the Foundation broadened its programme from medical science to human biology. This process of 'scientisation' reached a culmination in 1928, when the Foundation was restructured into a research-funding agency with divisions for medical, natural and social science.

By the 1920s, there were sharp internal divisions among Rockefeller officials over the quality of German research, the merits of German higher education, especially in medicine, and the extent that nationalism disqualified German professors as members of the international scientific community. As the Foundation's officers campaigned for rationalisation of Rockefeller philanthropy, the shift from pluralism to corporate unity resulted. In order to overcome internal divisions between officers over the value of German science, a series of special policies were adopted.

THE EVOLUTION OF A GERMAN PROGRAMME

The Foundation's wartime planning targetted promotion of social health and welfare with the elimination of social evils such as insanity, feeble-mindedness, VD, TB and infant mortality. After a brief phase of war relief work, such social aims were to become increasingly distant as the Foundation concentrated on medical research, and ultimately pure science. London was favoured as strategically placed for developing medical science in the British Empire.[8] In Europe, the Foundation worked to establish university medical schools and public health institutes in countries where these were lacking. Eastern Europe and the Balkans, areas which had hitherto looked to Germany for medical training, were priority areas. That Polish students were excluded from German universities was a matter of concern to the Foundation. In 1920 aid was given to the medical schools of Vienna, Prague, Budapest, Graz and Innsbruck.[9] The Foundation's officers were divided in their attitudes to postwar Germany. Anti-German feeling was still running high in America.[10] The stereotype image of the German professor had become one of a war-mongering imperialist, and the universities were condemned as a breeding ground for German nationalism.[11] Edwin Embree, who was responsible for European grants, distrusted Germans as nationalistic and anti-egalitarian. Moreover, he considered that Germany had over-invested in biomedical science, having at least twenty-two medical faculties. In October 1920, he judged that 'Germany will probably have to retrench bringing her system of universities into a right proportion to her means'. He consistently refused to support new universities like Cologne, Frankfurt or Hamburg.[12]

A few US academics were keen to re-establish links with their old German colleagues and teachers, at least to provide emergency relief. In 1920, the Foundation began a small programme of German grants for periodicals and laboratory equipment. In 1922, the Foundation initiated a survey of conditions in German universities. But before it could draw any conclusions, Abraham Flexner intervened. He attacked Embree's view on the need for consolidation of German higher education as 'certainly impracticable and quite unwise'. Inflation necessitated Rockefeller support for medical schools. His tone echoed the desperate pleas of German academics. The biochemist, Emil Abderhalden, claimed to have persuaded Flexner that a special policy of aid was needed for German science. Flexner wrote in July 1922 that 'German science is making such a fight for itself that if it dies it is going to die fighting ... this is important not only to Germany but to all mankind'. He argued that Germany still led the world in certain sciences like physiology, with men like Emil Meyerhof and Otto Warburg. Yet Flexner's priority was educational quality. He pointed out that foreigners were rushing from all parts of the world to German laboratories for their training. He regarded perpetuation of German science as a priority, which was to benefit the entire world. But the future of the German system was in jeopardy because talented young researchers had no career prospects.[13]

Flexner's proposal for immediate action met a chilly response. All but one of the trustees (Julius Rosenwald) favoured postponement of any decision until the Foundation's officers had decided on a general policy towards Germany. Gates gravely doubted the whole plan and John D. Rockefeller Jnr supported a conservative approach in the formulation of a long-term policy towards Germany.[14] Pearce, who visited Germany in November 1922 argued that the universities in central Europe could not be sustained:

> To attempt to hold them in their present and past state is futile and not our affair. The only thing we can do is to assist the oncoming men with such moderate aid as will not upset the scale of university expenditure or the general costs of living and will not interfere with the inevitable natural changes.[15]

Henry Eversole was a relentless critic of Pan-Germanist German professors. He even regarded the Soviet Union as created and propped up by Germany, so as to enable the spread of German economic power. He commented to Pearce:

> I believe that any feeding program except a selective one would be wrong in Germany at present. To be quite brutal, there is in Germany a certain, so called intellectuality, 'Kultur' if you will, that the world could jolly well do without; but at the same time we must not forget that there is in Germany a theoretical and practical scientific culture which if lost would put the world back, or rather retard certain scientific developments in the world for an indefinite number of years. This at least should be protected by the world.[16]

The Foundation assumed the role of guardian of world interests. But whether 'the world' needed education or scientific research was a moot point. Whereas Flexner's priority was education, other officers made research the priority.

The Foundation arrived at a compromise policy, designed to promote research and to compensate for what it regarded as unhealthy developments in German higher education. It decided against subsidising professors or universities, whether old or new, and declined to work through the new national scientific organisation, called the Emergency Fund for German Science, which was established in 1920. Instead, it wished to support the brightest young researchers in the medical sciences, and established a special committee in Germany for this task. Flexner agreed about avoiding the Emergency Fund. He condemned it as 'dominated by old men of rather a conservative turn of mind', slow and bureaucratic, and concerned to prop up the universities as institutions. It was administered by Friedrich Schmidt-Ott, the last Prussian Minister of Education (*Kultusminister*). Yet the Foundation overlooked how forward-looking the Fund was in certain ways. Its ability to involve leading professors on its committees instigated the modern system of a self-reviewing peer-group. It co-ordinated national resources and developed a coherent national science policy.[17] The Foundation's officers were adamant that the older generation of German professors was too nationalistic to merit support. They feared that German socialists, whom they characterised as anti-university, might level the accusation 'of plutocratic wealth aiding monarchist ideas'.[18] To avoid criticisms of the social implications of its policies, the Foundation was prepared to be interventionist when it distrusted the capacity of the recipient to use the funds in accordance with its ideals.

The Foundation established its independent committee with scientists who were younger, research-oriented and international in outlook. Vincent observed, 'They seem not to be typical Prussians of the old order.' The committee's aims were reflected in its official title: *Ausschuss zur Förderung des wissenschaftlichen medizinischen Nachwuchses (Hilfsausschuss der Rockefeller-Stiftung)*. The key figure was the Secretary of the new committee, Heinrich Poll. During November 1922, Pearce's discussions with Fritz Haber and Poll led to the idea of an autonomous committee.[19] Poll was a long-standing friend of Abraham Flexner, whom he had assisted in the inspection of Berlin medical institutions. For many years, Poll had a junior post under the biologist Oscar Hertwig, but had failed to gain a post at the Kaiser Wilhelm Institute for Biology. Poll had thus suffered from the lack of career opportunities in Germany for geneticists.[20] It was only in 1922 that he was given a teaching post in human genetics at Berlin, so that he could complement the lectures in social hygiene of Alfred Grotjahn. Poll shared the Rockefeller Foundation's long-term ideal of harnessing science to eliminate disease. He was an ardent eugenicist (although part-Jewish). He was a member of the Committee for Racial Hygiene advising the Prussian Ministry of Welfare. The other committee members were Max Matthes (professor of internal medicine at Königsberg), Max von Frey (professor of physiology at Würzburg), Max Versee (a hospital pathologist in Berlin), and Richard Willstätter (professor of organic chemistry at Munich). Haber represented the Emergency Fund, but soon resigned in March 1923 when it was made clear that the Rockefeller committee was to be independent of the Fund. Max Born, the physicist, was not appointed because the Foundation's officers decided to limit the scope of their programme to medical sciences. The US ambassador, who supported Flexner's scheme, did not participate because of the Foundation's desire to avoid being linked to government policies.[21]

The Fellowships were limited to 'the clinical branches only in their laboratory relationships'. University professors were disqualified from subsidies. The officers' evidence suggested that most poverty and worst prospects existed among intermediate-level researchers. The programme supported outstanding young *men*:

> The Berlin Committee decided that women should be considered in only very special cases, due to the fact that one of the principles of the whole scheme was to assist men who were ultimately going to hold important positions on the medical faculties, and that there is little likelihood of women holding important positions on the medical faculties for a long time to come.[22]

This was a harsh judgement, at a time when the proportion of women gaining medical qualifications was rapidly increasing and when there was a high proportion of women researchers in genetics. (In fact the Foundation appointed three German women as fellows for study abroad, but none were appointed by the German committee or Emergency Fund.) The novel feature about the German grants was that they could be held while remaining resident in Germany. There was a scale of tax-exempt grants. Recently qualified doctors could have $50–$150 a year; established young researchers could have $100–$300 a year. Five fellowships of $1000 could be awarded to researchers of exceptional merit. One fellowship went to Warburg and another to Meyerhof, once he had received the Nobel Prize. Both had full-time research posts with the Kaiser Wilhelm Gesellschaft. The Foundation's favouring of this autonomous conglomeration of research institutes contrasted to its distrust of university professors.

Poll was subjected to much jealous criticism. The Foundation initially took this as a good sign that he was standing up to the professorial mandarins. He was antagonistic to the Emergency Fund and to the Prussian Education Minister. Yet he was unable to deal with the administration of paying monthly cheques in an unstable currency, and a financial secretary was drafted in from the Rockefeller's Paris Office. Eversole criticised Poll for using the

Committee's patronage to expand university posts in human genetics. For example, he suggested that a teaching post be established in general biology and heredity at the University of Rostock, and offered to use Rockefeller funds to pay for the expenses of the candidate. The Rockefeller's officers considered that this violated their principle of non-intervention in domestic affairs. The Foundation began to normalise relations with Germany. It suggested that the Paris Office administer the Fellowship programme. The Committee argued that 'Germany could not be treated as other nations in Europe in regard to science, because the greatest scientists in the world emanated from Germany, which placed her on a different basis from other countries, especially as regards assistance.' Eversole explained that he wished to deal directly with each university faculty:

> Professor Poll was at first horrified at the idea, because he said that the German Universities were nothing but hotbeds of politics, and that the professors would play fellowships back and forth between them in a personal manner, and that the young scientists of real value would not be helped.[23]

As the economic situation improved, the Rockefeller Foundation tried to tip the balance of funds in favour of international fellowships.

Table 6.1 Rockefeller Foundation support for German science, 1922–39

	German grant ($)	Fellowships	International fellowships ($)
1922	65 000	194	
1923	100 000	262	35 000
1924	75 000	94	25 000
1925	20 000	79	30 000
1926	30 000		30 000
Total:	290 000		120 000

The distribution was as indicated in Table 6.1.[24] The year 1925 marked an interregnum with the programme administered by the Paris Office. In 1926, the fellowships programme passed to the Emergency Fund for German Science. When the Emergency Programme ceased in December 1926, the Emergency Fund retained the right to appoint fellows on similar terms to those awarded by the Medical Research Council. By 1939, it awarded twenty-four out of 169 German fellowships, the others being awarded as part of international programmes in the medical, natural and social sciences and the humanities. The Foundation's officers thus came to terms with the new structure of German science. Gregg accepted that 'Schmidt-Ott and Fehling [of the Emergency Fund] emphasise the need of Fellowships as the middle class cannot subsidise fellows or long-term research.'[25] The Depression caused a renewed crisis in German science funding. The Foundation allocated special Fellowship funds for an emergency programme from 1929. Gregg suggested the yearly sum of $21 000 over five years, to cover thirty men at $700 per year. By 1932, the Emergency Fund had received $300 000 for fellowships in medical sciences. The Nazi takeover of 1933 brought about a new crisis in the Rockefeller Foundation's relations with Germany. The Fellowship programme was scaled down by 1939. (See Figure 6.1.)[26]

The Fellowships Programme was a grandiose means of promoting an international research community, by providing the opportunity for foreign travel in order to develop qualities of 'future leadership and creative endeavour'. A specifically German programme with fellowships that could be held by Germans in Germany was problematic. The Foundation was uncomfortable with the idea that it was propping up a national educational system so that it could maintain routine functioning. The Foundation's officers found the German programme from start to end an irritant. Pearce and Gregg instead sought opportunities for 'creative philanthropy' where they could intervene to advance research programmes.

INSTITUTIONAL INITIATIVES

The normalisation of relations with Germany in 1925 made it possible for the Rockefeller Foundation to consider institutional investments there. These reflected changes in the Foundation's priorities, resulting from the restructuring of the Rockefeller philanthropic empire. Once the research-oriented Foundation emerged as supreme, medical education ceased to be a priority. The General Education Board's medical education programme was merged with the new medical sciences division. Abraham Flexner was disappointed that the Foundation decided to concentrate on

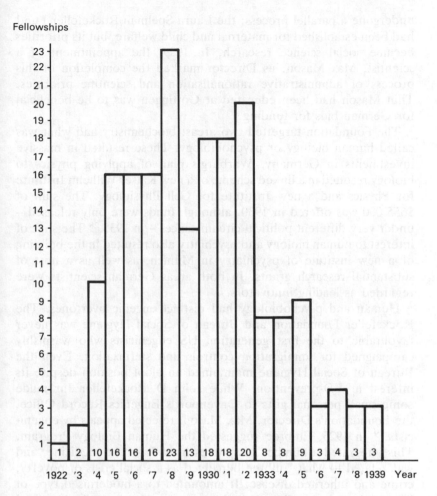

Figure 6.1 German Rockefeller Fellowships 1922–39
(includes Notgemeinschaft, International Education Board, Natural Sciences, Medical Sciences, Social Sciences, Humanities and Spelman Memorial programmes)

scientific research. He criticised this as philanthropy for the middle classes, and compared the change from education to science-funding as the abandoning of heavy artillery for scattered shot-gun fire.[27]

The Foundation rationalised its structure in line with its developing interests from medicine to all natural sciences. In 1928, it established divisions for medical, natural and social sciences. The latter had undergone a parallel process: the Laura Spelman Rockefeller Fund had been established for maternal and child welfare, but its priorities became social science research. In 1929, the appointment of a scientist, Max Mason, as Director marked the completion of this process of administrative rationalisation and scientific priorities. That Mason had been educated at Göttingen was to be beneficial for German bids for funding. The Foundation targetted two areas: biochemistry and what was called human biology or psychobiology. These resulted in massive investments in Germany. Warburg's plan of applying physics to biology resulted in a linked scheme of a new Kaiser Wilhelm Institute for Physics and a new Institute for Cell Physiology. The sum of $655 000 was offered in 1930, although funds were only released – under very different political circumstances – in 1935.[28] The shift of interest to human biology and psychiatry also resulted in the building of a new institute of psychiatry in Munich, as well as a host of substantial research grants. In both areas German scientists were regarded as leading innovators.

Human and psychobiology had distinct eugenic overtones. The Rockefeller Foundation and Bureau of Social Hygiene was never favourable to the first generation US eugenicists who waspishly campaigned for immigration controls and sterilization. Even the Bureau of Social Hygiene maintained an aloof position despite its interest in VD-prevention. While John D. Rockefeller Jnr made some small personal gifts to Davenport's Eugenics Record Office, the Foundation's Director, Max Mason, rejected appeals by eugenicists.[29] In 1925, Embree suggested the Human Biology Program. This integrated a number of spheres in biology and medicine, and was related to what Embree perceived as a social crisis of poverty, crime and inherited disease. It amounted to a modernised type of reform eugenics, in line with the newest advances in biology and medicine.[30] Kohler has shown how this was coolly received by Pearce and Simon Flexner, although it had the support of a Trustee, Raymond Pearl. They advised Fosdick not to support eugenics or mental hygiene. The Trustees declined to make a large-scale commitment, but agreed to a few projects. In December 1926, Embree was sent on a European tour with the brief of preparing a training programme for nurses. Instead, he developed his contacts with biologists in an attempt to pursue human biology.[31]

Embree resigned in 1927, frustrated and disappointed. But the human biology programme was kept alive by Alan Gregg, who became director of the medical sciences division in the reorganisation of 1928. He was keen to support psychiatry, and stressed its links to biology and medicine.[32] It was not until 1932 that a lasting appointment was made in the natural sciences division with Warren Weaver.[33] Only in 1935 did Weaver come up with an independent programme which applied physics and chemistry to biology.[34] It meant that until 1935 the natural sciences were still allied to what Gregg called psychobiology. Given the pervasive influence of hereditarian biology on psychiatry, it meant that the Foundation was in effect subsidising a modernised form of eugenics, although the term was not used. This conformed to international trends in medicine and biology during the inter-war period.

In 1929, the Foundation settled on four centres for neurology in Europe: Cornelius Kappers' Central Brain Institute in Amsterdam, Sherrington's Laboratory in Oxford, the German Psychiatric Institute in Munich and the Brain Research Institute of Oscar Vogt in Berlin. Both German centres combined the search for organic signs of mental illness with eugenic projects. This eugenic side became increasingly pronounced in German psychiatry. Pearce and Vincent were initially not interested in a proposal by the psychiatrist Emil Kraepelin, that the Rockefeller Foundation should contribute to a building to house the German Psychiatric Institute, which Kraepelin had founded in 1918. The Institute had initially been endowed with eleven million marks, contributed by Gustav Krupp von Bohlen und Halbach and James Loeb, an expatriate American of the Kuhn-Loeb banking family. Loeb mobilised his American-Jewish friends to support the Institute which had suffered badly as a result of the inflation. They, in turn, attempted to interest the Rockefeller Foundation. The Flexner brothers convinced Vincent of the virtues of Kraepelin's scheme.[35] Gregg was enthusiastic over how Kraepelin linked chemistry, experimental genetics, physiology and demographic and genealogical records. In November 1925, the Trustees agreed to contribute $2 500 000, and a further $75 000 in 1926, when presented with evidence that 'Munich is probably the best place in Europe to foster an outstanding institute devoted to investigation in psychiatry'. They were impressed by the support from the city of Munich and state authorities for a criminal biology data-bank, and district surveys of inherited diseases.[36] The Foundation contributed the lion's share to the building costs. After the Institute was completed in 1928, further grants followed. The most substantial of these, $89 000 from 1931 until 1939, was for a project to investigate the organic basis of mental disease by means of serology and neuro-histology.[37]

During 1929, the Foundation agreed to spend a sum of $317 000 for building an institute for brain research. This was integrated to a clinic, and directed by Oscar Vogt. Further special grants for equipment followed, for example $14 200 in 1932. Vogt researched into the cellular architecture of the brain, experimental genetics, neuro-pathology and psychology. These subjects had a social dimension, as he was interested in the location of individual variations in the brains of the supernormal, criminals and psychopaths. He encouraged experimental genetic research on inherited nervous diseases, recruiting the Russian geneticist Nicolai Timofeeff-Ressovsky. Vogt typified the progressive type of Weimar researcher, on the one hand keen to develop Pavlovian reflex theory, and on the other interested in heredity. Rockefeller officers admired the fact that his institute was integrated with a clinic. An ardent internationalist and sympathetic to socialism, he was dismissed by the Nazis in January 1935.[38]

In 1930, the psychobiology programme was supported with the argument that as infectious diseases were declining, a scientifically-based psychiatry should be developed.[39] Psychological and anthropometric studies of personality were envisaged in the social sciences. The Foundation increased grants to German eugenic projects. In 1929, it committed $125 000 for the period 1930–35 to fund a national German anthropological survey, co-ordinated through the Emergency Fund for German Science by the human geneticist Eugen Fischer. Populations, selected for either high eugenic worth or because of endemic diseases, were studied using a combination of social, biological, cultural and anthropological methods. It was hoped that 'knowledge as to the recurrence of degenerative traits and the distribution of hereditary pathological attributes should result from the study proposed'.[40] After the Nazi takeover in 1933, the Foundation's European officer, Kittredge, remained convinced of the complete objectivity of the survey. This was carried out by racial hygienists, whose views differed widely on racial questions. Most of these, such as Fischer, Hans F. K. Günther, Otto Reche, Ernst Rüdin, and von Verschuer achieved great influence in Nazi Germany, whereas others, such as Franz Saller and Vogt, fell foul of the authorities. Fischer's Kaiser Wilhelm Institute for Anthropology, Human Heredity and Eugenics received $6 052 for the period

1932–35. The money was used for research into hereditary diseases in twins.[41]

Psychiatry continued to be a major area of support in Germany throughout the 1930s. In 1937, $23 000 was granted to Kurt Beringer in Breslau for patho-psychology.[42] Werner Wagner, a neurologist in Freiburg, received major grants for the study of hereditary and mental disease, especially muscular dystrophy. Between 1930 and 1935, Walter Jaensch of the Charité hospital in Berlin received a $3000 grant for research on 'constitutional diseases in the psycho-physical field of medicine'.[43] In November 1933, smaller grants were awarded to the Munich psychiatrist, Oswald Bumke, for work on the 'psycho-physical constitution', as well as to the neuropathologist, Hugo Spatz. The grants were renewed annually owing to favourable reports by Daniel O'Brian, the Paris officer.

Whereas Gregg was alert to how certain projects on metabolic change were linked to the sterilisation and castration laws, O'Brian maintained a positive view of German science. In March 1940, he wrote in support of Bumke: 'With the traditional policy of the Foundation for neutrality and for maintaining international activities in an international way, I think it would be unfortunate if it was chosen to stop research which has no relation to war issues'.[44] In 1939, apart from two grants to Viennese social scientists, all other support for Germans was in psychiatry. The Paris Office was funding Bumke and Wagner, and the New York Office was paying money to the Freiburg neuro-psychiatric clinic. The one remaining visiting fellow to the USA was the psychiatrist, Robert Gaupp. By 1940, these psychiatrists were informed about the compulsory 'euthanasia' of the mentally ill. Recent research suggests that the psychiatrists in question were onlookers rather than instigators. The extermination of those branded as so mentally or physically crippled that their lives were 'valueless' was meant to be highly secret; the Rockefeller Foundation was thus unaware of this dark side to German psychiatry. Since 1933, the Foundation had been deeply concerned about Nazi antisemitism, the dismissal of scientists and the sterilization laws.[45]

Most problematic for the Foundation was the ten-year grant awarded to Felix Plaut and Walther Spielmeyer for neuro-histology in 1929. They worked at the German Psychiatric Institute, of which Rüdin became Director in 1933. By April 1933, there were complaints in the USA about Rüdin because of his involvement with the regime. His cooperation consisted in the preparation of a law enabling compulsory sterilisation. It was pointed out that the only money that Rüdin received from the Rockefeller Foundation was through the Emergency Fund grant for the anthropological survey.[46] The work of Plaut and Spielmeyer was mainly histological, attempting to relate nerve cell structure to mental disorders. Both fell foul of the regime after 1933. The Rockefeller's support was helpful in defending two persecuted researchers. Plaut and Spielmeyer poured out their worries to the deeply sympathetic and sensitive Gregg, who visited their Institute in June 1934. Spielmeyer was 'heartsick and ashamed of his own people', and wished to emigrate, but Gregg 'advised him to stay at it'.[47] In 1935, Spielmeyer died, apparently from natural causes, but so overwrought that suicide was suspected. Plaut was dismissed, and strenuous efforts were made to secure his emigration. Despite Rüdin's attempt to continue the funding, this was withdrawn. Funds for other projects, like the inheritance of homosexuality or of the disposition to goitre, were refused in 1938 'because of the present difficult situation in Germany on questions dealing with hereditary problems'.[48]

At the same time as the Rockefeller Foundation was seeking to sort out objective from ideological science, it was having to cope with the problem of the demand for jobs of dismissed German scientists. Its policy was to help those whom it had funded in the past by means of a pump-priming grant in the hope that the researcher would be taken over by an institution. It also established a research fund of $775 000 which gave 304 grants to 196 persecuted scholars.[49] But Poll, who was desperate to find a post outside Germany, could not be placed, and he died shortly after a fruitless visit to the USA (one suspects suicide). Gregg was deeply concerned that he was unsuccessful in helping him find a position.[50] Mounting public pressure forced the Foundation to take a low profile in Germany. The Foundation's European officers found it difficult to fathom politics. German researchers of Jewish descent themselves were deluded. Goldschmidt thought that Nazism was better than the alternative of Bolshevism and that Hitler would not be so bad if types like Joseph Goebbels could be eliminated. Otto Warburg thought the regime would not last longer than 1934. Some commented that Hitler was a moderating force.[51]

The more contact the officers had with Europe, the less clear-sighted they were. Once based in the USA, Gregg became more detached. After a visit in 1934, he commented: 'It might be the economic salvation of Germany to go communistic if that would break down their resistance to their natural markets in the east.

Germany is not much of a milieu for science in the near future.'[52] In 1937, Raymond Fosdick, the newly appointed President, insisted that the Foundation must not be involved in any way in funding racial research. The Foundation had to honour long-standing commitments; but Italy, Japan and Germany posed problems because of the racist character of research.[53] He felt that such totalitarian states could not support objective scholarship. The European officers continued to submit proposals from Germany which they regarded as fulfilling the criteria of objectivity. Finally, in June 1939, Fosdick ordered that no more major grants could be made to Germany. He declared that he had no objection to making grants to totalitarian states, but that it was clear that Germany and Italy could no longer meet the Foundation's requirements.[54]

At the same time, Weaver's new policy for applying physics and chemistry to biology began to take shape. Warburg was among those who had urged Weaver to take this direction, and indeed this was the rationale for funding his new institute. It might be suggested that the reductionism and positivism of this programme came as a welcome relief to the Foundation's officers. Psychobiology was a treacherous area at a time when the psychiatrists were in the vanguard of eugenics. The Rockefeller's long-standing connections with Warburg provided an important precursor for their major initiative on molecular biology. Here, again, German research affected fundamental issues in the Foundation's priorities.

NATIONALISM AND INTERNATIONALISM IN SCIENCE

Despite the rise of authoritarian regimes during the 1930s, international-nationalism remained a powerful force in science. The Rockefeller Foundation came to symbolise an ideal of international co-operation and of humanitarian science, while enabling individual researchers to develop international contacts on a personal level. Margaret Gowing has shown the precarious balance between the international-ism of the scientific community and national research organisations in the development of atomic energy. She has pointed out the importance of discoveries on an international level, as well as the vital part played by German and other European émigrés. At the same time, the development of nuclear energy was a challenging test for British, German, US and Soviet national science organiz-ations. The fear that Germany would develop a bomb was a major stimulus to British and US research. This sense of the superiority of German science can also be detected in the Rockefeller Foundation's policies.[55]

Rockefeller officers were confronted by a fundamental problem of disentangling positive scientific achievement from nationalist ideology. This problem was especially complex with regard to Germany, because of the high quality of teaching and research, and the often intense patriotism of scientists after the First World War. It was made all the more difficult by the Jekyll and Hyde behaviour of German scientists. When they appealed for funds for human genetics and psychiatry from state resources, they emphasised the social relevance of their studies. Only rarely did scientists express nationalist convictions to the Foundation. For example, in 1932, Claus Schilling's use of colonialist Pan-Germanic rhetoric disqualified him from funding, despite a strong recommendation by William Henry Welch (Schilling was to be executed for having undertaken malaria experiments at the Dachau concentration camp). When they approached the Rockefeller Foundation, scientists generally became internationalists, stressing the priorities of basic research and humanitarian aims. The judgement of many scientists was clouded by their nationalism. The Foundation's officers characterised them as wanting a return of the Hohenzollern regime. As Lambert, in January 1933, commented to Gregg, 'considering what that regime did for science, one should not be surprised at this'.[56] Such scientists did not understand the ultimate aims of Nazism until it was too late.

As Germany bequeathed a model of teaching and research that was taken up in higher education throughout the world, it was understandable that the Rockefeller Foundation should give the Germans special consideration. Yet at the same time it was unable to avoid the problems of nationalism. The first phase of special emergency measures beween 1922 and 1927 involved nurturing a younger generation of researchers. The hope that they would be free from the nationalist prejudices of established professors was not to be fulfilled. Among the younger generation were those who turned out to be even more nationalistic. The second phase of Rockefeller policy, that of expanding research facilities in psychiatry and human biology, was also to run into complications as these disciplines were often conceived of in eugenic terms. During the third phase of the Depression, from 1929, the Foundation worked in close co-operation with the German authorities. The final phase, from 1933, was that of a slow withdrawal from Germany, and support for expelled researchers. During all these phases, the Foundation's priorities were internationalist, and yet it could not avoid the national ideological and power structures of which German science was an intrinsic part.

The case of German funding reveals some of the complexity of the Rockefeller's large-scale interventive policies towards science and medicine. The Foundation was not able to alter course with the same rapidity as political and social change occurred. It was cautious in becoming involved in Germany, but once established, it was slow to withdraw. Officers were increasingly preoccupied with problems of objectivity and scientific excellence. The more they adopted scientific priorities and abandoned education and welfare, the less perceptive they were in judging the social aims of scientific projects. Gregg's great strength was that he could see the limitations of the scientific dimension, whether in psychoanalysis or in his concern with social conditions under the Nazis. He must be given credit for having greater insight into the risks of science than other officers. But Gregg did much to support the psychobiology programme. The Foundation's internationalism meant that it was helpful and loyal to refugee scholars, but it also meant that its priority was the quality of research, rather than the social context in which the research was conducted. While Rockefeller philanthropy was intended to promote the good of mankind, officials were at their weakest in judging the social context of science.

Acknowledgements

This research was carried out with a grant-in-aid from the Rockefeller University. I wish to thank the Director and staff of the Rockefeller Archive Center for the excellent conditions provided for researchers.

NOTES

1. D. Kevles, *The Physicists* (New York: Knopf, 1978). R. Olby, *The Path to the Double Helix* (London: Macmillan, 1974). R. E. Kohler, *From Medical Chemistry to Biochemistry*, (Cambridge University Press, 1982). R. Stevens, *American Medicine and the Public Interest* (New Haven: Yale University Press, 1971).

2. R.B. Fosdick, *The Story of the Rockefeller Foundation* (New York: Harper and Brothers, 1952).
3. R.E. Kohler, 'A Policy for the Advancement of Science: The Rockefeller Foundation, 1924–29', *Minerva*, XVI (1978) pp. 480–515, S. Cohen, 'Foundation Officials and Fellowships: Innovation in the Patronage of Science', *Minerva*, XIV (1976) pp. 225–40.
4. P. Abir-Am, 'The Discourse of Physical Power and Biological Knowledge in the 1930s: A Reappraisal of the Rockefeller Foundation's "Policy" in Molecular Biology', *Social Studies of Science*, XII (1982) pp. 341–82.
5. J. Ettling, *The Germ of Laziness, Rockefeller Philanthropy and Public Health in the New South* (Cambridge, Mass. and London: Harvard University Press, 1981).
6. E.R. Brown, *Rockefeller Medicine Men* (Berkeley: California University Press, 1979). H.S. Berliner, *A System of Scientific Medicine: Philanthropic Foundations in the Flexner Era* (New York: Tavistock, 1985).
7. A. Flexner, *An Autobiography* (New York: Simon and Schuster, 1960), pp. 100–8.
8. D. Fisher, 'The Impact of American Foundations on the Development of British University Education 1900–1939', PhD thesis, University of California at Berkeley, 1977.
9. Rockefeller Archive Center (hereafter RAC), C. Lewerth, 'Source Book for the History of the Rockefeller Foundation' (typescript, cited hereafter as 'History'), vol. 14, Medicine and Public Health 1919–1923, pp. 3500–5.
10. D. Kevles, '"Into Hostile Political Camps". The Reorganisation of International Science in World War I', *Isis*, LXII (1971) pp. 47–60.
11. P. Forman, 'Scientific Internationalism and the Weimar Physicists: The Ideology and Its Manipulation in Germany after World War I', *Isis*, LXIV (1973) pp. 151–80.
12. RAC MS History, vol. 15, pp. 3696–8.
13. RAC 1.1/717/8/46 Houghton to Flexner 10 July 1922. MS History vol. 15, pp. 3696–8.
14. RAC 1.1/717/8/46 Vincent to Flexner 31 July 1922.
15. RAC 1.1/717/8/46 Pearce to Gregg 14 November 1922.
16. RAC 1.1/717/8/49 Emergency Aid 1923, Eversole to Pearce, 11 November 1923.
17. B. Schroeder-Gudehus, 'The Argument for the Self-Government and Public Support of Science in Weimar Germany', *Minerva*, X (1972) pp. 537–70.
18. RAC 1.1/717/8/48, 22 December 1922. Pearce to Gregg.
19. RAC 1.1/717/8/47 Vincent to S. Flexner, 14 December 1922. Compare K. Macrakis, 'Wissenschaftsförderung durch die Rockefeller-Stiftung im "Dritten Reich". Die Entscheidung, das Kaiser-Wilhelm-Institut für Physik finanziell zu unterstützen, 1934–39', *Geschichte und Gesellschaft*, XII (1986) pp. 348–79, 350–1. Macrakis's study of physics complements this account of the biomedical sciences.
20. P.J. Weindling, *Darwinism and Social Darwinism in Imperial Germany*.

The Contribution to Cell Biology by Oscar Hertwig (1849–1922) (Stuttgart: Gustav Fischer, 1988).
21. P.J. Weindling, 'Die Preussische Medizinalverwaltung und die "Rassenhygiene"', *Zeitschrift für Sozialreform*, (1984) pp. 675–87.
22. RAC 1.1/717/8/47 Pearce to Vincent, 13 November 1922.
23. RAC 1.1/717/8/51 Report of 22 June 1924. Bundesarchiv Koblenz R 73/217 Rockefeller Foundation.
24. RAC. History, vol. 15, p. 3794.
25. RAC 1.1/717/16/152.
26. *The Rockefeller Foundation. Directory of Fellowship Awards for the Years 1917–1950* (New York, Rockefeller Foundation, nd).
27. A. Flexner, *Funds and Foundations* (New York, 1979) pp. 77–100.
28. Macrakis, 'Wissenschaftsförderung'.
29. G.E. Allen, 'The Eugenics Record Office at Cold Spring Harbor, 1910–1940. An Essay in Institutional History', *Osiris*, 2 ser., II (1986) 225–64. RAC Bureau of Social Hygiene 2/138, 3/178 and 204 Eugenics, 4/619–21 Germany.
30. RAC RG 1/Series 100/ Box 112/ Folder 1035 re criminology. RG 2 – 1929 Series 200/13 108. RG 1.1/200/204. BSH/Soc – 2/138.
31. Kohler, 'A Policy' op. cit., pp. 499–501.
32. I am grateful for discussions with Theodore Brown, Rochester, who is researching on Gregg's support of psychiatry and psychoanalysis.
33. R.E. Kohler, 'The Management of Science: The Experience of Warren Weaver and the Rockefeller Foundation Programme in Molecular Biology', *Minerva*, XIV (1976), pp. 276–306.
34. J.A. Fuerst, 'The Role of Reductionism in the Development of Molecular Biology: Peripheral or Central?', *Social Studies of Science*, XII (1982) 241–78. Abir-Am, 'The Discourse', op. cit.
35. RAC 1.1/719/9/54.
36. Ibid.
37. RAC 1.1/71/9/56.
38. RAC 1.1/717/10/64. P.J. Weindling, 'German–Soviet Co-operation in Science: the Case of the Laboratory for Racial Research, 1931–1938', *Annali di storia di scienze* (in press).
39. RAC 3/906/2/17 Staff conference 7 October 1930.
40. RAC 1.1/717/20/187 13 November 1929.
41. RAC 6.1/1.1/4/46. For human biology in Nazi Germany, see B. Müller-Hill, *Tödliche Wissenschaft. Die Aussonderung von Juden, Zigeunern und Geisteskranken 1933–1945* (Reinbek: Rowohlt, 1984).
42. RAC 1.1/717/12/84.
43. RAC 1.1/717/11/779.
44. RAC 1.1/717/12/98 O'Brian to Gregg, 26 March 1940.
45. E. Klee, *'Euthanasie' im NS-Staat* (Frankfurt a.M.: S. Fischer, 1983).
46. RAC 1.1/717/10/58, 14 April 1933.
47. RAC 1.1/717/9/56.
48. RAC 1.1./717/10/58. W. Scholz, 'Walther Spielmeyer (1879–1935) und sein Schülerkreis', in W. Scholz (ed.), *50 Jahre Neuropathologie in Deutschland 1885–1935* (Stuttgart: Thieme, 1961) pp. 87–107.
49. RAC 1.1/717/1/14.

50. RAC Gregg MS Diary 10 June 1938. The personal file on Poll has been withheld by Staatsarchiv Hamburg.
51. RAC, Warren Weaver, MS Diary May 3–June 13, 1933. 1.1/717/13/109.
52. RAC 1.1//717/9/56.
53. RAC, *Monthly Report* (October 1937).
54. RAC 1.1/717/16/150.
55. M.M. Gowing, *Britain and Atomic Energy, 1939–45* (London: Macmillan and New York: St Martin's Press, 1964).
56. RAC 1.1/717/11/69 Robert Koch Institute Berlin, 1.1/717/350/2369.

7   Science and Power in the Soviet Union

David Holloway

In her Spencer lecture, Margaret Gowing points to the long-standing relationship that has existed between science and politics. 'Today the intimacy between science and politics should be strong and apparent' she writes.

But, some say, this is a very recent relationship dating only from the Second World War, and contrasting with the innocent, academic paradise of prewar science. This belief in a paradise that has been lost and might be regained is, however, a fantasy at total variance with history, which shows on the contrary that the relationship is not only intimate but very old.[1]

Yet, as Professor Gowing has shown very clearly in her work on the British atomic project, this relationship entered a new stage during the Second World War, when scientists became 'very directly involved in the balance of power and the life and death of nations.'[2]

Margaret Gowing's comments apply with as much force to the Soviet Union as they do to Britain. The relationship between science and politics has, indeed, been particularly intense and troubled in Russia, ever since Peter the Great imported European natural science at the beginning of the eighteenth century. For over a hundred years there were many Russians who regarded the St Petersburg Academy of Sciences as an alien institution. It was only in the mid-nineteenth century that Russian scientists began to win international reputations, and Russian scientific institutions to rely on native rather than on foreign scholars. A more or less cohesive scientific community began to emerge then, with its social and psychological ties maintained by a network of learned societies, scientific circles and congresses.[3] This community was pervaded by a national consciousness that made it much more than an outpost of European science, and the growth of this consciousness was accompanied by the first priority disputes between Russian and non-Russian scientists. Yet science, even when it was assimilated into Russian culture, was regarded by many political reformers and revolutionaries as a Westernising force that would help to dispel superstition and thus to undermine the ideological basis of the

141

Tsarist autocracy. The Tsarist authorities, for their part, distrusted the scientific spirit because they regarded it as critical of authority. Thus science was seen by its friends and enemies alike as progressive and democratic.

The Bolsheviks' view of science was very much in the revolutionary tradition of the nineteenth century. They believed that science would inculcate rationality and civilisation, and would play a vital part in building a socialist society. They claimed, moreover, that Marxism was a scientific theory which shared with the natural sciences a materialist outlook and dialectical method, and they were convinced that, in a society organised on scientific principles, science and technology would flourish. Lenin used the slogan 'Communism = Soviet power + the electrification of the whole country' to convey the message that communism was to be created by a combination of social revolution and technological progress.[4]

From the very beginning of Soviet rule, therefore, an intimate relationship existed between science and politics, and in this chapter I want to touch briefly on some aspects of that relationship. Because Margaret Gowing's work has contributed so much to our understanding of how we came to our current nuclear predicaments, I want to look at Soviet science with particular reference to the history of atomic energy.

When they seized power, the Bolsheviks found that their enthusiasm for science and technology was not matched by political support from the scientific community. Most scientists had welcomed the February revolution of 1917 because they regarded the Tsarist autocracy as a brake on education and science, but they were suspicious of the Bolsheviks, who, they feared, might destroy learning rather than encourage it. The Bolsehviks recognised this and took steps to enlist the support of the scientific community. Their second Party Programme, adopted in 1919, declared that the greatest possible use should be made of scientific and technical specialists, 'in spite of the fact that in most cases they have inevitably been nourished upon capitalist ideology and trained in bourgeois habits'.[5]

The Bolsheviks sought the co-operation of scientists because they believed that science would contribute to the economic and military power of the Soviet state. Before the First World War, Russian science had been primarily an academic pursuit, and poorly supported by government. Scientists, moreover, did not have close ties with industry, much of which was controlled by foreign companies that relied on research done abroad, while Russian entrepreneurs showed little interest in financing science. But the war brought major changes, because dependence on industrial imports, including many chemicals essential for the manufacture of weapons, was recognised to be a factor in Russia's military weakness. The war stimulated scientific research, which came to be seen as an important part of government policy, and encouraged closer ties between science and industry.

The Bolsheviks did not have plans of their own for the organisation of science, and hence were willing to listen to proposals for using science to promote economic growth and self-sufficiency. They set up new research institutes and, in so far as resources allowed, supported scientific research without insisting on immediate economic results. In retrospect, the 1920s seem like a golden age. The Bolsheviks were content with collaboration on the part of the scientific community, and did not seek wholehearted political commitment. They did not infringe upon the intellectual autonomy of the Academy of Sciences. Soviet scientists travelled to the West, and Western scientists visited the Soviet Union. The Party and government shared the view of most scientists that Soviet science, while it should contribute to Soviet economic and military power, was also part of an international enterprise.

At the end of the 1920s, however, fundamental changes took place. Stalin, who had set the country on an ambitious industrialisation drive, sought to harness science more directly to economic policy. The Academy of Sciences lost its intellectual autonomy and was directed to meet the demands of industrialisation. The Academy was forced to elect Party members to its ranks for the first time. The 'ideology of pure science' came under fire, and science was now supposed to develop in response to the needs of the economy.[6]

It was, however, easier to demand that science serve industry than to ensure that it actually did so. By the mid-1930s, the Soviet Union was devoting a higher proportion of its national income to research and development than the United States was, but the authorities felt that they were not getting the return they needed.[7] The head of the science department of the Party Central Committee declared in 1936 that 'in the USSR, as nowhere else in the world, all the conditions have been created for science to flourish, for research to develop'.[8] The task facing the institutes was clear: 'to contribute in every way possible to the realisation of the Party's slogan, to catch up and overtake the economically and technologically advanced capitalist countries'. He complained, however that 'scientific research still lags behind practice', and similar complaints were heard from other officials at the same time. In the 1930s, the Soviet Union was beginning to confront a problem that Soviet leaders have grappled with ever since: how to stimulate technological innovation in a highly centralised planned economy?

The insistence that science contribute to industrialisation went hand in hand with tighter ideological control over scientists. Collaboration with the regime was no longer enough: the Party now sought political and ideological commitment. Scientific disciplines came under scrutiny from militant philosophers who wanted to root out any philosophical and political deviations that scientific theories might betray. Since Marxism–Leninism was a scientific theory, Marxist philosophers now claimed the right to judge whether theories in the natural sciences were really scientific or not. Scientific disputes could be resolved by appeal to philosophical authority, and hence ultimately to the authority of Stalin and the Party.[9]

Ideological controls created a dangerous environment for science, and the dangers were illustrated most clearly by the Lysenko affair, which destroyed Soviet genetics and caused great harm to Soviet biology more generally. David Joravsky has argued convincingly, however, that this affair should not be seen merely as a clash between natural science and dialectical materialism, but has to be explained in light of the terrible condition of Soviet agriculture after collectivisation.[10] Soviet plant breeders were unable to come forward with proposals for dramatic increases in grain yields, even though they were winning an international reputation for the scientific breeding of improved crop varieties. Their cautious realism was irrelevant to the momentous problems which faced agriculture. Trofim Lysenko, the 'barefoot professor', took advantage of this situation to make far-reaching claims for his own ideas, and to attack his opponents as anti-Marxist and anti-Soviet. According to a Soviet biography of Nikolai Vavilov, Lysenko's chief victim who died in the Gulag in 1942, 'the country needed wheat. And it was very much desired to believe Lysenko, and not his scientific opponents. His promises were all too alluring'.[11]

Ironically, Soviet biology suffered from the very importance given to science by the Soviet authorities. The belief that science could make a huge contribution to socialism was perverted into the conviction that there must be something wrong with a science that could not offer solutions to the problems the Soviet leaders faced in agriculture. The belief that the authority of the Communist Party rested on its scientific understanding of social laws underpinned the assertion that theories in the natural sciences could embody political or philosophical deviations, and this assertion opened the way to the ideological policing of science. It was this ideological context that enabled Lysenko to attack and defeat his scientific opponents.

The Soviet vision of science appealed to some foreign scientists, who were impressed by the support that science received, and by the fact that the Soviet Union was the first state to attempt self-consciously to plan research. The papers given by the Soviet delegation at the Second International Congress on the History of Science and Technology in London in 1931 made a deep impression on a number of British scientists who were interested in the relationship between science and society. J.D. Bernal, whose influential book, *The Social Functions of Science*, reflected his admiration for the Soviet Union, called it the 'most important meeting of ideas that has occurred since the Revolution'.[12]

But in retrospect it is clear that the politics of Soviet science was far more complex, far less rational and far nastier than Bernal or his colleagues understood at the time. It is true that the Soviet Union devoted large resources to scientific research and to the education of scientists. But far from exercising a rationalising influence on politics, science itself came to resemble Soviet politics. Because science was politicised, political techniques of argument could be used against scientific opponents: 'quotation-mongering' – the appeal to the writings of Marx, Engels, Lenin, or Stalin in support of one's arguments; and 'label-sticking' – the attempt to defeat an opponent's argument by associating it with a political or philosophical deviation.[13] These techniques were later condemned, after Stalin's death. As Nikolai Semenov (who won the Nobel Prize for Chemistry for his work on chain reactions) said in 1965, 'Lysenko and...his supporters...by using the conditions of the personality cult, have transferred the struggle against those with different ideas from the level of scientific discussion to the level of demagogy and political accusations.'[14]

Not all sciences suffered as biology had done. Lysenkoism, symptomatic though it was of the conditions of science under Stalin, was not the only possible fate for a scientific discipline. Physics fared much better. Quantum mechanics and relativity theory were criticised by some philosophers and physicists on the grounds that they were incompatible with dialectical materialism, but these attacks did not receive political backing, and physics in the laboratory was not affected.

In the 1920s and 1930s, the leading centre of Soviet physics was the Leningrad Physicotechnical Institute, which Abram Ioffe had established in 1921, with the support of the Soviet authorities. The express purpose of Ioffe's institute was to link physics with technology, for Ioffe shared the view, which had become widespread before the Revolution, that science and industry should stimulate each other's development. Ioffe's view of physics appealed strongly to the Bolshevik leaders of industry, and he was successful in raising funds to expand his institute in the 1920s. Ioffe travelled abroad almost every year to maintain contact with foreign physicists, and he sent the most promising of his junior colleagues to do research abroad. He was a good judge of ability, and brought many talented young physicists to work at the Institute. His Institute was later called the 'alma mater' and the 'forge' of Soviet physics.[15]

But the 1930s were a much more difficult decade for Ioffe. His goal of linking physics with production proved harder to realise than he had anticipated. His claims for the influence of physics on industry ('physics', he said, 'is the basis of socialist technology') had raised false hopes, and now disillusionment set in. At a special meeting of the Academy of Sciences in March 1936, he was taken severely to task for his institute's remoteness from industry and for his unwillingness to become more deeply involved in industrial production.[16]

Many of the criticisms levelled at Ioffe were justified, but not all of the difficulties with technology could be laid at his door, for innovation depended on more than the attitude of scientists. Another physicist, D.S. Rozhdestvenskii, asked at the Academy meeting why science was being used more effectively in capitalist industry than in the Soviet Union; his answer was that the Soviet Union did not yet have a powerful apparatus to take the place of the profit motive in directing science to productive uses.[17] The highly-centralised hierarchical planning system made innovation a difficult bureaucratic exercise, for it erected institutional barriers between research and production. Moreover, the practice of setting ambitious production targets for industry discouraged enterprises from introducing new products and processes, since these might interfere with current production and result in failure to fulfil the plan.

The difficulties of innovation modified Ioffe's view of the role that his Institute should play, and he focused increasingly on research that would have long-term rather than short-term applications. But conditions for research were also becoming more difficult in the 1930s. Ioffe regarded personal contacts with foreign scientists as essential for the development of Soviet science. By the middle of the 1930s, however, such contacts were being curtailed. Ioffe himself, who had done his doctorate at Munich University with Wilhelm Roentgen in the early years of the century, was not allowed to go abroad after 1933, and was no longer able to send his younger colleagues and pupils to do research in foreign universities and institutes. Peter Kapitsa, for whom Ioffe had arranged a place at the Cavendish Laboratory in 1921, was prevented from returning to Cambridge from a trip he made to the Soviet Union in 1934. Although personal contacts were not completely ended, visits by Western scientists became much fewer. Research was affected also by the arbitrary terror that Stalin unleashed on Soviet society in the late 1930s. Many physicists were arrested during the great purge, and some of them never returned from the Gulag.[18]

In spite of the repression and the restrictions on foreign contacts, Soviet physics flourished in the prewar years, thanks in large measure to Ioffe himself. Physics did not perish as biology had done; laboratories were not closed down in response to ideological criticism, and in spite of the emphasis on practical utility, research continued even if it did not promise inmmediate results. A strong nuclear group was formed at Ioffe's institute in the 1930s, for example, even though no one expected nuclear physics to lead to practical results in the foreseeable future.

At the end of 1932, a number of young researchers at the institute, excited by the discoveries of that *annus mirabilis*, decided to switch to nuclear physics. This group included Igor Kurchatov, who was to become scientific director of the Soviet nuclear program from 1943 until his death in 1960, and Lev Artsimovich, who later became known for his work on controlled fusion reactions. In spite of the pressure from the Party and government to do research with practical relevance, the physicists who chose to work on the nucleus were guided by their scientific interests and the excitement of the field, not by the criterion of utility. Many scientists and officials criticised this research, on the grounds that it was a waste of resources that could be more usefully employed in other fields. Ioffe, however, defended his young colleagues against these attacks, and obtained additional funding from the People's Commissariat of Heavy Industry, to which his institute was subordinate at the time. Nuclear research was supported by Nikolai Bukharin, who was (until 1933) in charge of industrial research at the People's Commissariat, and by Serge Ordzhonikidze, who was the Commissar. Bukharin was intrigued by the grandiose prospect that one day atomic energy might be harnessed for practical purposes, and Ordzhonikidze may have shared a similar vision.[19]

The role of Soviet physics was very different from that of Soviet biology, even though the Stalinist context, with its insistence on practical utility and its ideological policing, was the same for both. Biologists and physicists alike were criticised for not doing enough to help the Soviet Union achieve its economic goals, but one field was destroyed while the other prospered. There was no doubt an element of luck in this, but the main explanation for the difference seems to lie in the relationship between science and its practical application. The Soviet leaders declared Lysenko's agrobiology a success, because they found nothing to help them in standard biology. Lysenko's practical success (illusory though it was) was deemed to be proof that his theories were correct, while to defend genetics was tantamount to criticism of the policy of collectivisation. Lysenko's theories helped to convey the impression that the Soviet Union was creating the most advanced agricultural system in the world, when it was in fact compelling the peasants, with great brutality and ruthlessness, to provide the agricultural requirements of industrialisation.[20]

Soviet officials may have complained that Soviet physics was not doing enough to help industry, but industry was growing very rapidly nonetheless. A 'Lysenkoist' physics was not needed by the Soviet leaders to give the impression that Soviet industrialisation was proceeding apace. Besides, much of the work done by Soviet physicists was useful for industry: Ioffe's institute, for example, did a good deal of research for the electrical industry. Those parts of physics that came under ideological attack – quantum mechanics and the theory of relativity – survived because they were irrelevant to industry at the time, and did not get caught up in the dangerous nexus that existed between science and practical utility in the Stalin years.

In the 1930s, nuclear physics was the very model of an international scientific community, with discoveries in one country stimulating research in others. Soviet physicists felt themselves to be very much part of this community and, in 1933, Ioffe organised a conference on the nucleus in Leningrad, to which a group of foreign physicists, including Paul Dirac, Frederic and Irene Joliot-Curie, and Victor Weisskopf, came.[21] Even when contacts with Western physicists diminished, the Soviet nuclear physicists followed the Western journals very closely. They were intensely interested in the research being done abroad, and measured their own performance against that of their colleagues in Rome, Paris, Cambridge and other leading Western centres of nuclear physics.

When nuclear fission was discovered by Hahn and Strassman in Berlin at the end of 1938, Soviet scientists were just as excited as their colleagues in other countries by the discovery, and the research they did in the next two years paralleled that being done in the West. Soviet physicists made two important contributions during 1940: the discovery of spontaneous fission by G.N. Flerov and K.A. Petrzhak, and the theory of nuclear chain reactions developed by Ya.B. Zeldovich and Yu.B. Khariton. The papers by Zeldovich and Khariton were published in the main Soviet physics journal in 1940. The paper on spontaneous fission appeared in Russian and English in Soviet journals, and a cable announcing the discovery was sent to the American journal *Physical Review*, which published it in July 1940.[22]

Although Soviet physicists followed the foreign journals with intense interest, Western scientists took little note of what was being done in the Soviet Union. When Flerov and Petrzhak were nominated for a Stalin prize in 1940 for their discovery of spontaneous fission, the reviewer recommended to the prize committee that they not be awarded a prize, on the grounds that Western physicists had paid no attention to the discovery.[23] Soviet nuclear physicists very much wanted their work to be recognised by Western scientists, whose research they followed and admired so much, but this admiration was not reciprocated.

Kapitsa argued, in an essay on the great eighteenth-century man of science Mikhail Lomonosov, that because of his lack of personal contacts with European scientists, Lomonosov had not received the recognition he deserved. 'In order that a scientist's work become known', Kapitsa wrote, 'he must not only publish it, but in addition he has to convince people of its correctness and prove its importance. All this can be done successfully only with personal contact'.[24] The experience of Soviet nuclear physics in 1940 seems to show that Kapitsa was right, but there was more to it than Kapitsa suggested, for, even in the absence of personal contacts, Soviet physicists knew of Western research, while most Western scientists were unaware of Soviet work; and this reflected a deeper pattern in the relationship of Russia to the West.

Soviet nuclear research was proceeding on a broad front in 1940 and early 1941, but it was not specifically directed towards military purposes. Soviet physicists were aware, of course, that it might be possible to build a uranium bomb with immense destructive force, and Zeldovich and Khariton calculated the critical mass of uranium-235 needed for such a weapon. Nikolai Semenov, director of the institute where Zeldovich and Khariton worked, wrote to the government to draw its attention to the possibility of a bomb with unusual destructive force, but this letter elicited no response before Germany invaded on 22 June 1941.[25] Nuclear research was now brought to a halt. The nuclear laboratories were disbanded or took up other lines of research. The prospect of practical results seemed too remote to justify nuclear research when the country was reeling from the German attack.

Within two years, however, this hiatus was ended, for in 1942 Stalin decided to set up a Soviet atomic project, and by March 1943 the project was under way. At first glance the decision is surprising. Soviet physicists did not know more about fission in 1942 than they had done in 1941; their assessment of the possibility of a bomb had not changed; nor were the conditions for research any better than they had been after June 1941. What convinced Stalin of the need for an atomic project was information that other countries – Germany, Britain and the United States – were investigating seriously the possibility of building an atomic bomb.[26] This was the 'secret' of the atomic bomb during the Second World War: that other governments took it seriously enough to devote large resources to trying to build it.

As early as 1940, Soviet physicists had noticed that the Western journals were no longer publishing as much on fission, and had wondered why. But the crucial moment came early in 1942 when Georgii Flerov, now serving in the Red Army, visited the university library in Voronezh, where he was stationed. Piqued by his failure to win the Stalin prize, Flerov wanted to see whether there was any response to his discovery of spontaneous fission. He found that not only was little being published on fission, but that the big names in the field were not publishing on other topics either. From this he deduced that American nuclear research was now being done in secret, and was devoted to military purposes. He sounded the alarm by writing to Stalin that 'we must build the uranium bomb without delay'.[27]

The Soviet Union, meanwhile, had received information about the foreign interest in the bomb. In response to this intelligence, and to Flerov's letter, Stalin's chief adviser on scientific matters, S.V. Kaftanov, consulted various scientists about the possibility of an atomic bomb. Even though he met some scepticism, Kaftanov decided to advise Stalin to set up a small atomic project. Stalin agreed, and Kurchatov was appointed director of the 'uranium problem' at the end of 1942.[28]

The Soviet wartime effort did not compare in size or scope with the Manhattan Project, but it did lay the ground-work for future expansion. Kurchatov set up a nuclear laboratory outside Moscow, and assembled a group of scientists to work on the design of an experimental pile, on isotope separation methods, on plutonium production and on bomb design. Klaus Fuchs provided the Soviet authorities with a good deal of information about the progress of the Manhattan Project. The Soviet Union shrouded its own research in secrecy, so that the United States and Britain remained unaware of the Soviet effort.

In this context, the activities of the great Danish physicist Niels Bohr, about which Margaret Gowing wrote so revealingly in *Britain and Atomic Energy 1939–1945*, take on an added dimension.[29] After his escape from Denmark in September 1943, Bohr was informed about the British and American projects. He was immediately afraid that fundamental political differences between the Allies would lead to a breakdown in co-operation once Germany was defeated, and he foresaw that this might lead to a nuclear arms race between the Western allies and the Soviet Union. Bohr believed that, in order to prevent an arms race, the United States and Britain should inform Stalin about the existence of the Manhattan Project before the bomb was tested. Prolonged secrecy, in his view, would lead to distrust and suspicion, and thereby destroy the basis for international cooperation.

Bohr knew Soviet physics well: he had visited the Soviet Union, and several Soviet physicists had worked at his institute in Copenhagen. He knew of Soviet research on fission, and understood that Soviet physicists would appreciate the implications of that discovery. He suspected that the Soviet Union might already know of the Manhattan Project and have a project of its own in hand. He was reinforced in his view in April 1944 when he received a letter from Kapitsa inviting him to come and work in the Soviet Union. Bohr wrote a warm but innocuous reply, and showed the correspondence to the British security authorities. He felt it was now more urgent than ever for the United States and Britain to inform Stalin about the bomb. He won support for his proposal from leading advisers in Britain and the United States. He met both Churchill and Roosevelt to press his case, but he could not convince them of the wisdom of this course of action. Churchill was especially adamant that Bohr's advice be rejected.

It is difficult, even in retrospect, to know what effect an approach to Stalin might have had. Informing him that the Manhattan Project existed would not have told him anything he did not already know. At worst, Stalin might have treated the approach as a veiled threat, and reacted as he did in August 1945 when the full force of the atomic bomb was demonstrated in Japan. At best, he might have agreed to talks about international control of atomic energy, though it is hard to believe that he would have agreed to any form of international control that deprived the Soviet Union of the right to build its own bomb. The atomic bomb, as Vassily Grossman writes in *Life and Fate*, his great novel of the Soviet Union at the time of Stalingrad, soon came to be seen as the 'sceptre of state power',[30] and Stalin was intent, above all else, on building up the power of the Soviet state.

Even though his advice might not have averted the nuclear arms race, Niels Bohr showed a clearer awareness than anyone else of what Soviet physics could do, and hence of the danger of an arms race. If this awareness of the strength of Soviet science had been appreciated more widely in the West, the nuclear era might not have opened with the same degree of illusion on the Western side about the value of nuclear weapons and duration of the American nuclear monopoly.

The Soviet atomic project expanded during the war, and the Red Army's advance into Central Europe provided the Soviet Union with much-needed access to the uranium mines in Czechoslovakia. But the main turning-point came in August 1945, when the United States dropped atomic bombs on Hiroshima and Nagasaki. Stalin knew that the United States had tested a bomb successfully in July, but the bombing of the Japanese cities dramatised, much more clearly than news of the test had done, the destructive potential of the new weapon.

Stalin saw the American possession of the atomic bomb as a threat to the new power that victory over Germany had given to the Soviet Union. He was determined to acquire a Soviet bomb as soon as possible, and he quickly expanded the nuclear project into an all-out effort, under the direction of Lavrenti Beria, the chief of the police empire.

Beria was the logical man to put in charge: he was responsible for the German scientists brought to the Soviet Union at the end of the war, and he controlled the Gulag, whose prisoners mined uranium and built the new laboratories and factories for the project. But the most important reason for choosing Beria was that no institution would be more ruthlessly effective than the police apparatus at extracting the necessary resources from the war-ravaged economy. Factory directors who might be reluctant to release their best engineers were ready to accede to the demands of the NKVD (the People's Commissariat of Internal Affairs; after 1946 the MVD, the Ministry of Internal Affairs): this was the 'powerful apparatus' that Rozhdestvenskii had called for in 1936. Nor were the police unused to managing research and development programmes, for in the 1930s the NKVD had organised *sharashki*, prison design bureaux, in which engineers and scientists who had been arrested for crimes against the state developed weapons to defend the state.[31]

The leading scientists on the nuclear project were not arrested. They worked, of course, under conditions of great secrecy and tight security, and were accompanied by personal bodyguards wherever they went. But they had *dachas* and cars, and could look forward to high state honours if they succeeded in their work. The war had demonstrated the importance of science for military power, and Stalin accordingly raised scientists' pay and the level of investment in science.[32] In the months between August 1945 and March 1946, he initiated, besides the atomic bomb project, major research efforts to develop radar, rocket technology and jet propulsion.

Stalin and the other Party leaders did not regard scientists with any greater trust than before. Their suspicion was, if anything, heightened by their dependence on the scientists. People were encouraged to write letters of denunciation to the authorities. Kurchatov was the victim of such letters, and Beria would no doubt have dealt harshly with him if the nuclear project had failed. The atmosphere of the time is well conveyed by A.P. Aleksandrov, President of the Academy of Sciences from 1975 to 1986, who was one of Kurchatov's chief lieutenants in the late 1940s. Aleksandrov recalls that a group of five generals (probably MVD generals) came one night to the chemical separation plant of which he was the scientific director, and asked him what he was doing. He explained that he was working with plutonium,

> then they asked a strange question: 'Why do you think that it is plutonium? I said that I knew the whole technology for obtaining it and was therefore sure that it was plutonium and could not be anything else! 'But why are you sure that some piece of iron hasn't been substituted for it?' I raised the piece up to the alpha-counter, and it immediately began to crackle. 'Look,' I said, 'it's alpha-active'. 'But perhaps it was just rubbed on the surface with plutonium, and that's why it's crackling' someone said. I got angry, took that piece and held it out to him: 'Feel it, it's hot!' One of them said that it did not take long to heat iron. Then I replied that he could sit and watch till morning to see whether the plutonium remained hot. And I would go to bed. That apparently convinced them, and they went away.[33]

The late 1940s were perhaps the most difficult period for Soviet science. In 1948, Lysenko reached his apogee. At a special meeting of the Academy of Agricultural Science, he declared that the Party Central Committee had read and approved his report, and this silenced his scientific opponents. Lysenko was now able to purge research establishments and universities of those who did not accept his theories. Other scientific disciplines came under attack in the same period, though not with the same dire effect. The nuclear programme in particular remained unscathed, and Kurchatov resisted attacks on quantum mechanics and relativity theory.[34] If its irrelevance had saved physics in the 1930s, it was physics' importance for state power that saved it now. Stalin was not especially concerned about the state of agriculture (he tolerated a desperate famine in the Ukraine in 1947), and so it may not have mattered very much to him whether Lysenko was a charlatan or not. The nuclear programme was more important for the state, however, and Stalin was willing to let Soviet scientists use the same methods and theories as American scientists in building the bomb. Indeed, one of the main functions of atomic espionage seems to have been to reassure the Soviet leaders that their own scientists were working on the right lines.

The Soviet Union tested its first atomic bomb in 1949, and its first thermonuclear bomb in 1953. In 1954, the first atomic power station went into operation. The success of the project revived the idea, which Bukharin had done much to propagate, that the world stood on the verge of a scientific-technical revolution, which could achieve its full scope only in a socialist society. In July 1955, the Soviet premier, N.A. Bulganin, declared that 'the summit of the present stage in the development of science and technology is the discovery of methods of obtaining and using the energy of the atom. We stand at the threshold of a new scientific–technical revolution'[35] Soviet leaders now increased expenditures on science rapidly, in the hope that science would contribute not only to military power, but also to economic growth and social welfare. The nuclear programme had been a successful example of innovation. It may not have been a good model to emulate, however, except for high-priority, highly focused projects: poor technological performance has continued to plague the Soviet economy.[36]

The success of the nuclear project greatly increased the prestige of scientists, and Stalin's death in March 1953 gave them the opportunity to assert their authority. Scientists who had worked on the nuclear project took a leading role in throwing off some of the worst features of Stalinist science: they combatted Lysenko's influence, and pressed for freer ties with Western scientists. Most importantly, they reasserted the right of the scientific community to say what constituted science, and criticised the role that philosophers had played in policing science. The techniques of argument that had characterised Stalinist science lost much of their force, even though Lysenko retained some of his power with Khrushchev's support. But the unhappy experience of science under Stalin did not destroy the belief that politics should be, in some sense, scientific. In the 1950s and 1960s, two main currents of thought reflected the hope that science would now exert a beneficial influence on politics.

The first of these was a technocratic trend which saw in cybernetics and systems theory a way of injecting new elements of rationality into planning and administration. The second was a democratic current which saw in the 'republic of science' the model of a free and ethical polity. The opening paragraph of Andrei Sakharov's famous essay, 'Reflections on progress, peaceful coexistence and intellectual freedom' states, for example, that

the views of the author have been formed in the milieu of the scientific–technical intelligentsia, which shows great anxiety about the questions of principle and the concrete questions of mankind's future. In particular, this concern feeds upon consciousness of the fact that the scientific method of directing politics, economics, art, education, and military affairs has not yet become a reality. We consider 'scientific' that method which is based on a profound study of the facts, theories and views, presupposing unprejudiced and open discussion, which is dispassionate in its conclusions.[37]

Under Stalin the structure of authority and the norms of behavior in science mirrored those of Stalinist politics; after Stalin's death some scientists hoped to see their own newly-regained norms reflected more widely in social and political life.

It is impossible here to explore the extent to which those ideas have been influential in the post-Stalin years. But it should be noted that in the 1960s and 1970s some disillusionment with science and technology became apparent in Soviet literature, notably in works about life in the countryside. This attitude is also evident in dissident writings. Alexander Solzhenitsyn, in his 'Letter to the Soviet Leaders', called upon Russia to turn its back on the technological civilisation of the West and look inward for spiritual strength.[38] Alexander Zinoviev, in his satirical novel *The Yawning Heights* has one of his characters declare that 'when we base our hopes on the civilising role of science, we commit a grave error'[39] The relationship between science and politics is still a live issue in Soviet culture.

It is almost fifty years since nuclear fission was discovered. The nuclear age now has a history, and in her Rede lecture, *Reflections on Atomic Energy History*, Margaret Gowing notes that one of the tasks of the atomic energy historian is 'to illuminate current controversies – by showing how they derive from past choices, past events'[40] Yet a curious disjunction has existed between the historical analysis of atomic energy and the theories – whether prescriptive or descriptive – that people use in discussing current nuclear weapons policies. These theories make assumption – about the rationality of political leaders, about the effects of nuclear threats, and about the factors that shape policy – that need to be weighed more systematically against our historical experience with nuclear weapons.

Political scientists are now turning increasingly to nuclear history to see how their theories fare in the light of historical experience. This is a useful exercise, and may give nuclear history a greater role in informing our current debates. But this exercise also requires that serious history be written. We are fortunate, therefore, that the early stages of British nuclear history have been so well chronicled by Margaret Gowing, and that other historians, both official and official, have charted the early history of atomic energy in the United States.[41]

A full understanding of our nuclear past, and of its influence on our present nuclear condition, requires that the history of atomic energy in the Soviet Union be studied. This is not an easy task, because much of that history remains shrouded in secrecy. Yet some information has been published in the Soviet Union in recent years, and we have to make the best use of that material that we can. We need to understand what has shaped Soviet nuclear policy, and whether Soviet leaders have learned from their own nuclear experience – and if so, what they have learned. We need to know also whether the ways in which we now seek to understand Soviet policy make sense in the light of nuclear history. Soviet policy is often portrayed, for example, as a series of rational choices guided by military doctrine. What happens when we set this view of Soviet policy-making against what we know of earlier Soviet decisions?

Margaret Gowing writes that 'the history of the British atomic project is a microcosm of the history of Britain in the last forty years.'[42] The corollary is that the history of the British atomic project can be understood only in the wider context of British history. The same is true of the Soviet project. It makes no sense to look at that project in isolation from the rest of Soviet history, as though the Soviet project were no more than an adjunct to the American effort. I have tried to show in this chapter that Soviet science has to be understood in the context of Soviet culture and politics; and the same is true of Soviet atomic energy policy in all its ramifications.

NOTES

1. Margaret Gowing, 'An old and intimate relationship', in V. Bogdanor (ed.), *Science and Politics. The Herbert Spencer Lectures 1982* (Oxford: Clarendon Press, 1984) p. 55.
2. Ibid.
3. See Alexander Vucinich, *Science in Russian Culture. A History to 1860* (London: Peter Owen, 1963); and his *Science in Russian Culture 1861–1917* (Stanford: Stanford University Press, 1970).
4. See David Joravsky, *Soviet Marxism and Natural Science, 1917–1932*, (London: Routledge and Kegan Paul, 1961); Kendall Bailes, *Technology and Society Under Lenin and Stalin* (Princeton University Press, 1978);

Alexander Vucinich, *Empire of Knowledge* (Berkeley: University of California Press, 1984).

5. N.I. Bukharin and E. Preobrazhenskii, *The ABC of Communism* (Ann Arbor: The University of Michigan Press, 1966) p. 392.

6. On the transformation of the Academy, see Loren R. Graham, *The Soviet Academy of Sciences and the Communist Party 1927–1932* (Princeton University Press, 1967).

7. R.A. Lewis, 'Some aspects of the research and development effort in the Soviet Union, 1924–1935,' *Science Studies*, 1972, no. 2, p. 164.

8. K. Bauman, quoted in 'Soveshchanie v Narkomtyazhprome o nauchno-issledovatel'skoi rabote', *Sotsialisticheskaia rekonstruktsiia i nauka*, 1936, no. 8, p. 142.

9. This issue is explored most thoroughly by Joravsky, in *Soviet Marxism and Natural Science*.

10. David Joravsky, *The Lysenko Affair* (Cambridge: Harvard University Press, 1970).

11. S. Reznik, *Nikolai Vavilov* (Moscow: Molodaya Gvardiya, 1968) p. 288.

12. Quoted in Gary Werskey, *The Visible College* (London: Allen Lane, 1978) p. 146.

13. See my 'Scientific truth and political authority in the Soviet Union', *Government and Opposition*, Summer 1970, pp. 345–67.

14. In *Nauka i Zhizn'*, 1965, no. 4, p. 43.

15. M.S. Sominskii, *Abram Fyodorovich Ioffe* (Moscow–Leningrad: Nauka, 1964).

16. A report of this session is contained in *Izvestiya Akademii Nauk SSSR. Seriya fizicheskaya*, 1936, Nos 1–2.

17. Ibid., p. 60.

18. On the Kapitsa affair, see Lawrence Badash, *Kapitza, Rutherford and the Kremlin* (New Haven: Yale University Press, 1985). On the great purge see especially Alexander Weissberg, *The Accused* (New York: Simon and Schuster, 1951).

19. On the origins of Soviet nuclear physics, see A.P. Grinberg and V.Ya. Frenkel', *Igor' Vasil'evich Kurchatov v Fizikotekhicheskom Institute* (Leningrad: Nauka, 1984); on Bukharin's attitude, see George Gamov, *My World Line* (New York: The Viking Press, 1970) p. 121.

20. Joravsky, *The Lysenko Affair*.

21. The proceedings are in M.P. Bronshtein et al. (eds) *Atomnoe Yadro* (Leningrad and Moscow: Gosudarstvennoe tekhniko-teoreticheskoe izdatel'stvo, 1934).

22. *Physical Review*, Series 2, vol. LVIII, no. 1, 1 July 1940, p. 89.

23. S. Snegov, *Tvortsy* (Moscow: Sovetskaya Rossiya, 1979) p. 219.

24. 'Lomonosov and World Science', in P.L. Kapitsa, *Experiment, Theory, Practice* (Dordrecht: D. Reidel Publishing Co., 1980) p. 296. Kapitsa gave this lecture in 1961, and stressed that personal contacts, and freedom to travel abroad, were just as important in the 1960s as they had been in the eighteenth century.

25. I.N. Golovin, *I.V. Kurchatov* (Moscow: Atomizdat, 3rd edn. 1978) p. 50.

26. See my 'Entering the Nuclear Arms Race: The Soviet Decision to Build the Atomic Bomb, 1939–1945', *Social Studies of Science*, May 1981, pp. 159–97.
27. Golovin, *op. cit.*, p. 58.
28. Holloway, note 26 above, p. 175.
29. Margaret Gowing, *Britain and Atomic Energy 1939–1945* (London: Macmillan, 1964) pp. 347–66.
30. Vasilii Grossman, *Zhizn' i Sud'ba* (Paris: L'Age d'Homme, 1980) p. 535.
31. On the prison institutes, see G.A. Ozerov, *Tupolevskaya sharaga* (Frankfurt-am-Main: Posev 2nd edn. 1979).
32. On Stalin's science policy after the war, see Bruce Parrott, *Politics and Technology in the Soviet Union* (Cambridge: MIT Press, 1983) pp. 116–21.
33. A. Aleksandrov, 'Gody s Kurchatovyim', *Nauka i Zhizn*, 1983, no. 2, p. 23.
34. See Ya. Zeldovich in 'Vekhi atomnogo veka', *Nedelya*, 4 March 1984, p. 17.
35. *Pravda*, 17 July 1955.
36. See R. Amann, J. Cooper, R.W. Davies, (eds) *The Technological Level of Soviet Industry* (New Haven and London: Yale University Press, 1977).
37. A.D. Sakharov, *Razmyshleniya o progresse, mirnom sosuschchestvovanii i intellektual'noi svobode* (Frankfurt-am-Main: Passev-Verlag, 1970) p. 3.
38. Alexander Solzhenitsyn, *Letter to the Soviet Leaders* (New York: Harper & Row, 1974) pp. 19–26.
39. Alexander Zinoviev, *The Yawning Heights* (London: The Bodley Head, 1979) p. 209.
40. Margaret Gowing, *Reflections on Atomic Energy History, The Rede Lecture 1978* (Cambridge University Press) p.7.
41. My colleagues John Wilson Lewis and Xue Litai have completed a detailed study of the Chinese nuclear project which throws considerable light on a topic that seemed destined to remain obscure for a long time.
42. Gowing, *Reflections...*, p. 7.

8 Forty Years into the Atomic Age*
Sir Rudolf Peierls

In 1945, we heard a lot of talk about the 'Atomic Age', which had burst into the open with the attacks on Hiroshima and Nagasaki. How different are the public attitudes now from those at the birth of the Atomic Age! In Britain and the United States, at any rate, the dropping of the first atom bombs was greeted with joy at the ending of the war, and with pride at the achievements of the scientists and engineers. The joy was tempered by awe at the might of the new power, and horror at the suffering and devastation in the Japanese cities. The new weapon had made war so terrible that future global war appeared unthinkable. At the same time, the media were carrying stories about the bounty expected from the new source. Soon one had to discourage the wildest predictions, of electricity for practically nothing, of cars run on a pellet of uranium, of easy space travel. The scientists were given credit for what had been achieved, and for what was to come. They were respected, given support, and even sometimes listened to.

Now, forty years on, the mood has changed completely. Fear of nuclear war is a persistent nightmare. Nuclear power is regarded with suspicion by some and passionately rejected by others. In the United States, this opposition has led to a practically complete abandonment of plans for further nuclear power stations. In Britain, the opposition has been less strong (but very vocal); the protracted hearings at the Sizewell enquiry and the controversy over radiation effects at Sellafield were symptomatic. The recent disaster at Chernobyl in the Ukraine has added to the anxieties and greatly increased the strength of the opposition to nuclear power in any form. In France, where the lack of coal and oil deposits makes nuclear power more attractive, its development is continuing.

Along with the different reaction to 'atomic energy', the status of the scientists has changed. They are seen by many as the irresponsible inventors of evil new agencies, not caring about the damaging or dangerous effects of their activities.

There are, of course, many other branches of science and technology which have developed spectacularly in recent years, and

* Adapted with permission from a book review in *Minerva*, XXII (1984) pp. 285–91.

many of them, from computers and air travel to detergents and antibiotics, have had a far greater impact on our everyday lives than atomic energy. Some produce side-effects which arouse hostility and are blamed on the scientists. But in connection with the recent anniversaries, we shall look at atomic energy in particular.

One of the developments following from atomic energy is undoubtedly beneficial, but is not mentioned much in public debate. That is the use of radio-isotopes and neutrons for research and for medical treatment. The practical value of this is perhaps best demonstrated by the fact that it has been found worthwhile to build a considerable number of sophisticated nuclear reactors dedicated to research, with no relation to weapons projects or power. The privatisation of the British government-owned firm marketing radioactive isotopes has recently been in the news. But while the commercial aspects of this transaction were controversial, there is no disagreement about the value of the activities to which it relates.

But, to most people, 'nuclear' means either weapons or power, and around both of these feelings run high. Most of the passionate opposition to nuclear power comes from the possible hazards associated with it. These have three distinct aspects: radiation leaks during normal working, radioactive waste and major disasters.

The first of these, the possible health hazards from nuclear power stations working normally, should be easy to control. One difficulty is to maintain in an expanding industry adequate standards of caution and discipline. It is not possible to make the safety arrangements completely immune to human error. There have been some errors, for example, the recent discharge of excessive radioactivity into the sea at Sellafield. There is, as yet, no clear evidence of any injury to the public. Even if there was, it has to be remembered that the alternative energy sources, coal and oil, involve unavoidable accidents and pollution damage; compared to these, the health record of the nuclear power industry in this country is greatly superior.

Public opinion has some difficulty in accepting this conclusion, for two reasons. One is the fear of radiation as an insidious, invisible agent. The story is told that when the Atomic Energy Research Establishment at Harwell started, people in the neighbourhood were perturbed by the presence of a tall chimney from which there was never any visible emission. This suggested that something very sinister was being discharged. The problem was solved by arranging the discharge of some smoke or steam from the chimney. It now seemed normal, and the local fears were allayed.

The other difficulty is that much of the information about radiation levels and their effects comes from experts connected with the authorities operating the plants, and they may be regarded as interested parties. Here, matters are not helped by the past record of official statements, both here and in the US, which rather too readily gave assurances on the basis of inadequate information. Present controversies, in both countries, concerning damage to the health of military personnel during nuclear weapons tests add to the suspicion of official statements.

Radioactive waste is an unavoidable by-product of nuclear power, and since it will remain active for many hundreds of years, its disposal raises serious questions. It is easy to find radiation-proof containers, but it is not easy to be sure that the containers will not corrode or otherwise deteriorate over the centuries. Burying the waste requires certainty that movement of earth or underground streams will not carry radioactivity back to the surface or into wells or mines. Much research is being done on these problems, and it is fortunate that decisions can safely be postponed, since the amounts of waste produced so far can be kept in supervised holding sites for ultimate disposal.

The most emotive aspect of nuclear power is no doubt the possibility of catastrophic accidents. Nuclear reactors are not capable of causing an explosion similar to that of an atomic bomb, but a failure can spread radioactivity over a considerable area, as happened in the Chernobyl disaster.

This was by far the worst accident in the nuclear industry to date. The number of people killed or showing immediate injury is still very small compared to many mining disasters, but it differs in two ways: the delayed effects, in particular increased incidence of cancer in the population of the neighbourhood, and possible genetic effects, are very hard to estimate, but are no doubt serious. The other feature peculiar to nuclear accidents is the cost, both in terms of money and in human misery, of the precautions necessary to avoid more numerous casualties. The need to evacuate residents, to destroy contaminated crops and to replace the topsoil over large areas add to the seriousness of the accident. Some of the radioactivity has affected other European countries and led them into costly precautions.

Understandably, this accident has given rise to disquiet about all nuclear power stations. Should we expect a similar accident in our power stations sooner or later? It has been pointed out that the Chernobyl station is of a design not used anywhere in the West, and that it would not have passed the safety tests imposed, for example, in the UK. No doubt we face a period of intense discussion and re-examination of the nature of different reactor systems. Very possibly, the precise manner of the accident at Chernobyl could not be repeated in any of the Western designs, but then accidents rarely recur in exact repetition, because everybody learns how to avoid the last accident.

Chernobyl was very far short of the worst imaginable accident. Is it possible that even greater disasters could occur in nuclear reactors? No serious expert will claim that this is impossible, only that it is extremely unlikely.

The public are not accustomed to thinking in terms of probabilities, and to be told that enormous disasters are possible, even with an extremely small probability, is frightening. To put the matter in perspective, it has been pointed out that, on the basis of a 'worst-case' analysis, other parts of technology offer equally frightening perspectives. One example often quoted is that of a jumbo jet crashing on a crowded football stadium, an event which is certainly not impossible, if extremely unlikely. Another is an explosion of a large chemical plant. This has indeed happened, though perhaps not in the worst imaginable circumstances. These possibilities have not led to claims that planes no longer be allowed to fly, or that chemical plants be closed, only to an insistence on precautions that would make such disasters as unlikely as possible.

But how unlikely are the 'worst' nuclear accidents? There exists a considerable literature on this subject. A major breakdown of safety would require the simultaneous failure of several components, and since most of the relevant components are in use also in other industries, one can judge their failure rate from industrial experience. Several authors have made calculations on this basis, and while their estimates differ, they all find extremely small risks. However, this kind of analysis seems incomplete without taking into account the human factor.

At the time of writing, the causes of the Chernobyl disaster are still being discussed, but it is already clear that the behaviour of the operating staff, who switched off safety equipment while doing an unauthorised experiment, was at least one of the important causes. Human error, or to be more honest, human foolishness, also was the cause in the two important near-accidents, at Brown's Ferry and at Three Mile Island. I have heard it said that these only prove how safe is the nuclear industry, because, in spite of many things going wrong, there were no casualties and no spread of radioactivity. I do not find this convincing, because in both cases only luck prevented worse troubles.

The problem of eliminating human error is complex. For people whose normal occupation involves handling dangerous equipment, it is very easy to forget remote possibilities of danger, and to become casual about safety rules meant to forestall them. More study is needed of ways to keep personnel alert and careful, and ways of making equipment more foolproof. I expect that after Chernobyl all reactors will be fitted with devices which prevent operation with any vital safety equipment disconnected. But carrying automation too far also has its dangers because it prevents, or makes more difficult, an intervention by the operators in case of failure of the automatic control.

A further objection sometimes raised against nuclear power is that encouraging its development in other countries might lead them into developing a nuclear-weapons technology. This point is also controversial. Some say that a country whose technology is capable of producing nuclear weapons will be able to do so whether they have a nuclear power industry or not. The link between power and weapons would perhaps become closer if the 'breeder reactor' were to become widespread. This reactor is capable of making the raw material, uranium, go much further, and is therefore economically attractive, but it is technically more complicated and raises more difficult safety problems, because it uses highly enriched material, like a nuclear bomb. It requires a reprocessing plant, which extracts plutonium from the exposed fuel elements. Such a system therefore involves handling large quantities of plutonium, some of which is suitable for weapons, and the reprocessing is an essential and expensive part of a weapons programme. At present, France leads in the development of breeders, Britain has a prototype plant, while the American breeder programme seems to be in abeyance.

But the aspect of nuclear energy that gives rise to the most serious worry is undoubtedly the nuclear weapons. Already the decision to use the first available weapons on Japanese cities caused unending controversy. It was defended because it cost fewer lives, even fewer Japanese lives than would have an invasion of Japan, and it produced fewer casualties than the fire raids on Tokyo or Dresden. On the other hand, many argued (and I agree) that one could have tried to use the first bomb on a much more sparsely inhabited target to demonstrate its power, in the hope that this would be enough to bring Japan to surrender. In any event, the argument goes, the second bomb on Nagasaki, was surely unnecessary.

A number of scientists working on the atom-bomb project tried to urge against the use of the bomb on cities, at least initially. It is interesting that the centre of this agitation was in Chicago, where the research on the reactors was done, and not in Los Alamos, where the bomb was made. Perhaps the reason is that the Chicago laboratory had completed its urgent wartime task, and its members had more time for reflection, while those in Los Alamos were still working under great pressure. In any case, the Chicago paper, written on the initiative of James Franck and Leo Szilard, never reached the decision-makers.

After the war, there was great enthusiasm for the idea of international control of atomic energy. The United States was to give up voluntarily its temporary monopoly of nuclear weapons in return for an agreement by all other countries to develop nuclear energy only through an international agency. This plan, worked out by the Acheson–Lilienthal Committee with Robert Oppenheimer playing an important part in the drafting, was presented to the UN by Bernard Baruch, and became the 'Baruch plan'. It had undergone a subtle change of style: Baruch was aware of the need for the plan to be accepted by the American Senate, and therefore emphasised the points in America's favour, but this made it less attractive to the Soviet Union. However, this was not really important, because there never was a chance of such a plan being accepted. For the USSR to accept a plan proposed by the USA at a time when one power had nuclear weapons and the other did not, would have been humiliating, and they suspected that they would somehow be put at a disadvantage.

Next, the talk was of disarmament, and many liked to see this as complete disarmament, at least complete nuclear disarmament. Numerous international meetings, mostly under the auspices of the United Nations, discussed numerous proposed disarmament treaties without any real progress, and even today complete nuclear disarmament is claimed to be the ultimate aim. But the difficulty is that neither big power would risk dismantling their nuclear arsenals without reliable verification that the other side is complying with the treaty, since a few clandestinely preserved nuclear weapons would give an overwhelming military advantage if the other side had destroyed theirs. Therefore, any such treaty required an effective international inspection procedure, and this was unacceptable to the Soviet Union, for whom the restrictions on foreigners roaming around their country are an essential part of their security. It is by no means obvious that the required pervasive inspection would have been acceptable to the American Congress or industry.

By now the most that international negotiations are aiming at is arms control. This means treaties which would reduce the nuclear arsenals, or at least stop their expansion. There have been some marginal successes. The partial test-ban treaty has at least stopped the two major powers testing weapons in the open air, and therefore almost halted the radioactive pollution, a very desirable result, even if the treaty has not banned underground tests, and thus has not seriously slowed down the development of new weapons. The SALT I treaty put some slight restrictions on the numbers and types of weapons deployed. The 'ABM' treaty, negotiated at the same time, stopped the deployment of anti-ballistic missile systems, which would have led to further escalation of the arms race. Since then, no progress with treaties has been made, though the SALT II treaty, never ratified by the US Senate, has been observed by the two 'superpowers' on a voluntary basis, thus bringing some further slight restrictions.

Yet the arms race continues, in quality of weapons and the accuracy of their delivery, if not in numbers. By now, the stockpiles of weapons on both sides have reached grotesque dimensions. Everybody is convinced that nuclear war cannot be won against an adversary with nuclear weapons. Such a war would result in devastating damage to both sides. This is true, notwithstanding occasional assurances by governments that their country could fight a nuclear war and survive. These are statements to keep up morale.

The only purpose served by nuclear weapons in a real world is as a deterrent against nuclear attack. But then why accumulate the present excessive stockpiles and race to get more and better weapons? One may argue about just how much is needed for an effective deterrent, but is is beyond question that the present amounts are many times more than necessary. If one side has enough bombs to wipe out all the major cities of the adversary five times over, what would it matter if the adversary has enough to do so ten times?

There is one important proviso. In public debates the idea of a 'First Strike' is often bandied about. This term denotes an attack which wipes out the others' nuclear missiles and thus forestalls retaliation. If such an operation were feasible, it would make it vital to have large numbers of highly accurate weapons. In that situation, no country would feel safe unless it was guaranteed superiority, or at least parity in nuclear arms, and the arms race would have to continue to the limit of each country's technical and economic possibility.

Fortunately, the whole concept of a nuclear first strike belongs in the realm of science fiction. It ignores the existence of nuclear weapons carried by submarines; at present there is no effective way of dealing with these. Even if there were spectacular progress in submarine detection, it would be unlikely to lead to a possibility of disposing of these in a short time, which would be essential for a first strike. In addition, there are bomber planes carrying nuclear weapons, which, even during the short available warning time of a nuclear attack, could take off and survive.

Even ignoring submarines and bombers, a first strike would remain an uncertain speculation. It would rely on thousands of missiles functioning, all in a short time, and allowing for only a small failure rate. Such an operation is easily simulated on a computer, and the performance of the missiles studied on the test range, but the reliability in the heat of battle, and in a gigantic mass operation is something very different. One should remember that the American space shots, which are serviced by the cream of the nation's technical manpower, have frequently to be postponed because of the malfunction of some component, or have met with disasters. No government would stake the survival of their nation on the success of such a chancy operation.

In fact, none of the military experts believe in the feasibility of a first strike. How can one explain the continuing race for more and better weapons? It is easy to understand the motivation of the scientists and engineers in the weapons laboratories, who often initiate new technical ideas which satisfy their professional challenge. It is easy to understand the support from industrialists, for whom the arms race means more business. But why do so many politicians, and why does public opinion, support this wasteful and dangerous activity?

Is this a failure to appreciate the new situation created by nuclear weapons? In assessing the prospects of naval battles or of tank warfare, numbers are indeed vital, but one has to understand that nuclear weapons are not battleships. Or is it the naïve belief that the threat of retaliation will deter more if it is backed by greater numbers of – quite unnecessary – means of destruction?

Whatever the reason, it seems hard to get across the simple truth that each side could safely afford to freeze their nuclear weapons stocks at the present level, or even to reduce them by a considerable factor (though not below the minimum effective deterrent) without depending on equivalent action by the opponents.

There is indeed a movement, both in the UK and in the USA, advocating a 'freeze' of nuclear weapons, but usually it is not spelled out whether this is to be a voluntary or a negotiated freeze. A negotiated and verified freeze would be an excellent thing, but the negotiations to achieve it are not likely to be easier or more promising than other arms control negotiations.

The recent Soviet moratorium on weapons tests may show a realisation of the position, but it it so far of limited duration, unless the United States reciprocates. If, in the absence of such reciprocation, it is eventually allowed to lapse, this would show that again politics takes precedence over reason.

Recently, all these questions have been overshadowed by the 'Star Wars' programme, which aims at using lasers or particle beams or other new technologies for defence against missiles. This, in the words of President Reagan, would make nuclear weapons 'impotent and obsolete'. Few, if any, experts even in the United States administration believe that this aim, of giving complete protection to the whole country's population is attainable. Instead, there is talk about protecting missile bases or command centres and thereby strengthening the deterrent. Such a programme, while still speculative, may not be impossible to achieve, but would reinforce, rather than replace, the present reliance on mutual deterrence or 'Mutual Assured Destruction'. As I have tried to show, the existing deterrent does not need strengthening.

If we count the blessings of the 'atomic age', we must remember the many constructive applications of radio-isotopes and neutrons in research and in medicine. We may argue about the advantages of nuclear power, but at least we have the option of using or not using a new source of energy. Above all we must be aware of the possibility of nuclear war. We are fortunate that we are still here, and that for over forty years there has been no global war, a fact for which the credit must probably be given to nuclear weapons in making everybody frightened of war. This gives our world a certain kind of stability, but we must work for a better system which does not contain also the possibility of utter disaster.

9 Radiation, Language and Logic

Lorna Arnold

SOME LANGUAGE PROBLEMS

Ionising radiation affects us all, whether it comes from natural (cosmic and terrestrial) sources or from man-made sources. It consists of electromagnetic rays, of a shorter wavelength than light – the penetrating X- and gamma rays; and fast-moving particles – alpha particles (able to penetrate barely 0.1mm in tissue), beta particles (more penetrating) and neutrons. These radiations can ionise (that is, knock out electrons from) the atoms of materials through which they pass; in passing through living tissues, they can produce biological effects and may be damaging.

The hazards of ionising radiations from man-made sources, such as nuclear plant and radioactive waste, attract a great deal of public attention, occasionally heightened by media events – especially television programmes – or real-life events like the Three Mile Island and Chernobyl accidents.

More information is available about radiation than about any other occupational and public health hazards, and, of all the potentially lethal agents that human beings are subject to, few or none have been so closely studied. Yet it is not well understood by the public or by some of the journalists who profess to inform and explain.

It is true that the technical jargon is bewildering. Many people had learnt that radioactivity was measured in curies – evocatively named after a legendary scientific heroine, Marie Curie, 'the Radium Woman'. Some were aware that radiation was measured in roentgens, rads and rems, which were similar but somehow different. Then suddenly they vanish – even the curie – to be replaced by unfamiliar grays, sieverts and becquerels.[1] Moreover, grays and sieverts are large and usually have to be divided into thousandths (for example, milligrays) or millionths (for example, microsieverts).[2] Becquerels, by contrast, are very small – it takes 37 thousand million to add up to 1 curie, equivalent to 1 gram of radium – and in becquerels the estimated release of radioactivity from Chernobyl needs 18 noughts (50 megacuries or 1.8×10^{18} becquerels). All this is hard on members of the public, and on journalists too (including science correspondents[3], for the older professionals themselves jib at the

169

change, and many are still unreconstructed 'rads and rems men'. This is only the latest obstacle; communication was already difficult. Over-technical explanations to an unprepared audience are useless, but simplistic ones are unsatisfactory and unconvincing; the unavoidable fact is that the subject *is* complicated. The several kinds of ionising radiation have different characteristics and affect living organisms differently. Sources of radiation affecting the human body may be external to it or internal. There are complex pathways by which radioactive materials may get into the body; once there, these materials – which have different chemical properties – will concentrate in specific organs and tissues and, until they decay or are eliminated, will continue to irradiate them, perhaps for a lifetime.

As a result, the language of radiation, even without its mathematics, is not easy. If non-scientists like me pursue the subject, they will quickly enter a thicket of old and new terminologies: high LET and low LET radiation; RBE (relative biological effectiveness) and Q (quality factor); absorbed dose and dose equivalent; committed dose; genetic dose; collective dose equivalent commitment. They will encounter thresholds, dose-response relationships (linear, supralinear and linear-quadratic), stochastic and non-stochastic effects, and weighting factors. Then there are old tolerance doses, several 'maximum permissibles' – doses (MPDs), levels (MPLs), concentrations (MPCs) and body burdens (MPBBs) – and various limits and levels – annual, derived, authorised, reference, emergency and others. All around are risk assessments, risk factors, risk coefficients, cost benefit analyses, and concepts of justification, optimisation, ALARA (as low as reasonably achievable) and ALARP (as low as reasonably practicable). This luxuriant vocabulary has grown out of sixty years of practical experience; changing needs and conditions; wide-ranging research and increasing knowledge about biological and medical effects of radiation; and much national and international scientific discussion.

Popular writers often draw attention to the quantitative changes in international radiation standards and the progressive reduction of permissible doses,[4] but commonly ignore the underlying ideas; yet the figures, out of context, are liable to be misunderstood. This is especially so when commenting on the past, and in radiation matters the past is – literally – vitally important, since radiation effects many appear twenty or thirty years or more after the 'event'. It is the changing ideas and terminology, not the figures, that need to be understood and that these notes attempt to trace in broad outline.

BEFORE THE SECOND WORLD WAR

Early this century, radiation safety and the language of radiation were equally simple. After the discovery of X-rays by Roentgen in 1895, and of radioactivity by Becquerel in 1896, it was soon found that radiation could damage living tissues. By 1913, when the earliest safety rules were introduced, repeated irradiation had already led to severe injuries and even deaths among radiologists. Some protection – such as lead shielding, and restrictions on working hours – was possible, but standards could not be set, because no means of measurement existed. Radiation exposures were estimated by observing the appearance of a skin reddening or erythema; this might vary from slight discoloration to severe dermatitis. A 'tolerance dose' (a term borrowed from toxicology in 1925), and a means of measuring radiation, were both urgently needed to protect patients and hospital staff. Deaths among members of the medical services who for years had used radium and X-rays in the care of the sick and wounded had highlighted the problem, and scientists, and national committees, were working on it in several countries, notably Britain, the United States, France, Germany and Sweden. Then, in 1925, the first International Congress of Radiology took matters in hand.

In 1928, the Congress set up two bodies, the International Commission on Radiological Units and Measurements (ICRU) and the International X-Ray and Radium Protection Commission (IXRPC, forerunner of ICRP, the International Commission on Radiological Protection). The Congress also adopted a precise unit of X-ray exposure, the roentgen. This opened the way to quantitative safety standards and the first international 'tolerance dose' of 0.2 roentgens a day, approved in 1934. This was believed to be not more than one-tenth of the so-called erythema exposure for low energy X-rays and relied on the absence of any observable effect.

The scene was still simple. X-ray machines and radium were the only man-made radiation sources, and the world's entire stock of separated radium was only 2 kilograms.[5] Relatively few people, mostly hospital staff, were occupationally exposed; but women employed during the First World War to paint luminous dials, who had habitually pointed their brushes with their lips, later suffered tragically from severe blood disorders and cancers. There was still little or no chance of radioactivity escaping into the environment; outside the luminising industry, internal radiation hazards hardly existed. The hazard from external radiation in high exposures was realised, but nothing was known about long-term hazards of low exposures. Tumour induction, it was thought, could only follow high doses that had previously caused gross damage to tissue; it was not suspected that exposures too low to cause erythema or any visible effect might lead to cancer after a latent period of many years. Radiation was confidently used in many medical procedures – monitoring the skeletal growth of babies, 'stimulating' the ovaries of infertile women, and treating acne and ringworm – as well as for non-medical purposes – in beauty parlours to remove facial hair, and in shoe-shops to fit children's shoes. The ideas of a 'tolerance dose', and a 'threshold' below which no harmful effects would follow, were universally accepted.

A CRASH COURSE IN RADIOLOGICAL PROTECTION

With the Manhattan Project – the huge American atomic bomb enterprise of the Second World War – large numbers of people were occupationally exposed to radiation, and man-made sources of radiation multiplied unimaginably in variety, scale and intensity. A vast range of new radioactive substances came into being, all of them with their own chemical and physical characteristics, half-lives,[6] and patterns of radiations, more or less penetrating and more or less biologically damaging. Internal as well as external irradiation became a serious consideration; radioactive substances might be inhaled or ingested, and once in the human body, the radiation from them could not be switched off like an X-ray machine, stopped by shielding, or limited by reduced working hours or other means.

For the scientists, the Manhattan Project provided a crash course in radiation. It created the new multidisciplinary profession of 'health physics' or, more correctly, 'radiological protection'. 'Health physics' was a code name intended to conceal the connection with radiation and radioactivity, and therefore the possibility of nuclear weapons development.

It was supported by large-scale biological experimental work. The health physicists were concerned with the protection of the Project's workers, and they were brilliantly successful, with only two radiation fatalities during the war (neither due to radiation safety failures). The safety of the general population in case of major accidents was taken care of by remote siting of the atomic establishments, and radiological safety standards for the the public were not an issue.[7]

THE NEW COMMISSION – ICRP

The old International X-Ray and Radium Protection Commission, dormant since 1937, was reconstituted and enlarged in 1950 – under the more comprehensive title of 'International Commission on Radiological Protection' (ICRP) – to meet the pressing problems of the new atomic era. It was extremely active all through the decade, and published three sets of basic recommendations,[8] in 1951, 1955 and 1959. It had an independent status, since its members were chosen by their peers for distinction in relevant scientific fields, and were not appointed by governments or as national representatives. ICRP performed its task admirably and impartially in the crucial period when military and civil nuclear programmes were becoming established and growing rapidly, and that work provided a solid and internationally agreed basis for radiological protection for many years.

The first ICRP Recommendations in 1950 (published in 1951) owed much to American work; to the British Medical Research Council, with its Committee on Protection against Ionising Radiations and its 'tolerance panel'; and to important tripartite (Anglo/American/Canadian) scientific conferences[9] in 1949 and 1950. The 1951 Report recognised the carcinogenic and genetic effects of radiation, adopted a new and lower weekly permissible dose, introduced the new ideas of maximum permissible concentrations (mpc or MPC) in air and water, and listed maximum permissible body burdens (mpbb or MPBB) for the most important radionuclides. It abandoned the term 'tolerance dose', which might appear to mean a completely harmless dose. In tripartite discussions, the term 'permissible dose' had been proposed, but the British had argued for 'maximum permissible dose', on the grounds that observing the limit was not enough; exposures should be kept as far below it as possible. For some time ICRP used both 'maximum permissible' and 'permissible'. Eventually both terms were felt to be inappropriate for population exposures and indeed for any that were unplanned or essentially uncontrolled – for example, in accidents, or from worldwide fallout. They also prompted questions of who was permitting what to whom. In the 1970s, there was much discussion of 'acceptable' doses and 'acceptable' risks, as compared with other risks of everyday life generally accepted by the public. But was this a question – social and political, not scientific – properly one for the scientists to answer? Some of them thought not.

ICRP believed in 1950 that the limits it recommended were 'such as to involve a risk which [was] small compared to the other hazards of life'.[10] Nevertheless it foreshadowed ALARA and ALARP – see below – in strongly recommending that 'in view of the unsatisfactory nature of much of the evidence. . . coupled with the knowledge that certain radiation effects are irreversible and cumulative. . . every effort be made to reduce exposures to all types of ionising radiation to the lowest possible level'.[11]

During the 1950s, a mass of new knowledge about radiation began to accumulate: from laboratory experiments on a very large ('megamouse') scale in the United States and on a modest scale in Britain; from the study of the atomic bomb survivors of Hiroshima and Nagasaki; and from other clinical and epidemiological studies, of which one of the most influential was a British study of leukaemia incidence in patients who had received radiotherapy for ankylosing spondylitis, a painful and disabling spinal disease.

Many theoretical and practical questions were being discussed throughout the 1950s. For example, exactly what were all the effects of radiation? Did radiation exposure shorten life? What was the effect of dose-rate and intermittent exposures, and what repair and recovery occurred between exposures? Over what period should occupational exposures be assessed and controlled – a week, a month, or longer? What would be the results of lifetime occupational exposures at or near permissible levels? Was an overall lifetime limit necessary? Could higher exposures be permitted for older workers? What was the effect of irradiation on the unborn child? Were special limits necessary for women radiation workers? Were limits needed to safeguard against genetic as well as somatic damage? Should there be radiation limits for the general public, as well as occupational limits? If so, how could they be applied in practice to large numbers of people who could not all be monitored and controlled as radiation workers were? How much radiation were people exposed to from natural background sources, and from medical procedures?

The question of standards for the public arose in the middle of the decade, partly because it was apparent that the normal operations of atomic installations – with their inevitable radioactive effluents and emissions – would mean increasing the radiation exposure, however minimally, of members of the public. (After the 1957 Windscale accident, abnormal operations also had to be specially studied.) But it was the atmospheric weapon tests of the 1950s, creating widespread and even global fallout, that elevated radioactivity and public health into a major international concern.

Assessing and controlling these hazards, and trying to safeguard large populations, posed problems very different from those of radiation safety in nuclear laboratories and factories.

The concept of 'permissible dose' was defined in ICRP's next report as a 'dose of ionising radiation that in the light of present knowledge, is not expected to cause appreciable bodily injury to a person at any time during his life time'.[12] It further defined 'appreciable bodily injury' as 'any bodily injury or effect that a person would regard as being objectionable and/or competent medical authorities would regard as being deleterious to the health and well-being of the individual'.[13] Clearly, therefore, ICRP did not expect leukaemia or cancer to be caused by radiation doses at or below the permissible level.

ICRP now adopted two new units – the rad (a unit of absorbed dose which could be used for mixed radiations, whereas the roentgen could only measure X-rays and gamma rays over a limited range of photon energies), and the rem (a measure of 'dose-equivalent', expressing the dose in terms of biological effectiveness).[14] For the first time, too, the Commission proposed that the maximum radiation exposure of the general public should be one-tenth of the maximum occupational dose.[15]

By 1958, it had elaborated this idea and produced a complicated four-tier structure of MPDs: for radiation workers; for people working in the vicinity of controlled (that is, radiation) areas, or entering controlled areas occasionally; for adults living near nuclear establishments; and for the rest of the population.[16] Understandably, ICRP soon simplified this scheme.

The 1958 Recommendations (published in 1959) included an occupational MPD of 3 rems a quarter, subject to an overriding formula designed to limit the working lifetime total to 200 rems – in effect an average of 5 rems a year. The new double standard was stricter (an average of 5 rems and a maximum of 12 rems, instead of 15 rems a year) while permitting more flexibility in working conditions by extending the control period from one to thirteen weeks.[17] The 'permissible dose' for an individual person was again defined as

> that dose, accumulated over a long period of time or resulting from a single exposure, which, in the light of present knowledge, carries a negligible probability of severe somatic or genetic injuries. Furthermore, it is such a dose that any effects that ensue more frequently are limited to those of a minor nature that would not be considered unacceptable by the exposed individual and by competent medical authorities. Any severe somatic injuries (e.g. leukaemia) that might result from exposure of individuals to the permissible dose *would be limited to an extremely small fraction of the group*; effects such as shortening of life span, which might be expected to occur more frequently, would be very slight and would likely be hidden by normal biological variations. The permissible doses can therefore be expected to produce *effects that could be detectable only by statistical methods applied to large groups*. These recommendations are designed to limit not only somatic but also genetic effects . . . [My emphases][18]

BEYOND THE THRESHOLD

ICRP did not keep re-defining 'permissible dose' without reason. It weighed its words, and the changing definitions are worth examining. It has been said – because ICRP never thought low doses were without effect, and had warned that all exposures should be kept to a minimum – that the postwar ICRP had never accepted the idea of a 'threshold'. This is not so. Its pronouncements had certainly been cautious, and perhaps ambiguous. But 'effect' does not necessarily mean an observable effect on the organism as a whole; in 1954, the Commission, as we saw, *had* clearly stated that permissible doses were not expected to cause appreciable bodily injury (as defined), and in practice this implied a threshold. Doctors and health physicists generally understood matters so until 1958–59. But the 1959 Report signalled a significant change. 'Threshold' had gone (almost) the way of the old 'tolerance dose'. It was now the statistical probability, not the severity, of radiation injury that was significant. The theoretical and practical implications were far-reaching for both occupational and public health standards.

The new occupational implications were quickly perceived by health and safety staff of the Atomic Energy Authority. No longer – however infinitesimal the risk – could they give employees unqualified assurances of safety provided their radiation exposures were within ICRP limits. Nor – if an employee or ex-employee, with a radiation record within these limits, developed leukaemia – could they now be sure that the disease was not radiation-induced; only that this was highly improbable. The ICRP change reinforced the importance of reducing all occupational exposures as far as could be done in practicable terms.

However the threshold idea had not quite disappeared. It was still agreed that some thresholds existed, both for short-term effects of high radiation doses – in the range, say, of 25 to 200 rems – delivered instantly or over a brief period, and for a very few long-term injuries such as cataracts and skin damage. To bring about the latter effects, high cumulative dose-equivalents of the order of 1000 rems (10 sieverts) are normally required. Later these short-term and long-term effects were described as non-stochastic (not due to chance) because it was the severity, not the probability, of the damage that depended upon the dose received. Most of the harmful effects of low radiation exposures – cancers of various kinds – are stochastic; that is, the probability, not the severity, is related to the dose received.

A 1960 report by a Medical Research Council Committee on radiation hazards included an interesting discussion of thresholds:

> The use of the term 'threshold' is based on the concept that for particular forms of radiation damage a minimum dose can be established below which no effect will be produced . . . Any radiation exposure is likely to produce some changes in at least a few cells, although the normal processes of tissue repair may be adequate to reverse these changes if they are very slight or if they are caused at a very slow rate. The essential difficulty is to decide whether an apparent threshold is due to a genuine absence of effect at low doses or to a failure to observe the effect owing to the very low frequency at which it is occurring . . . The probability of harmful effects may be so small, or the delay in their induction so prolonged, as to make it impossible to design a sufficiently extensive study to demonstrate them.
> . . . It is often possible to study the effects of a considerable range of moderate and large doses. If, however, at these doses

a certain effect is found to be proportional to the dose received, it is not necessarily justifiable to infer that the same relationship would hold at lower doses or to conclude that a threshold did not exist at some dose below those studied.

In any case, the concept of a single 'threshold dose' applicable to all circumstances can hardly be valid. . .

Although we now have sufficient knowledge to make an approximate assessment of the damage to be expected from high and moderate rates of radiation exposure, we can at present only infer the degree of damage likely to be caused by low rates of exposure. . . We therefore think it prudent to continue to assume that even the lowest doses of radiation may involve a finite, though correspondingly low, probability of adverse effect. This may prove to be an unduly cautious estimate but. . . it is the only justifiable one in the present state of our knowledge.[19]

So, by 1960, a linear dose-response relationship was a prudent assumption; the true relationship was, and is, unknown. The linear hypothesis is still accepted by ICRP, in order to assess the upper limit of risk for purposes of radiation protection planning. Most scientists, including ICRP, believe that it over-estimates the probability of radiation injury at low doses, at least for most radiations; however, some argue strongly for other, non-linear, dose-response curves.

The linear hypothesis had very important implications outside the occupational field. As long as the threshold remained, it was reasonable to believe, first, that compliance with occupational MPDs ensured complete safety for a working lifetime (especially as most radiation workers incurred far less); then, that members of the public, exposed to far less radiation than the workers, were so much the safer, and needed no special standards, even allowing for the vulnerability of some groups – the old, the sick, babies and pregnant women. Once the threshold had virtually gone, this position was no longer tenable. With a threshold, it would not matter how may people were exposed to radiation below the threshold level. But if even a small exposure carried a finite long term risk of cancer, then the numbers exposed, and their total radiation dose, mattered – not simply the doses to individual people. The concepts of 'collective dose' and 'collective dose equivalent', 'risk co-efficient' and 'population detriment' followed logically. The probable excess cancer incidence would be the same whether (on average) ten million people received 1 millirem or one million received 10 millirems; in both cases, the collective dose equivalent would be 10 000 man-rems (100 man-sieverts).[20] The present ICRP risk coefficient[21] would indicate, in either of the hypothetical cases just mentioned, not more than one cancer fatality altogether (in, say, seventy years), which would not be recognisable as radiation-induced and would be statistically 'lost' among the numerous naturally occurring cancer deaths in the population – currently some 132 500 *a year* in England and Wales.

An offshoot of the collective dose equivalent was the 'collective dose equivalent commitment', designed to include not only past cumulative radiation exposures, but also future – 'committed' – exposures due to established practices, and to radioactivity already in the environment or incorporated in human bodies.

Consequences of the post-1959 'no threshold' situation included a strong emphasis on 'justification', the elimination of practices involving radiation exposures not justified by the benefits – pedoscopes in shoe shops and various other minor applications were abandoned – and an increased emphasis on keeping all other radiation exposures 'as low as reasonably achievable'. The latter principle is called (though not by ICRP) 'ALARA', and has evolved from ICRP's original 'lowest possible level', via 'as low as practicable' (1962) to 'as low as is reasonably achievable, economic and social factors being taken into account' (1977).[22]

ALARA has been controversial; some people consider it begs too many questions, and argue that it should be replaced by ALATA – as low as technically achievable. Since resources and priorities are involved, the answer lies in optimisation and cost-benefit analysis, but the argument then shifts to the definition of both costs and benefits.

In the United Kingdom, the term used is ALARP – 'as low as reasonably practicable'. The history of ALARP, and the fine distinctions between ALARP and ALARA, are interesting, but cannot be pursued here. In practice, the two principles amount to very much the same. The importance of ALARP or ALARA is that licensed nuclear operators may be required to reduce radiation doses (even when they are less than the regulatory limits) if a reduction is reasonably achievable or practicable; they may even be prosecuted for failure to do so.

From 1959 to 1987, the basic standards have not altered greatly, but the terminology has. The concept of 'dose limit' has changed significantly. It is no longer an indication of satisfactory performance, but marks, rather, the beginning of a region of unacceptability. In this country, causing an employee to exceed a dose limit is a criminal offence.

Relating to, and supplementing, the basic dose limits there are secondary quantities such as annual limits on intakes (ALI) and various derived limits. 'Authorised limits' are set not by ICRP, but by the appropriate national authorities or by managements. In addition, there is a network of 'levels', in general called 'reference levels'; these are not limits, but indicate that some action needs to be taken. There are 'recording levels', below which it is permissible to record that a measurement has been made but not to record details of the result. Higher than recording levels are 'investigation levels', at which some action has to be taken to find out more about the result obtained. The term 'emergency levels' – now called 'intervention levels' by ICRP – is self-explanatory.[23].

Limits and levels are thus quite distinct but may easily be confused. The diversity of all these concepts reflects the many ways in which the basic standards have to be applied in different circumstances – whether for planning and design purposes, in normal operations, or in on-site or off-site accidents and emergencies.

MISCONCEPTIONS

Not surprisingly, misconceptions and fallacies abound. The most rudimentary example of illogicality – 'radiation causes cancer, he was exposed to radiation, he died of cancer, therefore he died of radiation'–is probably one of the most common. A few less obvious examples follow.

For instance, ICRP limits are often regarded as sharp lines with safety on one side and danger on the other. This was a fallacy even in the heyday of the threshold. The lines are very fuzzy, but precise figures and limits are needed for design, management and regulatory purposes. The difference between 0.9 millisievert and 1.1 millisievert is not the difference between safety and danger, or health and sickness. But it may be the difference between lawful and unlawful.

As we saw, limits and levels are sometimes confused; so are dose limits and actual exposures. It is occasionally suggested, for example, that because some MPDs were higher in 1950 than in 1986, radiation exposures – and hence risks – were greater then. Whether they really were would depend, however, not on the MPDs but on the actual exposures and on the numbers exposed (that is, on the collective dose). Similarly, reductions in permitted doses (as distinct from actual exposures) would not *necessarily* mean improved safety.

The collective dose, or dose equivalent, and the risk factor, are often misunderstood or misused. Given a certain (estimated) collective dose, the ICRP risk coefficient will indicate, as an upper limit, a certain number of hypothetical cancer cases or fatalities. It is not a means of prediction, but is often so regarded; hence such erroneous statements as I read in my Sunday newspaper recently – 'the government has said that there will be more than 40 cancer deaths in Britain because of Chernobyl'.[24] I have even heard the ICRP's risk coefficient criticised as an arrogant claim that the Commission can predict radiation-induced cancers in precise figures (rather than in ranges).

The dose-response relationship is also misapprehended. The hypothesis of a linear relationship, down to zero dose, is a prudent assumption for planning purposes, not a valid scientific fact. There is no proven clinical evidence of injury to human beings from low doses of radiation below ICRP limits, indeed below doses of about 1 sievert. Certainly, cases of radiation-induced cancers cannot in the present state of knowledge be distinguished from other, non-radiogenic, cases; epidemiological studies on a sufficiently large scale may or may not indicate an excess of cancer incidence in people exposed to low doses of radiation, but cannot identify individual cases.

Misunderstandings arise from the very words 'hazard', 'probability' and 'risk'. They have neutral meanings in scientific safety assessments. But in everyday speech they – unlike 'fortune', 'chance' or 'luck' – are ill-omened; they seem to imply that something 'hazardous' and 'risky' (that is, 'dangerous') is 'probable' (that is, 'very likely to happen'), where usually the very opposite is the reality. Endless trouble is caused too by those facile and misunderstood words 'safe' and 'safety', but to follow this linguistic trail would take us far outside radiological territory into a much wider world of occupational risks and environmental hazards. The problems of radiation and radioactivity are not unparalleled; some similar problems may be found in less publicised fields. But the history and philosophy of radiological protection is of special interest, not only to scientists and doctors but also to students of language and logic and of the moral and social sciences.

NOTES

1. The roentgen and becquerel were named after the discoverers of, respectively, X-rays and radioactivity. Sieverts and grays are named after Swedish and British radiologists, R. Sievert and L.H. Gray. 'Rad' was abbreviated from 'radiation absorbed dose'; 'rem' from 'roentgen-equivalent-man'. The new (Système Internationale) units were introduced in order to standardise radiation measurements with a range of other physical measurements.
2. 1 gray = 100 rads. 1 sievert = 100 rems.
3. Even a scientific journal, in an article explaining the new SI units, made an error of three orders of magnitude in converting the curie to becquerels (*Nature*, CCCXXI, (1986) p. 195) and corrected it in the next issue.
4. The ICRP limit for whole-body exposure of male radiation workers has, broadly, been reduced from 1 roentgen a week (1934), to 0.5 roentgens a week (1950), to 0.3 rem a week (1954), to 5 rems a year (1965).
5. I.e. 2000 curies. Expressed in becquerels, this amounts to 7.4×10^{13} (or 74 million million).
6. Half-life – the time taken for the activity of a radioactive substance to decay to half its original value.
7. However, it is now known that in the early years Hanford (the site of the plutonium production reactors, in the State of Washington) released 1 million curies of radioiodine and kilogram quantities of plutonium to the environment, causing 'Chernobyl sized' doses to milk drinkers in the vicinity (*Nature*, CCCXXIII (1986), p. 569).
8. *British Journal of Radiology*, XXIV (1951), pp. 46–53. *British Journal of Radiology*, supplement 6 (1955). *Recommendations of the International Commission on Radiological Protection (Adopted September 9, 1958)* (London: Pergamon Press, 1959). Among many detailed reports published since 1959, ICRP issued important general recommendations in 1966 (*ICRP Publication 8* and *ICRP Publication 9*) and in 1977 (*ICRP Publication 26*) (all published by Pergamon Press, Oxford).
9. In Canada, at Chalk River, Ontario, in 1949; in England, at Buckland House near Harwell, in 1950.
10. *British Journal of Radiology*, XXIV (1951) p. 46.
11. *Ibid.*
12. *British Journal of Radiology*, supplement 6 (1955) pp. 7 and 15.
13. *Ibid.* p.15.
14. In these units the absorbed dose and dose equivalent are numerically equal for beta and gamma radiation, but not for neutron and alpha radiation, which are ten and twenty times more biologically damaging.
15. *British Journal of Radiology*, supplement 6 (1955) p. 10.
16. *Recommendations of the International Commission on Radiological Protection (Adopted September 9, 1958)* (London: Pergamon Press, 1959) p.10.
17. *Ibid.* pp. 11–12.
18. *Ibid.* p.9.

19. *A Second Report to the Medical Research Council on the Hazards to Man of Nuclear and Allied Radiations*, Cmnd 1225 (London: HMSO, 1960).
20. To put this figure in perspective, the average annual dose from background radiation in the United Kingdom is 2 millisieverts. The annual occupational dose limit for a radiation worker is currently 50 millisieverts; a reduction has just been recommended (1988).
21. 10^{-2} Sv^{-1} for radiation induced cancer fatalities. For radiation induced cancer incidence, non-fatal as well as fatal, the risk coefficient is obviously higher – about three times higher in practice. Risk coefficients have been much discussed in recent years by ICRP and other bodies – including the American BEIR Committee (the National Academy of Sciences Committee on Biological Effects of Ionising Radiation) and UNSCEAR (the United Nations Scientific Committee on Effects of Atomic Radiation) and are of course open to revision.
22. Subject to the overriding requirement that appropriate dose-limits must not be exceeded. See *ICRP Publication 26* (Oxford: Pergamon Press, 1977).
23. See *ICRP Publication 42, A Compilation of the Major Concepts and Quantities in use by ICRP* (Oxford: Pergamon Press, 1984).
24. This would have read more correctly 'there might be up to about 40 deaths (or possibly none).'

10 Labour and the Origins of the National Health Service

Charles Webster

As a consequence of a recent flurry of research initiatives, the early history of the National Health Service has been charted in meticulous detail.[1] Notwithstanding increasing availability of documentation in the public records, or greater elaboration of the narrative, interpretations have remained remarkably consistent with the classic study produced by Eckstein in 1958. Eckstein's authority has been further enhanced by Addison's account of the wartime background to the welfare legislation of the 1945–51 Labour administration.[2]

The National Health Service would appear to vindicate the 'consensus' approach to the development of social policy. From this perspective, the inefficiency and incompleteness of the patchwork of health services formed by accretion over the previous century was increasingly evident during the interwar period. Advances in medical science underlined the need for radical reconstruction of the health services. Beginning with the famous Dawson Report (1920), medical experts produced plans for a comprehensive health service to be administered on hierarchical and regional lines. The gathering consensus during the Second World War around Keynesian economic theory and Beveridge's ideas on social security created conditions for the realisation of plans developed over the previous two decades by the medical profession and its associates.

The National Health Service, therefore, appears to provide a model demonstration of the translation of technical expertise into social advance. The rational, humane and economic merits of the solution advocated were sufficiently self-evident for the scheme for a comprehensive health service to attract the broadest consensus. Delay in formulating an acceptable plan was the result of disagreements concerning the most appropriate means for realising an optimum service. The technocratic explanation of this major development in social policy conveniently disposes of the need to invoke ideology or class conflict. Indeed, even ministers, leading politicians and political parties are reduced to the status of onlookers. The documentary record invites the conclusion that the essential action involved bureaucrats and medical interest groups. Their negotiated conclusions seem to have been adopted with little change, first by coalition ministers, and then by their Labour successors. The approach pioneered by Eckstein possessed the utility of dispelling the tenacious American myth that the National Health Service represented a dangerous lurch towards socialisation in the welfare sector. Consistent with this bias, Eckstein minimised the contribution of the labour movement in health planning. Even the adoption of a comprehensive health policy by the 1934 Annual Conference is not regarded as an event of significance. In this context, Eckstein concludes that 'The Dawson Report. . . had appeared more than a decade before. The BMA had published a fairly radical program of medical reform four years earlier. The Labour Party was certainly not in the vanguard of the agitation. It joined the team, at best, in the middle of the game'.[3] The recent literature, although adding detail concerning labour involvement, has not significantly challenged the Eckstein interpretation. It is therefore timely to review the evidence concerning the role of the Labour Party and the labour movement in the emergence of the National Health Service.[4] The result of this exercise is useful for various reasons. First, it will help to resolve the apparent paradox that the mass movements of the left were irrelevant to a critical development in social policy which is popularly regarded as the brainchild of Aneurin Bevan and the postwar Labour government. Secondly, vindication of a role for labour reintroduces ideology and class conflict, casting doubt on the adequacy of the standard pluralist and technocratic explanations of this and other innovations in the welfare field. Finally, by shifting the emphasis from 'consensus' to 'conflict' and 'compromise', the way is cleared for a less suprematist idea of the National Health Service. Such demythologisation is a necessary preliminary to a more realistic assessment of the balance of benefit and loss under this famous experiment in social welfare.

From the time of its origins, the Labour Party was necessarily involved in problems of health care, primarily because Labour was committed to the abolition of the Poor Law. Since medical relief was one of the main aspects of poor law administration, substitution of health services free from the taint of poor relief was an inescapable element in Labour social policy. Creation of a comprehensive 'State Medical Service' developed from existing public health services was a major priority of the Webbs and their Fabian associates. This policy found expression in the influential Minority Report of the Royal Commission on the Poor Laws (1909).[5] The Socialist Medical League formed in 1908, and the State Medical Service Association dating from 1912, were professionally dominated groups working for the objectives of the Minority Report.[6] Therefore, even before the First World War, the Labour Party worked actively for extension of municipal health services. The Labour Party therefore supported legislation to develop maternity and child welfare services, the school medical service and a school meals service. The last was resisted by administrators within the Board of Education on account of its encouragement of 'socialist proclivities' among local authorities.[7] Such services were cultivated by socialists because they represented real concessions to the working classes, as well as being a vehicle for the redistribution of wealth. On the other hand, there was much opposition within the labour movement to the introduction of contributory health insurance, which was regarded as an unsound principle for the provision of health care, and a likely obstruction to the future development of public health services. In rousing Labour MPs' hostility to the insurance schemes in parliament, Beatrice Webb noted that 'what we are trying to achieve is to direct the sickness insurance scheme into a big reconstruction of public health'.[8]

The increasing power of Labour as a party of local and national government was accompanied by a growing commitment to the extension of public health services. During the First World War, the Labour Party supported reform of the machinery of government and the establishment of functional ministries as a preliminary to an anticipated drive towards social reconstruction. The new Ministry of Health created after the First World War was expected by Labour to superintend the abolition of the Poor Law and the extension of public health services.[9] Christopher Addison, the first Minister of Health, soon went over to the Labour Party.[10] In the light of impending administrative reforms, the Labour Party established its Public Health Committee in 1918. The substantial policy document issued by this committee in 1918 indicates that Labour was not in arrears of the Dawson Consultative Council.[11] Indeed, the Dawson Report of 1920 may be regarded as a counterblast to Labour proposals, written from the perspective of a medical élite desperately searching for a means to salvage the general practitioner from impending redundancy.[12]

Labour groups in the London boroughs, Bradford and Sheffield were pioneers in the field of public health even before the First World War. The record of Labour in local government between the wars was uneven owing to the effects of the depression, and because of limitations of insight among councillors and their officers. Those Labour authorities attempting to optimise welfare services faced intransigent opposition from central authority and local bureaucrats.[13]

During the 1920s there was a notable decline in Labour central leadership on the health front. In general election manifestos, health tended to be covered by pledges concerning housing and social security. Notwithstanding production of a scattering of health policy pamphlets, the Party's Public Health Committee was relatively inert, while the State Medical Service Association lapsed. Formation of the Socialist Medical Association (SMA) in 1930 reversed the decline and created a new forum for mobilising the expertise of socialist doctors. This group was probably founded to counteract the new planning initiative of the British Medical Association (BMA), which issued in 1930 and reissued in 1938 its *A General Medical Service for the Nation*. The BMA thereby became committed to making the future extension of health services dependent on National Health Insurance provision.[14]

The SMA was antagonistic to contributory insurance and it reinforced Labour commitment to extension of public health services. Eckstein and others have exaggerated the indebtedness of Labour to schemes evolved by the BMA, and they have overlooked the barriers to consensus between the two approaches. Although small compared with the BMA, SMA membership was not insignificant, rising to 1500 by 1943. The SMA exercised an influence disproportionate to its numbers, and its effect was even felt within the BMA. On account of communist infiltration, the SMA became a vehicle for expression of ideas concerning health representing a broad front of the left.

Members of the SMA assumed influence in local health affairs and health administration especially in London. For instance, the SMA prepared a health policy statement for the London County Council (LCC) election. After Labour assumed control of the LCC in 1934, Somerville Hastings, President of the SMA, became chairman of its Hospitals and Medical Services Committee. Thereafter, the LCC was very much a pace-setter in the field of the municipal health services, but in addition, Labour-controlled authorities such as Finsbury and Tottenham were responsible for major initiatives, including the development of health centres.[15] These health centres symbolised the utility and forward-looking character of the schemes for which the SMA was working. The taste for expansion and experimentation rapidly caught on in local authority circles just before the Second World War. The leading Labour local authorities were straining towards the establishment of comprehensive services, and they were looking to the political parties and the health departments for leadership.

The 1932 Leicester Labour Party Conference dutifully supported a motion prepared by the SMA President advocating a complete State Medical Service, 'giving everything necessary for the prevention and treatment of disease and open to all'. The main lines of SMA policy were first publicised in *A Socialised Medical Service* (1933), and they were subsequently pursued with tenacity by the Association. Proposals contained in this SMA pamphlet were echoed in the policy document approved by the Southport Conference in 1934. Through the SMA, Labour thus became pledged to: (a) a comprehensive service provided free to all; (b) employment of all staff, including the medical profession, on a full-time salaried basis; (c) administration under a new form of multi-purpose, elected, regional government; and (d) placing the centre of gravity of the service in a comprehensive system of publicly provided health centres.

All but the first point of policy were offensive to the BMA. Consequently, the 1934 policy statement and its later echoes aroused instinctive fears within the medical profession concerning the alien motives of Labour administrations. The same degree of alarm was not communicated to the public. Socialist thinking on health and welfare was effectively publicised through such media as the Left Book Club and Penguin books.[16] Such semi-popular statements from the left dominated the field. They heightened alarm over the state of the British health services, while suggesting that greatly enhanced standards of health care were a reasonable and realistic expectation.

The socialist case for health was echoed at the popular level, most notably in a special issue of *Picture Post* devoted to the 'Plan for Britain'.[17] It is therefore not surprising that in advance of the publication of the Beveridge Report, tests of public opinion discovered widespread public demand for a state medical service of the kind advocated by the Labour and Communist Parties. Such responses were recorded by the British Institute of Public Opinion, Mass Observation, the Ministry of Information, and the Nuffield College Social Reconstruction Survey.[18] Equivalent views were transmitted to the Beveridge Committee by the Trades Union Congress and the Nuffield College Survey. It is difficult to resist the impression that Beveridge was carried onwards by an inexorable tide of public opinion, at least with respect to his conclusion that the new system of social security should include a comprehensive health service. The Penguin Special by the distinguished consultant Aleck Bourne reflects SMA thinking concerning the detailed administration of a new comprehensive health service. Although the SMA traditionally favoured a 'completely unified' hospital service, it had stopped short of advocating state or municipal control of the voluntary hospitals. However Bourne concluded that 'we have confidence that as between a semi-bankrupt system of unco-ordinated individual existence and a unified State system with local autonomy, the latter is far preferable and offers the only solution for the future of British hospitals'.[19] Bourne's plan for a comprehensive municipal health service involved:

1. The transfer of all matters of health from other government departments to the general charge of the Ministry of Health.
2. The general and special health services of the country should be worked, under the aegis of the Ministry, by the Local Authorities through Health Committees.
3. The Health Committee is a committee of the Local Authority, and must have jurisdiction over a sufficiently wide or populous area to ensure adequate funds and efficient service.
4. The Health Committees should be appointed by the County Councils and the County Borough Councils, and all health services should be placed under their control.
5. From the Central County or County Borough Health Committee should be appointed a series of sub-committees responsible for sub-divisions of the health services   tuberculosis, maternity and child welfare, school children, hospitals, infectious diseases, health in factories, mental disease and all other health activities.
6. While the County or County Borough Medical Officer should be head of these activities, adviser to the Central Health Committee, and generally responsible for the working of all the health services of his area, each sub-committee would have its own medical officer who would perform a similar function for his own department. All the medical officers to the sub-committees would form a County or County Borough Medical Committee under the chairmanship of the principal Medical Officer of Health to the Central Health Committee.

7. National Health Insurance should be put under the management of the Central Health Committee and the Insurance Committees abolished.

8. The Poor Law Authorities should be abolished and their institutional and domiciliary work (by their District Medical Officers) should be taken over by the Health Committees of the Councils.

9. The 'Health Area' could not always coincide with county boundaries. Such areas (e.g. Rutland) would combine with a neighbouring authority while large unwieldy areas would be split.

10. A closer relation of the general practitioner and specialist with the Public Health Central Committees. One of the chief agencies for ensuring this liaison would be by their increasing work in the Central Committee's various hospitals, clinics and diagnostic centres.

Bourne claimed that his scheme was agreed by 'nearly all bodies and individuals who have discussed the question of administration'.[20] This latter point represents a miscalculation with respect to his colleagues in the medical profession, yet it suggests that confidence in the existing system was declining and that municipalisation of the health services was emerging as the main logical choice for the future.

The SMA was in a good position to dominate Labour health planning when the Party resuscitated its Public Health Advisory Committee in November 1938, and when in July 1941 the National Executive Committee established a range of sub-committees to prepare for postwar reconstruction. The Public Health Reconstruction Committee was chaired by Somerville Hastings. Together with David Stark Murray, also of the SMA, Hastings dominated the proceedings. It is therefore not surprising that Labour's definitive policy document, *National Service for Health* (April, 1943), closely reflected SMA aspirations. By virtue of the continuity of SMA influence, the major health resolution of the 1943 Annual Conference closely followed the pattern laid down at the 1934 Conference.[21]

Recent research has uncovered evidence concerning tentative steps towards comprehensive health planning by officials within the Ministry of Health before the Second World War. Office meetings held in 1937 and 1938 show that officials were reacting to policy initiatives within the Labour Party, and to developments taking

place in London, associated with the rise of LCC hospital services
and the decline of the voluntary sector. At the first office conference
on health service planning, it was noted that health service reform
was likely to become an election issue in the near future.[22] Officials
then came directly face to face with Labour in the course of
mounting an emergency operation to save the London voluntary
hospitals. At a major conference convened by the Ministry to bring
all the relevant parties together, the LCC delegation was led by
Herbert Morrison, backed by powerful henchmen, Charles Latham
(the Labour leader of the LCC), and Somerville Hastings. The LCC
representatives appeared coldly indifferent to the plight of voluntary
hospitals. Morrison looked on extension of financial support as the
thin end of the wedge to 'whole financing of voluntary hospitals
from public funds', an outcome that the LCC was not willing to
contemplate.[23] This meeting made evident the effectiveness with
which a determined local authority could invade the acute hospital
sector, and within the space of ten years threaten the viability of
the prestigious teaching hospitals. The Ministry of Health thus went
into planning for postwar hospital administration with the clear
understanding that major local authorities were capable of driving
the voluntary sector into bankruptcy, and indeed the LCC seemed
to be relishing this possibility. It seemed likely that the other Labour
authorities, and perhaps also non-Labour ones, such as Surrey and
Middlesex, might imitate this habit. The department itself, although
driven by the voluntary lobby to accept the principle of partnership,
was responsive to the LCC position and it was frankly recognised
that the voluntary system was 'approaching demise'.[24] Although not
finally accepted in 1939, the policies of municipalisation and
nationalisation were freely discussed, and they were recognised as
logical, simpler and administratively more satisfactory alternatives
to subsidy of the voluntary sector.

The LCC was deeply suspicious of the motives underlying schemes
for hospital regionalisation emanating from the voluntary sector.
The Medical Officer of Health to the LCC warned the Ministry that
Morrison, Latham and Hastings were opposed to obligatory grants
to voluntary hospitals. Furthermore, representation on governing
bodies of voluntary hospitals would be a condition of LCC subsidy.
The Ministry was told that Hastings in particular was advocating a
'full blown State Medical Service'.[25] LCC alarm at the counter-
offensive from the voluntary lobby caused Latham to write an
inflammatory article for the *Star*, accusing the advocates of

regionalisation of being Fifth Columnists plotting to rob the democratically elected authorities of their hospital service.[26] Although the government stopped short of advocating municipalisation of the hospital service, in the first public statement on postwar hospital policy delivered by Ernest Brown in October 1941, local authorities were promised statutory responsibility for planning and a senior, potentially dominant, role in the partnership.

Labour was very much in mind when the department was considering wider questions of health planning. In May 1940, almost a year before the government's Reconstruction Committee was convened, it was noted that statements by Arthur Greenwood, the newly appointed Minister without Portfolio, suggested that there would be a recapitulation of the First World War Ministry of Reconstruction, with committees on all aspects of policy.[27] The alternatives spelt out to the Permanent Secretary in January 1941 included a 'State Medical Service' run either by major local authorities, or by elected regional councils.[28] It was recognised that a comprehensive health service would be associated with 'considerable schemes of social reform'. Politically, it was necessary to 'expect such schemes. . . the whole pressure is towards equality of treatment and benefit'. It was stressed that a full rate and exchequer financed service was 'supported by a considerable weight of vocal political opinion'.[29]

Thus, at the outset of wartime planning, it was appreciated that the Labour Party was likely to take a strong stand on behalf of socialised medicine. Officials noted that a broadening band of opinion was being converted to the socialist line. First, progressive views were being voiced in the *BMJ* by John Ryle, the Cambridge Regius Professor of Physics, although it was felt that 'his reputation for Leftist tendency deprives him of a good deal of the influence' that he might have exercised on the profession.[30] Secondly, a new organisation, Medical Planning Research, representing the views of younger and scientifically-minded doctors, came out forcefully in favour of full-time salaried service in health centres. Thirdly, the small, maverick, TUC-affiliated Medical Practitioners Union, not to be outdone by the SMA, produced its own scheme for socialised medicine, similar in most respects to the SMA model, but involving the creation of Area Authorities concerned only with health, and not elected or local authority controlled.[31] Finally, and most important of all, innovatory tendencies were evident within the Medical Planning Commission, a body convened by the British

Medical Association with a view to representing the ideas on post-war reconstruction of all major medical organisations. The SMA was accepted into the Medical Planning Commission and it found allies, especially among the representatives of the Society of Medical Officers of Health. Because of these leftist influences, the Draft Interim Report of the Medical Planning Commission turned out to be a more radical document than had been anticipated. Although not accepted by the majority of the Commission, arguments in favour of the full-time salaried alternative were fully stated. The most conspicuous feature of this report was the firm support given to group practice in health centres, and this was carried to the point of providing a full description of a model health centre. The Ministry regarded this latter feature as a sign of an 'enormous advance in medical opinion' and confirmation that the profession was moving in the direction of official thinking.[32] In fact, the Medical Planning Commission Report soon proved to be an embarrassment to the profession and it was quietly buried by the BMA.

Taking heart from the Medical Planning Commission Report, officials produced their initial scheme for a general practitioner service. This coincided with SMA doctrine in advocating a unified service administered by county councils, county boroughs or combinations of these; provision for the whole population, rather than for 90 per cent as the profession wanted; and employment on a full-time salaried basis for general practitioners working in health centres, group practice in health centres being the established pattern for development. Concessions were made to tradition by accepting private practice outside health centres, and by proposing strong professional advisory committees.[33] There was thus only a fine measure of distinction between the preferred scheme of the Ministry and the draft policy documents of the Labour Party.

In framing proposals for Ministers, officials were undoubtedly influenced by the Labour commitments in the field of health. Appointment of non-Labour Ministers of Health was insufficient to restrain Labour influence. Neither the National Liberal Ernest Brown, nor his successor, the Conservative, Henry U. Willink, were weighty political figures compared with Thomas Johnston, the Labour Secretary of State for Scotland, who also possessed the advantage of office for the whole wartime period. Responsibility for framing the new health service was, of course, a joint responsibility of the Ministry of Health and Scottish Department of Health. Further opportunities for Labour intervention occurred at the level of the Reconstruction Priorities Committee, which included Bevin and Morrison. In October 1943, they were reinforced by Attlee. Both Bevin and Morrison were experienced in the health field. The former had been building his own industrial health empire in the Ministry of Labour and he was concerned that this development should stay within his department. Morrison had presided over the growth of health services in the LCC. Attlee was less obviously experienced with health policy, but he was fully conversant with the problems of social security. He was briefed by both the SMA and by Dr Stephen Taylor, who became a Labour MP in 1945, and who was instigator of Medical Planning Research. In agreement with Taylor, Attlee was opposed to any 'glorified panel service'.[34] The Labour triumvirate was the most cohesive force in the Reconstruction Priorities Committee. Indeed the strength of this partnership was a worry to Churchill.

The Labour members were no doubt gratified to find that the proposals presented by Brown coincided closely with their own thoughts. Morrison, in particular, must have been pleased with the forthright support for local government control:

The comprehensive service must be one and indivisible in each area of the country. The alternative course of removing the existing health services from the local authorities would go far to discredit and destroy local government. It follows that the new services, including any substitute for the National Health Insurance medical benefit, should be treated as local government services.[35]

Labour objections were reserved for features inherited from the ministerial statement on hospitals of October 1941. In line with traditional local authority objections to precepting, Morrison opposed proposals for joint boards, which he regarded as weakening the influence of major local authorities. Bevin momentarily adopted the opposite position, suggesting that the health service might be administered on a national basis, with local interests being represented on advisory committees.[36] Morrison stuck stubbornly to his line, arguing that major local authorities were facing death by a thousand cuts. He circulated a memorandum criticising the joint board proposal because it was 'thoroughly bad in principle, to cut at the root of local government, and to be contrary to sound principles of financial planning'.[37] By September 1943, Morrison had worn away the opposition. Sir John Anderson, as chairman, invited the Minister of Health to present the alternatives of single authorities and joint boards in his forthcoming White Paper. In agreeing to this concession, the committee was no doubt influenced by the political advantage of securing local authority support for the scheme. Bevin suggested that, if adopted, the joint authority alternative should be presented as a temporary expedient pending local government reorganisation.[38]

The debate returned to general practice when the Minister of Health reappeared with watered-down proposals following the chastening experience of negotiation with an actively antagonistic profession. Now Attlee criticised the inconsistency of the initial acceptable plan for 'grouped and non-competitive practice in publicly provided health centres, with the current proposal for the old system of panel doctors receiving capitation fees'.[39] Brown fell back on the argument for gradualism, but he agreed that the White Paper would emphasise that health centres were a main objective of policy, presumably with the intention of leaving it implicit that service in health centres would involve some kind of move in the direction of non-competitive practice.

During the final stages of preparation of the White Paper, Woolton became Chairman of the renamed Reconstruction Committee and Willink Minister of Health. The Labour leaders appreciated that the White Paper would be a compromise, but they were most unhappy about the outcome. Publication was held up for a month in January 1944 while they pressed their criticisms. The White Paper was too indefinite. Labour wanted a firm declaration of government policy, not a provisional document. Morrison was still not satisfied that the single local authority alternative was sufficiently clearly stated. Attlee wanted an affirmation of the complete separation between public and private practice. Both he and Morrison objected to the right being granted for all doctors in the scheme to take private patients, and they opposed paying non-health-centre doctors on a capitation basis. Bevin and Morrison felt that insufficient emphasis had been placed on health centres, while Bevin wanted it made clear that health centres would aim to take away work from hospitals and so correct one of the failings of panel medical practice. The Labour members were also displeased that no positive view was expressed concerning the prohibition of the sale and purchase of medical practices. Finally, with respect to the short version of the White Paper, Attlee objected to any sentiment contemplating the continuation of voluntary hospitals as more than a short-term expedient.[40]

Woolton tried to respond to this formidable list of complaints without introducing major concessions. The Labour team allowed itself reluctantly to be pacified, but their wrath was revived when Churchill, at the instigation of Beaverbrook, went back on the Cabinet agreement to publish the White Paper by reopening discussion on private medical practice, the status of voluntary hospitals and the terms of employment of consultants. The infuriated Attlee reminded the Prime Minister that Labour members had accepted much that was unpalatable about the White Paper, to the extent of risking censure within their own party. He warned that any resumption of discussions would unavoidably force them to renew demands for a full-time salaried service and other policies 'far more repugnant to Conservative feeling'. Woolton sensed danger, warning his Conservative allies that the White Paper had indeed been difficult for Labour to swallow. Although further Cabinet discussion was held, Churchill allowed his mind to be settled without demur and the White Paper was published on 17 February 1944.[41]

Hastings described the White Paper as a 'watered-down version of the Labour Party's scheme'.[42] It was accepted by the 1944 Conference, but as an 'obvious compromise'. In the meantime, Willink returned to his negotiations amid mounting fears within the labour movement that further unwelcome concessions were being made by the Minister to the profession and the voluntary hospitals. Already in May 1944 the Labour Party circulated *A National Health Service*, recapitulating party policy and including a diatribe against concessions to vested interests.[43] The Reconstruction Committee was left out of things. However, following a series of press leaks, Bevin asked about progress on controversial issues. He was informed about some of the minor concessions made by Willink.[44] Of these, the sale of practices was the only point brought before the Reconstruction Committee. Behind the scenes, Willink was preparing a new White Paper, as well as draft legislation, all of which was abandoned on political grounds with the approach of the 1945 election.

In the run-up to the general election of 1945, Labour capitalised on its fidelity to the 1944 White Paper. Confidence of the public in Labour's commitment to social welfare undoubtedly contributed to the landslide victory. In government Labour enjoyed the best of both worlds, attacking Willink's apostasy, while regarding itself free to depart from the White Paper and draw up fresh proposals.

It is well known that Aneurin Bevan departed from the 1944 White Paper in two major respects, first by abandoning unified organisation at the periphery and instead adopting a separate form of organisation for each of the three main branches of the service. Secondly, he bravely grasped the hitherto little considered option of nationalising the entire hospital service and evolving for it a new form of administration. Once these decisions had been reached, it was a relatively straightforward operation to fill out the legislation by cannibalising the abandoned Willink Bill and earlier drafts.

Having heard rumours of Bevan's intentions, the SMA attempted as best it could to square his plans with their traditional policy. Stark Murray reminded Bevan of SMA support for 'regional elected authorities administering a national plan and employing whole time salaried officers in Health Centres and large hospitals'. He regarded Bevan's Regional Hospital Board structure as a reasonable temporary expedient pending local government reform, providing that boards were 'nominated by Local Authorities, the Minister, and possibly health workers'.[45] Nationalisation of voluntary and municipal hospitals caused no difficulty with the SMA. Understandably, the main point upon which this organisation exerted pressure was health centres, which had been virtually extinguished in Willink's later schemes, but which were expected to regain prominence in Bevan's Bill. During the preparation of the Bill, SMA leaders peppered Bevan with comment and criticism, mainly on minor points, their major disappointment relating to failure to prevent backsliding on the question of full-time salaried service. Perhaps the most telling criticisms of the Bill from the SMA direction came from the experienced medical administrator Horace Joules, who attacked the proposal to exempt teaching hospitals from the regional hospital structure, and also argued that the adoption of paybeds would have a widespread and deleterious influence on the hospital service.[46] But despite having twelve members in Parliament, the SMA was no longer a force to be reckoned with and there is no evidence that its wisdom exercised any particular charm for Bevan.

Bevan's difficulties on his own side lay rather with the LCC and the local authority associations. Under Bevan's scheme, local authorities were not only to be deprived of their central role in a unified service, but they were also to be stripped of hospital services, which in many places had been built up with great success and were the object of much pride. Many of these areas were Labour strongholds and Labour's local politicians were not inclined to sacrifice the powers of their prestigious Health Committees without a struggle.

Divergences of opinion concerning the local government issue prevented Bevan's imaginative Bill from being greeted with unreserved acclaim within the Cabinet. Wrangling lasting from October 1945 until March 1946 spoiled the glamour of the occasion, and it aroused doubts about other aspects of the NHS Bill.[47] This legacy of disagreement resulted eventually in open conflict between Bevan and his critics, so exposing the infant National Health Service to damage from within the Labour government, and depriving Labour of the full electoral advantage of this substantial measure of social reform.

The above review of Labour involvement in health policy before the inception of the National Health Service provides a corrective to the interpretations stemming from the work of Eckstein. Labour emerges as a more formidable presence than is customarily recognised, and it was by no means a latecomer in the field of health policy. Before 1920, Labour contributed to the debates on Poor Law reform, National Health Insurance, post-First World War reconstruction and the Ministry of Health. Labour's proposals for a State Medical Service formulated between 1909 and 1934, placed the party ahead of its political rivals, and at least in a position of parity with planners representing medical interest groups. Between 1930 and 1945, the Socialist Medical Association was a highly effective publicist for socialised medicine. During the same period, Labour local authorities worked steadily towards establishment of comprehensive municipal health services.

Accordingly, it is arguable that 'classic' planning initiatives from Dawson onwards were not entirely spontaneous, but were at least in part reactions to mounting pressures emanating from the labour movement. Notwithstanding this pressure from the left, before the Second World War, retrenchment-minded governments sanctioned only minor improvements in services, and their planning initiatives were slight in scale. The emergence of the Labour Party into a position of authority in the wartime coalition government, together with the need to conciliate the civilian workforce, revolutionised attitudes towards the social services and stimulated a new mood of realism with respect to planning. Reflecting the general stampede towards social reconstruction, there emerged a rash of planning initiatives in the field of health, in the course of which leftist organisations restated their demands for a free, comprehensive health service provided by public authorities. In response, medical organisations swam along with the tide, attempting as best they could to protect the position of their respective vested interests. The subsequent protracted and acrimonious negotiations, conducted first with the coalition government and then with the postwar Labour government, extended almost without a break from 1943 until 1952. This trial of strength illustrated the brutal power of vested interests to extract compromises from elected government. In the course of these changes, the policies for socialised medicine evolved by the Labour Party over three decades were abandoned to such an extent that the National Health Service was reduced to an empty shell. Although, for the sake of pride, formally represented as a socialist measure, in reality the National Health Service had become the captive of corporate interests. It has taken a great deal of assiduous effort on the part of political theorists to designate this situation as a permanent and beneficial consensus.

NOTES

1. H. Eckstein, *The English Health Service, its Origins, Structure and Achievements* (Cambridge, Mass.: Harvard University Press, 1958); F. Honigsbaum, *The Division in British Medicine. . . 1911–1968* (London: Kogan Page, 1979); J.E. Pater, *The Making of the National Health Service* (London: King's Fund, 1981); R. Klein, *The Politics of the National Health Service* (London: Longman, 1983); D.M. Fox, *Health Policies, Health Politics, The British and American Experience, 1911–1965* (Princeton University Press, 1986). Honigsbaum is exceptional among these studies in drawing attention to the activities of left-wing organisations.
2. P. Addison, *The Road to 1945* (London: Cape, 1975).
3. Eckstein, p. 108.
4. Literature pertinent to the perspective of this review includes: R. Miliband, *The State in Capitalist Society* (London: Weidenfeld and Nicolson, 1969); V. Navarro, *Class Struggle, the State and Medicine* (Oxford: Robertson, 1978) albeit marred by inaccuracy; I. Gough, *The Political Economy of the Welfare State* (London: Macmillan, 1979).
5. B. Webb, *Our Partnership*, ed. B. Drake and M.I. Cole (London: Longmans, 1948) pp. 316–491; N. & J. MacKenzie, *The First Fabians* (London: Weidenfeld & Nicolson, 1977); H.V. Emy, *Liberals, Radicals and Social Politics, 1892–1914* (Cambridge University Press, 1973); J.R. Hay, *The Origins of the Liberal Welfare Reforms, 1906–1914* (London: Macmillan, 1975); M. Freeden, *The New Liberalism* (Oxford University

Press, 1978); R. McKibbin, *The Evolution of the Labour Party 1910–1924* (Oxford University Press, 1974).

6. Minute Book of the State Medical Service Association 1912–1918, Socialist Medical Association Archive, Brynmor Jones Library, Hull University. D. Stark Murray, *Why a National Health Service?* (London: Pemberton, 1971) pp. 7–19. Honigsbaum, pp. 54 and *passim*.

7. L.A. Selby-Bigge to W. Runciman, 29 April 1908, PRO, Ed 50/8.

8. *Our Partnership*, p. 470, 6 March 1911; B. and S. Webb, *The State and the Doctor* (London: Longmans, 1910); 'The Working of the Insurance Act: Interim Report of the Committee of Enquiry instituted by the Fabian Research Department', *The New Statesman*, 14 March 1914.

9. N. and J. MacKenzie (eds), *The Diary of Beatrice Webb*, vol. III (London: Virago, 1984) pp. 274–82, 290–1; K. Morgan, *Consensus and Disunity. The Lloyd George Coalition Government 1918–1922* (Oxford University Press, 1979); M. Cowling, *The Impact of Labour 1920–1924* (Cambridge University Press, 1971).

10. K. & J. Morgan, *The Political Career of Christopher, Viscount Addison* (Oxford University Press, 1980).

11. B. Moore and C.A. Parker, 'The Case for a State Medical Service Restated', *The Lancet*, 1918, ii, pp. 85–7, 20 July 1918. Labour Party, *The Organisation of the Preventive and Curative Medical Services* (1918); Labour Party and TUC, *The Labour Movement and Preventive and Curative Medical Services* (1922). Labour documents of this vintage are not cited by Eckstein.

12. Consultative Council on Medical and Allied Services, *Interim Report on the Future Provision of Medical and Allied Services*, Cmd. 693 (HMSO, 1920), discussed in C. Webster, 'Designing a National Health Service 1918–1942' (unpublished).

13. Webster, 'Health, Welfare and Unemployment during the Depression', *Past and Present*, number 109, 1985: pp. 204–30.

14. Minute Book of the State Medical Service Association, 1929–31 records the decision of the Association not to amalgamate with the SMA. DSM 1/1, 1930–34, Brynmor Jones Library, Hull University, records the establishment of the SMA in October 1930, after a preliminary meeting held in September 1930. The aims of this body were, (1) a 'socialised medical service, free and open to all', (2) dissemination of the principles of socialism within the medical and allied services, (3) stimulation of health questions in the labour and trades union movement. The SMA is discussed by Stark Murray and Honigsbaum.

15. P. Coe and M. Reading, *Lubetkin and Tecton: Architecture and Social Commitment* (London: Arts Council, 1980) pp. 140–4; Finsbury Borough Council, *Finsbury Health Centre* (Finsbury, 1938).

16. Gollancz, Left Book Club: G.C.M. M'Gonigle and J. Kirby, *Poverty and Public Health* (London, 1936); W. Hannington, *The Problem of the Distressed Areas* (London, 1937); H. Sigerist, *Socialised Medicine in the Soviet Union* (London, 1937). See also such related Gollancz publications as C.E. McNally, *Public Ill-Health* (London, 1935). Penguin: A. Bourne, *Health of the Future* (Harmondsworth, 1942); D. Stark Murray, *The Future of Medicine* (Harmondsworth, 1942). These

Penguin Specials by members of the SMA were backed up by such Pelicans as M. Spring Rice, *Working-Class Wives* (Harmondsworth, 1939).

17. *Picture Post*, vol. x, no. 1, 4 January 1941.
18. For further details, see Webster, *Problems of Health Care: The British National Health Service before 1957* (HMSO, London, 1988) Chapter II, section (ii).
19. Bourne, p. 141.
20. Bourne, pp. 127–8.
21. Labour Party Archive, London, Public Health Sub-Committee memoranda, beginning RDR8, October 1941, 'The Health Centre in the Organisation of the Medical Services' by D. Stark Murray; and RDR16, November 1941, 'A Scheme for a State Medical Service' by Hastings. SMA, *The Socialist Programme for Health* (1943).
22. Office Conference, 7 February 1938, 'Development of the Health Services', PRO, MH 80/24.
23. Joint Conference with LCC, 27 January 1937, MH 79/513, MH 80/24.
24. Sir A.S. McNalty to Sir George Chrystal, 'Proposed National Hospital Service', 21 September 1939, MH 80/24.
25. Memorandum by Dr Allen Daley, 28 February 1941; Daley to Sir A. Rucker, 4 March 1941, MH 77/22. Notes on meetings between officials and LCC representatives, 29 August 1941 and 4 September 1941, MH 77/25.
26. *The Star*, 12 August 1941.
27. Sir Edward Forber, 'Post-War Hospital Policy', 8 May 1940, MH 80/24.
28. E.D. MacGregor to Sir John Maude, 20 January 1941, MH 77/22 and MH 80/24.
29. MacGregor to Maude, 20 January 1941.
30. H.A. de Montmorency to Maude, 7 March 1942, MH 80/81.
31. Medical Planning Research, 'Interim General Report', *The Lancet*, ii, pp. 599–622, 21 November 1942. Medical Practitioners Union, *The Transition to a State Medical Service* (August, 1942).
32. Medical Planning Commission, 'Draft Interim Report', *British Medical Journal*, i, pp. 743–53, 20 June 1942. Note on MPC Report by Dalrymple Champneys, MH 80/1.
33. Ministry of Health Draft, 'Medical Practitioner Service', September 1942, MH 77/177, MH 80/24.
34. SMA deputation to Attlee, 11 November 1943, MH 77/63. Attlee to Willink, 11 October 1943 (communicating views of Taylor), MH 77/42.
35. Minister of Health and Secretary of State for Scotland, 'A Comprehensive Medical Service', PR (43)3, 2 February 1943, PRO, CAB 123/45, MH 87/13.
36. Committee on Reconstruction Priorities, PR(43) 16th meeting, 30 July 1943, CAB 87/13.
37. Morrison, 'Administration of the New National Health Service', PR(43)49, 17 August 1943, CAB 87/12.
38. Committee on Reconstruction Priorities, PR(43) 18th mtg, 8 September 1943, CAB 87/12.

39. PR(43) 24th mtg, 15 October 1943, CAB 87/12.
40. Reconstruction Committee, R(44) 3rd mtg, and R(44) 4th mtg, 10 January 1944, CAB 87/5.
41. R(44) 13th mtg, 4 February 1944; notes on Attlee's response to the White Paper, January 1944; Woolton to Churchill, 1 February 1944; Attlee to Woolton, 1 February 1944; Attlee to Churchill, 10 February 1944; Woolton to Eden, 10 February 1944: CAB 124/244. War Cabinet, M(44) 17th mtg, 9 February 1944, CAB 65/41. P. Addison, *The Road to 1945* (London: Quartet, 1977) pp. 239–42.
42. Labour Party, *A National Health Service: The White Paper and After* (May, 1944).
43. Hastings, 'Public Health', in H. Tracey (ed.), *The British Labour Party*, 3 vols. (London: Odhams, 1948), ii, pp. 130–41, p. 137.
44. Bevin's concern was almost certainly touched off by the *Daily Worker* exclusive, 'Government Abandons Health Plan', 27 March 1945. Willink to Bevin, 26 April 1944, MH 77/119. See also *Daily Mirror*, 28 March 1945.
45. Stark Murray to Bevan, 23 January 1946, MH 77/85.
46. For exchanges between Bevan and the SMA, August 1945 to March 1946, MH 77/51, 63, 85, 119, and SMA Archive, Brynmor Jones Library, DSM 1/25.
47. Pater, pp. 105–64; K.O. Morgan, *Labour in Power 1945–1951* (Oxford University Press, 1984) pp. 152–63; Webster, *Problems of Health Care*, Chapters IV and V.

11 Economists and Engineers
Sir Alec Cairncross

Margaret Gowing is one of the few economists of her generation who has shown a particular interest in engineering. Her study of the development of the atomic bomb is a commentary on events of the highest importance, in which technical, political and economic influences interacted in a way that economists should be particularly well equipped to explain, but rarely investigate. It is just such a mixture of influences that has come to dominate life in industrial countries; and it is increasingly futile to limit attention to any one of these influences to the exclusion of the others in explaining the past or providing for the future. Conversely, in the assessment of situations and projects and in framing recommendations for action, it is increasingly necessary for those who analyse economic, social and political factors to co-operate with those whose province is technology.

It cannot be said that there is at present much co-operation or mutual understanding between these two groups, of which the leading representatives are economists on the one side and engineers on the other. In my experience, economists commonly take little interest in engineering and engineers are apt to view with suspicion the activities of economists. It seems appropriate in a volume in honour of Margaret Gowing to ask whether this need be so and to review what unites and what divides economics and engineering as fields of study.

One thing both have in common is that they aim or should aim at a practical outcome. The engineer's aim is to get something done, or done better, whether he is designing (or repairing) a machine or a structure of some kind. He takes over information of all kinds as to what is wanted and what is possible and uses it to build something that will work: not something abstract and logically consistent but something tangible and visible. The economist, in his own way, is also interested in getting things to work, or work better. But the things that concern him are not machines and physical structures but economic and social systems and the successful harnessing of human effort to achieve desired results.

Another thing that engineers and economists have in common is an interest in efficiency. But technical efficiency is not the same as economic efficiency: a beautifully functioning machine may be

203

outrageously expensive and not at all efficient in terms of cost. A commercial concern is primarily interested in what is cost-effective, not what is elegant or imposing; it is likely to prefer engineers who aim at economic efficiency (as it is said American engineers are trained to do), rather than perfectionists who pay little regard to cost (as I have heard employers complain of British engineers).

Like all subjects claiming to be scientific in approach, both economics and engineering make extensive use of models and measurement. The degree of reliance on these, however, varies widely. Among engineers, I am told, there are those – chiefly Americans – who like to model and measure everything in sight while others – for example in Germany – go to the other extreme, practice in Britain being somewhere in the middle. Perhaps much the same could be said of economists.

However that may be, both subjects inevitably make use of theory. To do otherwise would be to forswear the use of reason and reflection. But in engineering the path from theory to artefacts is usually short and the assistance given by theory is easily put to the test. Economists, by contrast, have developed a very complex theory on the basis of a few simple postulates as to human behaviour. There is, however, a stronger compulsion for engineers to move on to the solution of immediate practical problems, whereas economists like to linger at the level of theory and devote much of their time to elaborating it. It is easy for them to lose their way and pursue lines of thought and analysis that have no conceivable application. Even when they turn to so-called 'applied economics' they continue to build logical structures or models on the basis of hypotheses, the only difference from 'pure theory' being that the models relate more closely to the use of policy for specific purposes. Although logical profundity and theoretical prowess command a special prestige, economics does not exist for the articulation of theory, except in so far as this improves our understanding of how the economic system works and assists in the improvement of economic performance.

Theory by itself does not supply the answer to practical problems. The problems are embedded in the world of fact, not hypothesis; in the uncertainties of real life, not the certainties of theory. All that theory can do is to alert us to the implications of the facts once established and suggest questions that direct our attention to the relevant facts. But the facts themselves are usually uncertain, incomplete, and subject to different interpretations. The questions admit of answers only on the basis of assumptions that may be mistaken or as expressions of probability given the uncertainties.

If economists and engineers could speak with certainty, there would be no more to be said. There would be no room for disagreement and no need for dialogue. But precisely because both deal in uncertainties, more than one answer can be given and there is need to debate the answers. If all that can be said is 'it is likely that this will happen', not 'this *will* happen', the natural thing to ask is 'how likely?' It is there that the trouble begins. How is the likelihood to be conveyed by an expert in one subject to an expert in another or by both to someone who is expert in neither subject but has to make the ultimate decision?

Before we pursue that question, let us remind ourselves just how uncertain economics and engineering can be as a guide to action. In economics there are major disagreements in such matters as the role of the money supply in causing inflation or the virtues of national economic planning. When membership of the Common Market was at issue, half the profession seemed to be on one side and half on the other. Even at a less political and more technical level, there is usually a fairly wide spread between economic forecasts covering a year or so and much larger differences for longer periods. What economist could have predicted forty years ago that West Germany would now enjoy the highest standard of living in Western Europe or East Germany the highest in Eastern Europe?

Similarly, in engineering there must always be a question whether any device designed by an engineer will work satisfactorily, whether a structure will stand the usage intended, whether a machine will meet the performance requirements, what faults will emerge in the design and what will go wrong between design and construction. The uncertainty may be negligible, as it usually is, once the design is well established. Or it may be overwhelming as it often is with new designs. Who can tell whether a new type of aeroplane, for example, will be successful until it has flown? Nobody foretold that the Lancaster would be a much more successful bomber than the Halifax: nobody *knew* until statistics were collected of bombs dropped per aircraft lost. Nobody could even be sure that the Lancaster, given its origins in the two-engined Manchester, would be a satisfactory four-engined aircraft. Or, to take a more recent example, nobody could be sure, even after the Concorde had flown for the first time, that its payload would ever be appreciably above zero, much less make it worth operating commercially.

In the natural sciences, it is usually possible to reduce or eliminate uncertainty by repeated experiments. But the scope for experiment is limited in engineering, especially the engineering of large one-off jobs like the building of bridges and other structures. It is, however, often possible to conduct experiments on small-scale models and draw conclusions for large-scale construction. Uncertainty then attaches only to the process of scaling up and a good engineer may be able to work out rules that allow him to scale up with considerable assurance. In much the same way, engineers can make use of prototypes or pilot plants to try things out. These rarely have any counterpart in economics, where experimentation is virtually non-existent and it is necessary to rely on the force of logic and careful examination of past history. The economist has usually to make do with hunch and that strengthening of the judgment that comes from intimate and extensive familiarity with the way things work.

Very often, too, there is a difference in the handling of uncertainty. The engineer is taught to leave a margin for contingencies, but knows that all such margins are costly and that it is only bad engineers who never find that the margin they recommend was insufficient. As a director of British European Airways once told me, every additional hour's flying experience enhances a pilot's skill and his passengers' safety, but one cannot on that account prolong the training process indefinitely. Economists may engage in risk analysis, but it rarely falls to them to decide what risks to take. If they stray from the comfortable certainties of theory, it is usually as advisers, not decision-takers on whom the final responsibility rests. Their advice is likely to be hedged around with 'ifs' and 'maybes', given this and given that. Even economic forecasts may be more successful in suppressing uncertainties than in expressing a judgment on them.

There is little or no overlap between the work of economists and engineers in dealing with macro-economic problems such as inflation and unemployment. Collaboration between them is usually called for in connection with large capital projects of all kinds. The engineer has then to assess the technical uncertainties and may join with the economist in assessing the commercial uncertainties, while the economist advises on the wider economic and social implications.

The proposal to build a Channel Tunnel, for example, needed extensive investigation by engineers to establish the feasibility and probable cost of the work. This not only raised issues as to tunnelling equipment, geology of the sea-bed, ventilation and so on, but made it necessary to consider the whole communications system by rail, road, air and ferry between Britain and France. These, too, had their technical aspects. But, like the Tunnel project, they also had commercial aspects and beyond that they raised political, social and economic issues. All of these introduced their own elements of uncertainty.

If the project was to be treated as a purely commercial one, some of these matters could be ignored and the issue reduced to one of prospective return on estimated outlay. It might then seem that it would be for the engineer to advise on the cost and the economist perhaps on the return. But things are rarely so straightforward. The engineer's estimate is unlikely to be accepted without further question. He will be asked how firm it is, what allowance he has made for delays, unforeseen snags, strikes, increases in labour and material costs, and so on. If he has made allowances for any of these, the allowances may be challenged by non-engineers who feel at least as well equipped to judge what is appropriate. Any estimates he makes of operating costs will inevitably depend on the volume and type of traffic and here again his estimates will be open to challenge, just as traffic forecasts also are open to challenge by those who start out by trying to estimate operating costs and the sustainable level of fares.

Estimates of cost raise a much larger issue. Cost of what? In the Channel Tunnel case there is no single project, but a host of variants, each claiming to out-perform the others. The options include a single tunnel, twin tunnels, a submerged tube and a bridge. Each of these in turn can be varied, for example as to terminal facilities and links to the road and rail system on both sides of the Channel. There are various possibilities of proceeding in stages or varying the period of construction. There is also the possibility of deferring construction for one or more years: a project deferred is a different project from one begun right away and needs separate assessment. What initially might seem a single project can rapidly sprout new shapes and develop into a quite different project. This makes it all the more necessary, in a review of the project, to ensure co-operation and mutual understanding between the different kinds of expert engaged in evaluating it.

Changes in the shape of a project affect both cost and return. There can be no sharp division, therefore, between two sets of advisers, one advising on cost, one on return. The engineer has to advise on the full range of alternative projects, including some that may be put up by the economist on commercial grounds. All of his estimates as to cost and construction are subject to a margin of error. Yet it is rare in such circumstances to find any indication from the engineer of the margin he would regard as reasonable. So all those to whom his estimates are passed feel free to exercise their own judgment, although the matter is one on which they claim no professional competence (other than recollection of past errors on other projects).

The danger is that the engineer may fasten his attention on too limited a range of possibilities and overlook others. He may also fail to take stock of the problem of co-ordination between his activities and those of other experts and present an assessment that is not easily married with other assessments that deal with a different set of uncertainties. He may not convey what is firm and what is doubtful in his estimates, what contingencies would greatly alter these estimates and what can be largely disregarded, what major assumptions underlie the estimates, and so on. In this respect, he is in exactly the same position as an economist presenting a forecast. The forecast by itself tells only half the story; the text surrounding it may be just as useful to the decision-taker who has to marry the forecast with other considerations.

The engineer's difficulties in estimating cost are, if anything, less formidable than those of the economist in estimating financial return. For one thing, the work of construction is finite and involves a single estimate. The financial return, on the other hand, stretches out into the future from data nobody knows for sure. Each year carries its own uncertainties and, in each, these affect both operating cost and utilisation. Whatever help market surveys may afford, great uncertainty must attach to the use that will be made of a tunnel immediately after completion in six or seven years' time and, still more, in ten or twenty years' time. Who can tell how many foot passengers, car owners, lorry drivers and coach operators will elect to use the Tunnel and how much freight will pass through it? Any answer must depend on a whole series of unknowns. What fares will the Tunnel be able to charge and how would traffic respond to variations in fares and freight charges? Would these fares be the same at all times and seasons or varied with the time of day, day of the week, and season of the year? What competitive pressure on fares and freights will the Tunnel face from sea-ferries and air transport? What kind of ships will be in operation, how fast will their turn-round times be, how low may their costs have fallen, or alternatively, if oil prices go through the roof again, what effect will that have? By how much will traffic have grown and how will it be shared between competing transport services?

These are, for the most part, questions calling for commercial judgement and it is not necessarily from an economist that an answer is sought – if indeed the questions are asked. They may be put to a businessman or a banker or engineer or sometimes to all three. If they *are* put to an economist, he has the advantage of a wider understanding of how market forces operate and may foresee repercussions that others might overlook. But his judgment can be challenged, just as the engineer's can be; and he owes it to those whom he is advising to make as explicit as possible the basis on which he reaches his estimates.

A project of the magnitude of the Channel Tunnel, involving two countries and two governments, is unlikely to be embarked upon without an assessment of a different kind in which wider issues and other uncertainties have to be evaluated. Governments will wish to satisfy themselves that the resources devoted to the project are not disproportionate to the benefits and that those costs and benefits that do not enter into the financial outlays and returns still yield a balance of social advantage. It is at this point that the need for the services of an economist is more likely to be felt.

There are, for example, effects on the environment and on employment that have to be assessed. How significant would be any loss of employment in Dover or any addition to road traffic through Kent? How would the balance between the south-east and other regions be affected? Is it likely that the consequences would be so adverse as to disturb a judgment on purely financial criteria or make it desirable to revise the project or attach conditions to its operation? Even from a narrower, economic point of view, there may be costs and benefits of importance to society but irrelevant to a financial evaluation. The Tunnel might, for example, offer savings in time or other advantages to travellers to which there is no counterpart in the payments they make and hence in the receipts of the tunnel operators. If fares remain unchanged, but travel is faster or more convenient, the gain accrues entirely to consumers and so does not affect the calculations of the promoters. Similarly, there may be social costs in road traffic congestion that fall on road users, not on the tunnel operators.

A question of particular importance to economists in comparing social costs and benefits is how to find a common measure for present and future magnitudes. Where a project is privately financed, the promoter may discount all future outlays and revenues at what he judges will be the cost of the capital he raises. But where the Government is finding the finance or is asking for a comparison of *social* costs and benefits, there is no easy way of establishing the rate at which future costs and benefits should be discounted. Market rates may be a poor guide to social time preferences; and who can be sure that today's discount rates will still look appropriate tomorrow?

From the political point of view, there are other uncertainties. Does it matter who owns the Tunnel or whether control passes to citizens of some other country? Will the cost of construction be raised by government efforts to steer contracts to suppliers of this nationality or that, to particular locations or enterprises? Will the two governments concerned agree to refrain from control over fares and methods of operation? Is it certain that assurances of that kind will be honoured if, say, the competition of the ferries ceases?

These are, for the most part, questions likely to be raised by an economist; not that an economist can be relied upon to provide an answer that is more than a guess. Economists are not necessarily better than other people in judging uncertainties, except to the extent that the uncertainties are rooted in economic forces. The first business of an economist is to raise questions, not to claim undue authority in answering them.

The piling of one set of uncertainties, assessed by one group of experts, on another set of uncertainties, assessed by a different groups of experts is characteristic of the evaluation of large projects like the Channel Tunnel. Whoever makes the final evaluation has to judge uncertainties conveyed to him by somebody else – probably with a different intellectual background – and is obliged, therefore, to begin by evaluating, not the project itself but the judgement of his advisers. If the first group consists of engineers and the second of economists, it is not surprising if both are a little ill-at-ease in this relationship.

The Channel Tunnel is not altogether typical of large capital projects, but it does bring out the many issues that may arise in which the technical, and the commercial and economic are com- mingled. Even with less complex projects like a power station or a steel works, the same combination is inescapable. As the Sizewell enquiry demonstrates, the questions that arise transcend the purely engineering aspects and can so multiply that a public enquiry into them can go on almost indefinitely. But if the enquiry shows the importance of social and economic factors, it also brings out their interconnection with engineering practicalities. The choice of project must be one that engineers agree to be feasible. But economists, whose subject has been described as 'the logic of choice', would also insist that it should be consistent with other choices and objectives.

To elaborate: modern civilisation rests more heavily on abundant energy than on anything else in the natural world. Most forms of energy – coal and oil in particular and electric power derived from them – are exhaustible: not perhaps immediately, but within a relatively small number of generations. There can be no guarantee that some form of energy other than nuclear power will take their place, although undoubtedly there are alternatives on a relatively small scale and at higher cost. There is therefore a risk whichever way we turn: either that some disaster may flow from the use of nuclear power or that we may fail to develop a more acceptable substitute form of energy on a sufficient scale and endanger the standard of living that we now enjoy. In assessing the risks, we need the best technical information; but we also need the best economic information, for example, as to the penalty in terms of living standards that forgoing nuclear power would involve.

Once again, we are faced with a problem in communication. How does one expert, conversant with the potentialities and risks in one area, convey these to the layman or to another expert conversant with the potentialities and risks in another area? Engineers and economists have to be capable of conveying their respective judgments to one another when each judges by quite different standards and is alert to quite different risks. Yet if they cannot communicate with one another, how can they hope to communicate with the lay public or with their political representatives?

It is true, of course, that not many economists are ever involved in decisions about large capital projects and perhaps the same is true of engineers. But let us take any form of technical change designed to improve industrial efficiency. This is something about which both groups are very much concerned, but which gives rise all the same to much misunderstanding. Engineers who try to improve efficiency think in terms of inputs and outputs. An increase in output per unit of input means a rise in productivity and represents industrial progress. But both inputs and outputs are heterogeneous;

and some reductions in inputs or increases in outputs may be of negligible significance compared with others. In order to make comparisons, one needs a common measure; and the only satisfactory measure is money. Yet one constantly finds pseudo-measures like output per acre or per unit of energy or per head that may be useful checks, but are not true measures of efficiency, as cost in terms of money of unchanged value would be. It is not a lesson easily absorbed by a non-economist that value and efficiency are as dependent on what people elect to spend their money on as they are on the amount of effort that has gone into production.

This points to one of the biggest differences between engineers and economists. Engineers are usually production-orientated; and production stops at the factory door. Economists, on the other hand, tend to be market-orientated and start from sales rather than production. Generally their eyes are on demand, and the need to meet what the consumer wants and will pay for. They do not disregard supply and the forces governing productive efficiency, which exert increasing pressure over time. But they do not as a rule study the technical constraints on production any more than they spend much time explaining why people want the things they want. Their interest is in the human responses to productive opportunities, whereas to the engineer human behaviour is usually of secondary interest. This makes for an element of impatience in the engineer's approach to a project when it excites social or political attack that holds it up. Economists are perhaps more inclined to accept the need to take account of human reactions, since such reactions are the stock-in-trade of their subject.

This difference comes out strongly with technical change. Any new product or process has not only to be tested and proved: it has also to be *sold*. An inventor who makes a novel contribution on the side of production may fail miserably on the commercial side in trying to raise finance or find buyers for his product or process. Solving the engineer's problem does not solve the economic problem of innovation.

What could be done to improve matters? One obvious course would be to equip engineers who mean to spend their lives in industry with a better understanding of the market forces with which they will have to contend. This means broadening and lengthening their course of study to include economics and management. To some extent, there has always been such an option, and it is now more commonly provided and taken. It is still true, however, that

British engineers take shorter courses of study than engineers in most other countries.

Another possibility would be to invite young engineers and economists to collaborate in joint projects as part of their undergraduate course of study, appropriate subjects being suggested by their teachers.

Teaching economics to engineers, however, is not easy. For many of them the subject is too amorphous and seems too much like common sense which they feel they already possess. They are apt to show impatience with the subject, unless it can be expressed in precise mathematical terms, which they take to be characteristic of any discipline claiming to be scientific. The rest may be dismissed as 'just common sense' or 'platitudinous', because it seems too amorphous and lacking in rigour. But as Walter Heller used to put it: 'never underestimate the power of a platitude'. It is precisely the simple aphorisms of economics that are most easily and foolishly ignored: for example, 'there is no such thing as a free lunch' 'you can't have your cake and eat it', 'real costs are opportunities forgone'. On the other hand, the equations and functions that so appeal to the engineer may misrepresent the waywardness and incalculability of human behaviour.

I once asked a colleague who lectured in engineering what he had learned from the course in economics he took as a student. His reply was, 'bad money drives out good'. He was disappointed to be told that even this was by no means always true.

I suspect that it needs a different kind of textbook to get economics across to engineers and that economists are too intent on talking to one another to cater adequately for a specialist audience with the preoccupations of engineers. Equally, engineers don't seem to have learned how to communicate elementary technology to economists. Yet there is a great deal of simple factual information that is invaluable in understanding production problems, but is very hard to acquire except from an unusually articulate engineer.

I can think of several key figures in different countries who were at home both in economics and in engineering: Lord Roberthall, for example, who studied engineering in Australia before turning to economics and serving for fourteen years as the chief economist in British government service; Robert Bryce who came to study economics at Cambridge as an engineer in the 1930s and returned to Canada to become the leading civil servant and government economist of his generation; A.W. Phillips, the Australian who invented the Phillips curve and designed a machine to simulate the workings of the economic system; it, too, kept breaking down. There have also been outstanding engineers – the late Lord Hinton, OM, was a striking example – who regarded engineering and economics as inseparable and took it to be the business of an engineer to find the cheapest and simplest way of producing the results required.

There are fewer cases on record of the reverse process: of economists who have sought to master engineering or at least acquire a working knowledge of engineering terms and processes. One such case is that of Duncan Burn, who was almost alone amongst the economists of an earlier generation in his familiarity with industrial technology. It can be difficult to acquire such a familiarity without frequent contact with engineers or an opportunity to work alongside them for long periods. It was something that happened in war-time, when economists found themselves in production departments. But in peace-time, few universities offer a course for economists on the technology of modern industry.

What economists and engineers need if they are to collaborate is more practice in interrogating one another. Each wants to size up the other's judgment. Each is on the look-out for what may go wrong and is curious to discover the source of the other's misjudgments. They can learn from one another to distinguish eventualities that matter from others that can be dismissed; to bear in mind possibilities their own discipline does not fasten on to; to attach meaning to what begins as jargon.

To my mind, training of engineers (and perhaps economists too) should give far more attention to what is liable to go wrong. Case studies of large-scale projects tend to deal with the planning stage only and cover up the later history when things did not turn out as planned. Few of those connected with such projects want to parade their mistakes. Yet everybody knows that we learn more from our mistakes than from anything else. A good engineer and a good economist could usefully be told plenty of horror stories as part of their training. They need to think as much about the uncertainties as about the certainties.

Contact and communication between the two groups is important not only to improve the usefulness of both but as a means of promoting more rapid economic growth. The junction between the two disciplines, between the technical and the economic aspects of innovation, is the weak spot of the British economy and the sooner we try to train engineers and economists who are at home in each other's discipline, to understand one another, and to work with that understanding, the better for our future as an industrial nation.

Acknowledgement

I am indebted to Dr. J.J. O'Connor and Dr A.M. Cairncross for helpful suggestions in the preparation of this chapter.

12 Public History in the United States: a Retrospective Appraisal
Richard Hewlett

In 1986, historians in the United States marked the tenth anniversary of the public history movement in that country. During that decade, what was initially considered a new and experimental use of history grew into a widely accepted sub-discipline that seems to be making a lasting imprint on the profession in America, and to a lesser extent in Britain and Europe. This paper describes the evolution of the public history movement in the United States and appraises its impact on the profession.

Although the term 'public history' is in use in both the United States and Britain, it has different meanings on opposite sides of the Atlantic. In Britain, the term is often applied only to activities designed to influence public policy and opinion, but it does not include history written for private purposes.[1] In Britain, historians with academic ties seem to write most of the works that are called public history, so that the distinction between public history and traditional history is based on its purpose. In the United States, the term encompasses a broad range of activities and is often employed to cover anything done by an historian, archivist or historic preservationist who is not on the faculty of an academic institution. Thus in America the distinction is largely based on the historian's institutional affiliation.

AMERICAN ORIGINS

The American distinction clearly reflects the evolution of the historical profession in the United States over the last century. Until the 1880s, only a few writers of history in the United States had received formal professional training in history. The most famous American historians of the nineteenth century were gentlemen scholars like Francis Parkman, George Bancroft and John L. Motley. Although Bancroft and Motley studied history at German universities after graduating from Harvard, none of the three relied upon history for his livelihood or had any academic affiliation. A knowledge of history, as distinct from its methodology, was the mark of an educated man, and history was a subject that educated amateurs could read and even write with enjoyment. Amateurs established the American Historical Association in 1884 and dominated it for four decades. History belonged to the educated public and was not the private preserve of a professional élite.[2]

During these same years, however, the larger American universities were establishing graduate schools based on the seminar system adopted with great success in Germany. For graduate training in history, this innovation meant adopting the rigorous rules of evidence and methodology commonly associated, but not always accurately, with Leopold von Ranke. By these standards, only a few teachers at the college level and almost none at the secondary level could qualify as professional historians. For leaders of the new graduate programmes in history in the few American universities that offered them, the setting of professional standards and the upgrading of training for history teachers became a crusade. Influential professors of history, such as George Burton Adams of Yale, William A. Dunning of Columbia and Albert Bushnell Hart of Harvard, began in the 1890s to take over control of the American Historical Association from the less scholarly amateurs. The transition was slow, at least in comparison with the rapid transition that had occurred in the social sciences from amateur to professional control. As late as the First World War, more than two-thirds of the members of the Association were amateurs or teachers at the secondary level.[3]

The imposition of professional standards continued after the war, under the leadership of J. Franklin Jameson, who had taught in graduate history departments at Brown University and the University of Chicago before moving to the Carnegie Institution in Washington, DC, where he became director of research and continued to serve as managing editor of the *The American Historical Review* for two decades. In 1928, he was appointed head of the manuscripts division of the Library of Congress and, as the profession's first Washington lobbyist, led the successful campaign to establish the National Archives. These institutions provided the professional base needed to support the growing graduate programmes in history in the universities.[4]

THE HEGEMONY OF ACADEMIC HISTORY

By the time the Second World War ended, the dreams of these academic historians had been more than fulfilled. Hundreds of war veterans, entitled to a free education under the GI Bill of Rights, flocked to the graduate schools to become historians. Membership in the American Historical Association grew rapidly, and the *Review* had become the journal of record for the profession. The National Archives had become a research centre rivalling the great institutions of Europe. The doctor's degree was now the hallmark of professional competence, and the quality of historical research and writing greatly improved.

In some respects, however, the professional movement was too successful. By the 1950s, the professors had driven most of the amateurs and independent historians from the field. The professional associations no longer seemed to need the financial support of wealthy amateurs, and the academic orientation of the associations left the independents with little reason to continue membership. The result was that academic historians, with their preoccupation with teaching and research, often focused on topics of interest only to themselves and other academics. Although the number of professional journals and scholarly history books published each year in the United States rapidly increased, their contents were directed more to the needs of academics than to those of society at large.

The isolation of academic historians in the United States became more complete in the two decades after the Second World War. While the historians did not change their ways, Americans outside the profession were revising their ideas about the meaning and value of history. The enormous forces for change unleashed in the postwar period made even the early decades of the century seem too remote to serve as a guide for the present. In twentieth-century America, with its consumer-oriented society and planned obsolescence, the past could be rejected as utterly out of date. The rapid accumulation of scientific knowledge could be interpreted as signs of unprecedented progress which was carrying modern society into a world that had little resemblance to the past. The revolution in physics, led by Einstein, as one scholar has put it, 'denied the idea of a universally definitive sequence of objective time' and killed 'any hope of arriving at an ultimate temporal order'.[5]

For many Americans, however, the successive shocks inflicted by the world energy crisis, the Vietnam War and Watergate shook their faith in the nation's destiny as reflected in its history and brought into vogue the popular slogan that history was 'irrelevant'.

As one American historian put it in 1965:

> We are passing through an era of historical nihilism. 'The past does not exist', cries one of the characters in Jean Paul Sartre's *La Nausée*. 'The world we are living in is totally new,' pontificates Robert M. Hutchins. We are, as it were, in flight from history. We have ignored the fact, familiar to us in earlier, more sober times, that only history can explain how the present has come to be what it is.[6]

The postwar 'baby boom' in the United States masked the effects of this popular disillusionment with history. In 1962, the American Historical Association confidently predicted the need for more college teachers, and the average number of PhDs produced annually rose from 319 during most of the 1950s to 881 in 1969 and 1213 in 1973. By the early 1970s, however, the number of undergraduates taking history courses was in decline, graduate school enrolments were in turn depressed, cutbacks were occurring in the number of teaching assistantships, and the number of teaching positions open to new PhDs had sharply fallen. A 1977 study by the American Historical Association showed that of 1605 historians seeking employment, only 52.5 per cent were successful, 37.4 per cent found jobs that were only temporary, and another 32.1 per cent found jobs outside teaching, many in fact in positions unrelated to their historical training. As historical publications on every side proclaimed, the history profession was in a state of crisis.[7]

A PROFESSION IN CRISIS

Some of us who had left academia when we received our doctorates began to sense during the 1960s that the profession was losing touch with the society it was intended to serve and that in some respects we who were working as historians outside the universities were in greater demand than were teachers. With the job crisis of the 1970s, many professors were coming to the same conclusion. Deeply troubled, some of them turned to us for advice. The outsiders for the moment, it seemed, had become the messengers of salvation.

As we met with the faculties of graduate history departments, we found that the professors commonly asked two questions: one, could we find or create jobs for historians who could not get teaching positions; and two, what kind of training should historians have to make them employable in non-teaching positions? The answer to the first question was clearly negative. There was no way that we could suddenly produce jobs in our government agencies, historical societies and corporations for new PhDs trained to be teachers of teachers. All we could suggest were curriculum changes that would make new graduates more employable outside academia.

FIRST DEFINITION

There was, however, a positive response to the crisis of the 1970s. In 1976, Robert Kelly and his colleagues at the University of California in Santa Barbara offered, as they called it, the first 'Graduate Program in Public Historical Studies.' 'Public History', they stated with revolutionary enthusiasm,

> is a many-faceted new field of history. It stands for a convenient way of bringing together a number of endeavors which are not now present in the standard historical curriculum, but which are essential for relating historical skills to the larger society. If history is to be done for the public benefit, which is the hallmark of the new Public History, then components, or sectors, of Public History need to be identified.[8]

Their list of 'sectors' included: Government, Research Organisations, Information Media, Historical Preservation, Historical Interpretation, Archives and Records Management and Teaching of Public History. Carnegie-Mellon University and other institutions were also drafting public history programmes about the same time.

BUILDING AN ORGANISATION

Responses to the job crisis also came from historians outside academia. Most of these were historians in agencies of the federal government, which then employed close to 1000 professional historians. The Second World War had brought scores of first-rate historians into military service, and many of them had remained in federal service after the war. The large staff in the Army historical office continued to produce more than eighty volumes of highly acclaimed history of the US Army in the Second World War. Historians in the Departments of State and Agriculture, the National Archives, the Library of Congress and several federal agencies had produced work that commanded the respect of the profession, but for the most part these historians worked in isolation within their own organisations and had little sense of collegiality with each other or with academics.[9]

Federal historians had a rare opportunity to break out of this strait-jacket of isolation in 1977 after five professional historical organisations joined together to form the National Coordinating Committee for the Promotion of History. The new committee, with its headquarters in the offices of the American Historical Association in Washington, set out to promote historical studies, especially in the schools at all levels, to broaden historical knowledge in the general public, to restore confidence in the discipline and to demonstrate to both government and private industry the advantages of hiring professional historians.[10]

In addition to setting up state committees to organise historians at the local level, the Coordinating Committee established resource groups in several employment areas, one of which was the federal government. This resource group, consisting of a dozen experienced federal historians, quickly started several projects to promote the interests of federal historians and to encourage federal agencies to establish historical programmes. Among other things, the group tried to raise the civil service standards for federal historians, prepared a directory of federal historical offices and activities and organised annual all-day professional conferences for government historians. More than 150 historians attended the first conference in September 1977, and interest and enthusiasm grew rapidly as the once-isolated historians began to work together. In 1979, they formed a formal organisation, the Society for History in the Federal Government, which continued the annual conferences, undertook additional projects, published revisions of the directory and issued a quarterly newsletter, appropriately named *The Federalist.*[11]

At the same time the federal society was in gestation, a broader organization of public historians was in the making. Patterned tentatively on the American Council of Learned Societies, the new National Council on Public History drew on professional associations and private institutions for its support and membership. Several historians who led the way in creating the federal society also helped to create the National Council. The new organisation also had strong support from the graduate history departments, which were interested in training public historians. Especially important was the leadership provided by the University of California at Santa Barbara, which accepted the proposal that *The Public Historian* should become the official journal of the National Council. The journal, plus the three-day professional meetings held annually, gave the new organisation all the trappings of a professional historical society and within a few years won the recognition of the academic community of American historians. This explosion of interest in public history in the last years of the 1970s spawned a panoply of projects and activities that have touched every aspect of the profession at every level in the United States.[12]

PROFESSIONAL STANDING

Now that the three major organisations promoting public history have completed a decade of substantial growth and evolution, it is clear that public history in the United States is more than a fad or temporary diversion from the mainstream of historical studies. If public history is to have a permanent place in the historical discipline, at least in the United States, it seems in order to assess its impact as well as celebrate its success.

Despite what might be called the initial 'success' of the public history movement in America, many historians are still troubled by the very concept of public history. Most of us still have in the back of our minds the image of the classic historian. He or she is a scholar steeped by years of study in one historical era or subject. In the United States he almost certainly has a PhD. Safe in a tenured position, he is free to examine the documentary evidence of his period and to present, either in lectures or historical essays, formal expositions of what he finds new and significant in his research. The products of his labour, he hopes, will be well balanced, judicious, accurate reflections of what he has learned, written perhaps for no other purpose than satisfying his own curiosity or for his own enlightenment. He tries to lift his presentations above mere chronologies of facts to reveal hitherto unseen relationships and insights that will enrich our understanding of the past. And, finally, he attempts to bring his work alive by casting it in good prose with all the style and grace that he can command. We can hope that our profession will never discard this model, for without the classic historian we would soon have no enduring history.[13]

But, we may ask, how does the public historian measure up against the classic model? In answering that question, we must first determine what public history really is. The definition that Robert Kelly and colleagues at Santa Barbara offered (and which has been largely adopted in America) is not very precise. They said that public history is history done for the public benefit; and when we consider the eight sectors that they laid down for public history, we run into some strange applications of the historical discipline. There are historians who spend much of their time with hammer and nails helping to restore historic buildings. Others write sections of environmental impact statements that must be filed with government agencies before new industrial plants can be built.[14]

SKILLS OF THE PUBLIC HISTORIAN

In the light of our model of the classic historian, it is difficult to maintain that these people are producing history. They are not engaged in a formal exposition of history. Many of them have only a master's degree in history, some only a bachelor's. They do not seem to be engaged in the judicious weighing of evidence and the presentation of a new synthesis that enriches the human spirit. Unlike our classic historian, who presumably is free from the diversions and restraints of everyday life, public historians are bound by the demands of their clients and probably by a deadline as well. Furthermore, we may ask, are they doing anything that really demands the special qualifications of an historian?

This question is difficult to answer, but it can be argued that, more often than not, people who are engaged in what may seem to be activities peripheral to history are often making a valuable contribution to society as historians. This conclusion stems, not from a logical extrapolation of some commonly accepted definition of what an historian is, but, rather, from direct observation of what public historians are doing. There is strong evidence that historians are performing services which other specialists can provide neither so well nor so efficiently. Two examples will suffice:

Several years ago, in response to public concern, the US Government decided to assemble in one location all the documents that could be found in federal, state, local and private collections relating to the possible biological effects of radioactive fallout from nuclear weapon testing.[15] It seemed reasonable to assign this project to a corporation that had established itself over many years as pre-eminent in the study of the biological effects of radiation. The corporation in turn selected experienced engineers to visit the record repositories and select documents relevant to the new collection. After visiting eight or ten repositories, the engineering team came up with a modest list of documents. It did not take government officials long to determine that the listing had hardly begun to identify all the relevant documents. So the government brought in a corporation specialising in historical research to make a new survey. These historians in time identified hundreds of thousands of documents in more than a hundred repositories. So mammoth is the inventory that six years later not all of the documents have yet been processed and made available to the public.[16]

How can this difference in performance be explained? Certainly it cannot be attributed to deficiencies in the competence or diligence of the engineers who did the original search. Rather, the knowledge and skills of the historians made the difference.

In the first place, the engineers were not likely to know where the pertinent documents might be found, so they limited their search to the collections of organisations that were obviously involved in activities related to weapon testing or the study of radiation effects. The historians, however, saw the much larger network of government and private research organisations that were likely involved. They also found that the records of one collection identified other collections that would be useful.

Secondly, the engineers had no experience in searching the great mass of records that find their way into the documentation of modern scientific enterprises. Overwhelmed by the magnitude of the task, the engineers thought it reasonable to confine themselves to the most obvious files and then only to sample them to try to locate high concentrations of pertinent materials. The historians, from their knowledge of how large record collections are organised, could identify many more record groups of possible value, and they knew how to scan thousands of pages within these groups quickly and accurately.

Third, the engineers tended to identify only those documents that contained specific words and phrases related to radiation effects. The historians were able to see the more subtle implications in seemingly unrelated documents, and sometimes these proved more revealing than those with explicit connotations. Historians were superbly, if not uniquely, suited to this task.

Historians have also performed well in the area of legal research. Law firms, particularly those involved in class action suits that may result in judgments in the millions of dollars, frequently find the need for in-depth research in historical records. This kind of research has customarily been assigned to law clerks or paralegals. But law firms have found that this approach sometimes results in the kinds of deficiencies that occurred in using engineers in the radiation effects project. The paralegals are not used to working in large volumes of records. They often find the work demeaning rather than challenging. More important, they are often too literal in evaluating the relevance of documents, while historians are more apt to see the less obvious implications and the relationships between documents. Finally, and this is one of the crosses historians still have to bear, law firms can find historians who will do this work at hourly rates that paralegals would scorn.

So vast is the domain staked out by the public historians that it would be futile further to pursue this assessment of their work in the more peripheral aspects of their craft. It is perhaps more revealing to examine the accomplishments of public historians in areas considered most central to the discipline.

GOVERNMENT SERVICE

The first of these is government service, a role of the historian that has become traditional in both the United States and Europe. Going back at least to the First World War, the military services have from time to time tried to draw from the history of one conflict the lessons that will avoid the same errors in the next. What has changed is that professional historians have gradually replaced military officers in preparing these studies. Likewise, historians have earned a key role in assembling, editing and publishing state papers, particularly diplomatic records. Only since the Second World War, however, have professional historians been employed to write institutional histories of government agencies and executive departments. Most often, such histories have been commissioned by agencies created since 1945, and for that reason these institutional histories also describe the evolution of policy decisions that are still of public concern. No better example can be found than the magnificent volumes on the British atomic energy programme written by Professor Margaret Gowing of Oxford University.[17]

Histories of this calibre, both in Britain and the United States, have done much to establish the historian as a professional in the eyes of government officials.[18] But they are, and perhaps always will be, the exception rather than the rule. There is an ever-increasing number of federal agencies in the United States which have historical offices, but most of them do not support research and writing leading to major historical works of the kind that our classic historian would recognise.

Many federal historians work alone in their agencies and they face severe handicaps. They have no colleagues with whom they can share problems or ideas. Once their superiors discover their analytical and writing skills, they are often burdened with drafting speeches or doing other chores that have little relation to history. Many are only part-time historians and spend what few hours they have for historical work preparing administrative histories or annual summaries of activities. Often employed at junior civil service grades and with little administrative experience, the lone historian in a government agency may have little, if any, professional standing and no practical way to establish his identity as an historian.[19]

Even when the staff consists of several people, agency historians may face similar obstacles. Often their skills in historical research are employed to produce data for budget hearings or operational reports. At most, they may hope to produce short articles or studies of agency programmes sufficiently removed from current concerns to allay the anxieties of agency officials. In many agencies, the possibility of writing a serious institutional history or providing historical perspective for a current policy issue seems hopelessly remote.

The historian's role in policy-making is a subject that has received considerable attention in the United States. It is easy to cite glaring examples of policies that failed because government officials did not understand the historical background of the problem they were facing. And it is abundantly clear that government officials continually use, or misuse, history to justify or rationalise their actions, whether or not they have the services of a professional historian. Such observations suggest that the historian should have a vital role in government decision-making.[20]

Historians who have been studying the decision process in the federal government, however, have quite rightly pointed to the dangers of superficial analysis and particularly of faulty analogies to earlier events. These historians, perhaps with more realism than some of us want to admit, assume that government officials will continue in the future to use 'history' without the help of historians. Under such circumstances, fear of the faulty analogy threatens to preclude any attempt to use the past to understand the present.[21]

In pressing home this point, historians may be doing both the profession and the nation a disservice. They may be rejecting the possibility that good historical analysis can lead to sound results. Part of the problem is that some of the doubters have little conception of how historians are already contributing to the policy process. They may envision the historian participating as an equal with cabinet officials or agency heads in the highest councils of government, perhaps even with the power of veto if the historical assumptions underlying a policy decision appear faulty.

The role that government historians are playing is more modest, less dramatic and probably much more practical. In fact, it almost always happens that as federal historians gain intellectual control over the historical records of their agencies, they are called upon to prepare histories of current policy issues. True, these studies are often narrowly circumscribed by the shortage of time or the presumed need for secrecy. Often they are never published, and they may be ignored or misused. But the alternative is almost never 'no history' but 'history without historians'.[22]

What some critics fail to understand or appreciate is the substantial commitment that the federal historian must make to achieve the status of a participant in the policy process. It can take years of lonely persistence to gain access to policy papers, skillful administrative gymnastics to survive in the bureaucratic jungle and extraordinary patience in waiting for the day of recognition to come.

Would our classic historian make a career commitment to a federal history project in the face of such limitations? Probably not. Have most public historians, or even federal historians, been willing to make a similar commitment? Only a small percentage have in the past, but the numbers are increasing as the climate for professional work improves. The Society for History in the Federal Government and the national professional historical associations in the United States are all helping to bring the federal historian back into the fold and, most important of all, to secure his professional identity in the federal service.

CONTRACT HISTORY

If the government historian is working on the fringes of the profession, those who have ventured into commercial enterprise may be considered intrepid, if not foolhardy, explorers of unknown territory. It is true that, over the last forty years, a number of American historians have written impressive histories of large corporations.[23] But most of these scholars have been professors who have done their work from the outside, supported by their university salaries while on sabbatical and not by the corporations they were writing about. Such a relationship can still result in good history, but it is not the only possible arrangement.

Ultimately more interesting, and perhaps more useful, is a direct relationship between the client and the historian. Just as governments can benefit from the services of historians, so can private corporations, law firms, medical research institutions, and professional societies.[24]

In some respects, the historian's relationship with a private organisation can be more direct than with the government and thus easier to define. A private company, unlike the government, can hire any historian of its own choosing willing to do the work, and the relationship can be defined with a short letter of agreement or even with a handshake. The scope of the work, the product and the time frame in which it is to be completed can be clearly specified. Once completed, the product is the property of the client, and the historian moves on to other work.

As a practical matter, however, few historians can make it on their own in contract work. Good historical research and writing take time, and while the individual is working for two years or more for one client, his other prospects fade away. Clients, particularly those with long-term projects, fear that unforeseen exigencies may prevent the individual historian from completing the work. Not many historians have the practical business experience needed to administer contracts. One solution is to create a firm of professional historians who have the broad range of talents necessary to run a corporation and the specialised knowledge required to do historical research in several fields.

THE HISTORICAL RESEARCH CORPORATION

The historical research corporation is a new entity in the profession in the United States, but it has already demonstrated that it has many advantages over the single scholar. The corporation can offer clients a broad range of services in all the sectors of public history. It can provide these services in a business environment familiar to clients. With staff in reserve, it can insure the client against the hazards of relying on a single individual. It can, with luck, increase the size of its staff in order to meet the needs of many clients simultaneously in different localities. Perhaps most important of all, historical research corporations seem likely in the future to offer employment as professionals to a significant number of public historians.

The corporate movement in public history in the United States is little more than five years old, and hence any prognosis must be tentative. On the positive side, there appears to be an enormous untapped potential for historical research and writing in the private sector. The demand seems to be growing steadily for historical services in all areas of public history. For the most part, clients are surprised and delighted to see what historians can produce.

On the negative side, while historians can see the huge potential for services to private institutions, it has never occurred to most prospective clients that historians could be of any value at all. Even when a few executives do find the possibility interesting, they have little idea of how the historical firm might go about its work, what services it might offer or how to judge the value of those services. The result is that years may elapse between the first expression of interest and the signing of a contract. One obstacle to agreement is often the client's sense of values. Some corporations think nothing of spending vast sums for newspaper advertising but find that they cannot 'afford' five thousand dollars to put their historical records in order.

It seems, then, that firms offering historical services face a monumental task of educating the public to understand the value of historical work. Yet it is by offering these services, by responding to the demands of the market, that the educational process will be accomplished. And, unless we agree with our classic historian that history with a purpose is no history at all, must we not admit that it is a legitimate, if not obligatory, function of the historian to make historical talents and knowledge available for the benefit of society at large?

Seen from the inside, the history firm has its heartening and discouraging aspects. One of the joys of working in such a company is offering professional employment to talented historians who, for no fault of their own, have no chance of pursuing an academic career. Many of the projects are stimulating and exciting, but much of the work is drab and unimaginative. Salaries are low, if not by academic standards, then by those that prevail in the commercial marketplace, and that is where history firms work. For historians, professional status still depends on publications, and all too often the decision to publish rests solely with the client. It is often difficult to match the client's requirements with the specialities of available staff; and despite the accomplishments of public history programs in the universities, too many graduates are still being trained to be teachers rather than public historians.

We may ask ourselves what it is that drives public historians to leave the comfortable and cultivated surroundings of the classic historian for the unknowns, frustrations and even the dangers of the outside world. Originally it may have been economic necessity, but many who have chosen to follow these uncharted paths to historical study have done so out of a sense of adventure. Some, no doubt, are seeking to assuage the nagging doubt whether historical work, in the end, has any social utility at all. Most seem motivated by the conviction that many of the terrifying problems facing the world today can never be resolved without a sound understanding of how they arose in the first place. Only by addressing the problems of our society will we know whether the conviction is sound.

APPRAISAL OF CURRICULUM

The curriculum changes that were commonly proposed by Professor Kelly and others in the 1970s focused on new skills more than on historical knowledge. Those of us who had directed history projects outside the academy saw the need to break away from the tradition of solitary research and writing, because many of our projects were too large and on too short a time schedule to make it possible for one historian to do all the research and writing. We thought public historians should also have some practice in working with scholars in other disciplines, and to that end we urged that public historians take at least a few courses in the social sciences or public or business administration. Because much of the work coming to public historians in the United States then seemed to be related to contemporary history and science and technology, we thought that historians might well have some training in those areas. Above all else, however, we needed historians who would take non-academic work seriously, who understood the inflexibility of deadlines in working under a contract and who could quickly adapt to working on a subject not of their own choosing. Strangely enough, these attitudes toward research and writing were often the rarest characteristics in recent history graduates.

Thus public history programmes usually stress practical training in a variety of tasks to develop skills that go far beyond those required for conventional library-centred research and formal exposition. Students learn how to work effectively in team research with other historians and specialists in other disciplines. Most programmes require students to arrange an internship in a local government agency or business, where they can learn first-hand how to work with clients. In addition to conventional graduate history courses, students are encouraged to take courses in other subjects such as public or business administration, planning and statistical analysis.

The distinctive feature of public history is that it is project- or issue-oriented rather than author-oriented. That is, the nature of the product – its size, shape and content, the completion date and the ultimate disposition of the product – are determined not by the author, but by the client. For this reason, public history curricula often seem more concerned with developing skills in interpersonal relations and management than with conventional research and writing.

A guide recently published by the National Council on Public History listed seventy-eight American colleges and universities offering courses in public history.[25] Of these, fifty offer programmes leading to undergraduate or graduate degrees. Impressive as these numbers are, the spectrum of courses offered may give us reason for concern. Thirty-six of these institutions offer courses in archives and records management; twenty-nine in historic preservation; twenty in operation of historical museums; but only twelve offer courses in editing and publishing, and only eight in policy analysis (or what is called public history in Britain).

The statistics suggest that teachers of public history have not yet moved very far beyond the initial response to the crisis of the 1970s, when the principal concern was to find jobs for new graduates. Those of us who are out in the market-place see a highly dynamic, rapidly changing situation, in which new ideas for applications of public history are bubbling up around us. From this perspective, the course offerings in public history seem a bit stale and unimaginative. Teachers of public history need to take a new look at the subject and begin to plan for the future.

It is too early to say whether the curricula now offered in the universities will establish a lasting learning pattern in the discipline of history. Certainly, conventional historians have reservations about some aspects of the programme, and perhaps even some of those teaching public history in the universities feel uncomfortable with some of the results.

In the long run, we can judge the curriculum only by the performance of graduates of public history programmes. On the one hand, many graduates have acquired a certain mind-set and orientation that make it relatively easy for them to adjust to the rough-and-tumble environment of a history services corporation. They have skills that are directly applicable in the work that public historians do. Graduates from conventional history programmes often have much to unlearn before they can be useful. On the other hand, public history graduates too often lack the historical perspective and the fundamental skills in evaluation of evidence, imaginative synthesis and critical writing that we expect from professional historians.

These observations may suggest that too much stress is being placed on 'cook-book' skills at the expense of solid training in the discipline of history. Perhaps the solution lies in incorporating into conventional graduate programmes the kinds of learning experiences that public history programmes are now offering. It is probably an exaggeration to claim, as Professor Kelly and his colleagues at Santa Barbara did, that they were defining a new field of history. Public history may only constitute a new set of skills which increasing numbers of historians will find useful in the future.

PUBLIC HISTORIANS AND SOCIETY

A special problem for public historians is that they must write about the society in which they live. It is conceivable, though unlikely, that a public historian might be requested to write a study that would involve understanding the effect of mortmain legislation in medieval England. To prepare an accurate and useful paper, the public historian would have to learn enough about thirteenth-century England to place the mortmain statute in its proper perspective. But he or she would also have to be certain that what was written about the subject was pertinent to the client's needs. Most historians, of course, must learn to live in two societies at the same time, but the conventional historian can decide for himself which aspects of his research he wishes to present to his readers. For the public historian, that decision may be dictated by the client.

The public historian is more often than not placed in a predicament that medievalists do not ever have to face: having to write history about the recent or immediate past. Here the public historian has only one society to consider, but because he or she is so much a part of it, it is the most difficult one to interpret. How he can maintain objectivity in writing about his own times is a matter that continues to concern most public historians.

The imposition of the client's needs and interests can make things difficult for the public historian. The client's statement of the assignment can presuppose a faulty interpretation of history. Then the historian faces the difficult task of 're-educating' the client before he can proceed with his study. Sometimes the assignment confines the historian to the most pedestrian aspects of the subject, while the fresh insights that he discovers may fall outside the scope of his paper and cannot be used.

STANDARDS AND ETHICS

With clients looking over their shoulders, public historians have from the beginning been concerned about what some have called a question of ethics. If the client has so much to say about the product, how can the historian protect himself against client demands that will undermine the integrity of his history?

Fortunately, public historians have not had to face these ethical questions alone. In the last few years, several historical associations in the United States have discussed professional standards openly and frankly. In the spring of 1986, the American Historical Association issued a draft revision of the ethics statement adopted in 1975. The revised statement contains an extensive section on the

'Rights and Responsibilities of the Historian in Society'. This section deals exclusively with the 'responsibilities distinctive to public history'.[26]

The Society for History in the Federal Government was the first to draft such a statement for public historians. In 1985, the Society adopted a set of principles and guidelines that define the mutual responsibilities of the historian and his administrative supervisor and what each may expect of the other. The statement acknowledges that many persons called 'historians' in the federal government have no professional training and that not all of the work produced by federal historians is history in the classic sense. But the statement does urge that well-trained historians be treated as professionals and that administrators make full use of their talents, not only in writing serious history, but also in contributing to policy studies.[27]

As public historians move into new kinds of assignments, they inevitably encounter new situations that may threaten the integrity of their work. The nature of the threat, however, is not essentially different from that faced by historians in the past. For both public and academic historians, instances of plagiarism or falsification or suppression of evidence are rare. A truly professional historian is no more likely to buckle under the improper demands of a client than he is to similar proposals by the publisher of his books or to the dean who will recommend him for a tenured appointment.

For convenience, we tend to speak of these matters as 'ethical' problems, but in most instances, they involve definitions of mutual responsibility and expectations on the part of historians and their clients. It is surprising how often prospective clients go out of their way to respect the integrity and independence of the historian. Attempts by clients to 'buy' an historian's endorsement of their own version of 'history' are probably rare, and these proposals can be quickly rejected.

There are practical ways to avoid conflicts between the client's interests and the integrity of the historian. One is to reach agreement at the start that the historian's product will be a manuscript and not a published work. Within the constraints on scope and schedule imposed by the client, the historian is free to select material from all available sources and to come to his own conclusions. If, at completion, the work is acceptable to the client, it can be published as the work of the historian. If the historian cannot accept the client's revisions of the manuscript, then the client cannot use the historian's name on any publication using his work.

A second way to avoid difficulties is to acknowledge that not everything an historian produces is history. Thus the historian does not have to insist that an historical preface for a budget presentation be anything more than factually accurate. It need not be exhaustively researched, fully documented and include a careful weighing of all the evidence pro and con. Nor is it necessary to treat a ceremonial address for an institutional anniversary as a formal piece of historical work. Yet the production of such materials can be an appropriate use of the historian's skills.

Recently, some public historians have encountered problems in working with members of the legal profession. Lawyers in the United States have found the talents of historians especially useful in research for class-action suits against the federal or state governments. When the same historians are asked to appear in court as expert witnesses, some attorneys have asked them to suppress evidence unfavourable to the attorney's case or to be evasive in cross-examination. Historians have been successful in rejecting these suggestions, but it would seem desirable to include relations between lawyers and historians in our statements of principles and guidelines.[28]

Ultimately, the public historian must face the fact that his career is determined by the needs and interests of his clients. Presumably, as one acquires stature as a public historian, there will be increasing opportunity to select the more interesting and significant topics, but it may be difficult to build the sort of coherent careers that traditional historians have enjoyed. There is one further complication: the public historian is likely to be required to work on a wide variety of subjects, some of which will be completely new to him. This situation can be frightening or stimulating, depending on the personal inclinations of the historian.

Over the long term, this situation may not prove tenable. Either public historians will, in time, have to limit their portfolios to a few specialties, or they will have to work closely with academic historians who have done extensive research on matters related to their clients' assignments. We can hope that the profession would move toward the second option. Academic historians should be included more often as consultants in public history projects to provide background, perspective and valid analogies for public historians who are struggling with difficult and complex topics.

The public historian has a perspective on his profession and his world that is quite different from the traditional view. Certainly, the public historian cannot aspire to the idyllic career that he imagines some academic historians enjoy. Nor can he expect that his way of doing history will ever become the norm for the profession. He may, however, find consolation in the fact that what he produces not only gives him personal satisfaction, but also has a positive and measurable value in the society in which he lives.

NOTES

1. Avner Offer, 'Using the past in Britain: retrospect and prospect', *The Public Historian*, VI (1984) pp. 17–20; Gary S. Messinger, 'The liberal arts in Britain: some lessons for America', *Academe*, LXIX (1983) pp. 21–7.
2. Michael Kraus and Davis D. Joyce, *The Writing of American History* (Norman: University of Oklahoma Press, 1985), pp. 97–108, 136–47; John Higham, *History: Professional Scholarship in America* (Baltimore: Johns Hopkins University Press, 1983).
3. Joan Hoff Wilson, 'Is the historical profession an "endangered species"?', *The Public Historian*, II (1980) pp. 4–9.
4. Ruth Anna Fisher and William L. Fox, eds, *J. Franklin Jameson: A Tribute* (Washington, DC: Catholic University of America Press, 1965); Victor Gondos, Jr, *J. Franklin Jameson and the Birth of the National Archives, 1906–1926* (Philadelphia: University of Pennsylvania Press, 1981).
5. John T. Marcus, *Heaven, Hell and History: A Survey of Man's Faith in History from Antiquity to the Present* (New York: Macmillan, 1967), pp. 233, 235, as quoted in Stephen Vaughn, *The Vital Past: Writings on the Uses of History* (Athens: University of Georgia Press, 1985), p. 4.
6. Donald M. Dozer, 'History as Force', *Pacific Historical Review*, (November 1965), as quoted in Vaughn, *The Vital Past*, pp. 266–7.
7. Arnita Jones, 'The National Coordinating Committee: Programs and Possibilities,' *The Public Historian*, I (1978) pp. 49–52.
8. Editors' Preface, *The Public Historian*. I (1978) pp. 6–7.
9. Richard G. Hewlett, 'The practice of history in the Federal Government', *The Public Historian*, I (1978) pp. 29–36. The Office of the Chief of Military History, Department of the Army, has produced eighty-three volumes in the series, *The United States Army in World War II*. Samuel E. Morison, the distinguished American historian and reserve rear admiral during the war, wrote a series of volumes of combat history for the US Navy. The Department of State continued publication of its series of documents on *The Foreign Relations of the United States*. Wayne D. Rasmussen directed historical research at the Department of Agriculture for almost fifty years and is recognised as the dean of agricultural history in the United States. Richard G. Hewlett and his colleagues at the Atomic Energy Commission completed two volumes

of the official history of that agency during the 1960s.

10. Arnita Jones, 'The National Coordinating Committee', p. 52.
11. Records documenting the formation of the National Coordinating Committee and the Society for History in the Federal Government are held by the American Historical Association in Washington, DC.
12. Records documenting the formation of the National Council on Public History are in the archives of the Council and are held by the Executive Secretary at West Virginia University, Morgantown, W. Va.
13. Philip D. Jordan, 'The usefulness of useless knowledge', in Vaughn, *The Vital Past*, pp. 45–54.
14. For examples of other applications of public history, see: Ronald W. Johnson, 'The historian and cultural resource management', *The Public Historian*, III (1981) pp. 43–51; Donald H. Ewalt, Jr and Gary R. Kremer, 'The historian as preservationist', ibid III (1981) pp. 5–22; Edward Weldon, 'Archives and the practice of history', ibid., IV (1982) pp. 49–58; Paul Soifer, 'The litigation historian: objectivity, responsibility, and sources', ibid., V (1983) pp. 47–62.
15. US Congress, House Committee on Interstate and Foreign Commerce and Senate Committee on the Judiciary, *Joint Hearings on Health Effects of Low-Level Radiation*, 96 Cong., 1 sess., Serial 96–41 (Washington: Government Printing Office, 1979), pp. 71–85; US Congress, House Committee on Interstate and Foreign Commerce, *Hearing on Low-Level Radiation Effects on Health*, 96 Cong., 1 sess., Serial 96–129 (Washington: Government Printing Office, 1979), pp. 7, 11, 157, 164.
16. History Associates Incorporated, *Guide to Archival Collections Relating to Radioactive Fallout from Nuclear Weapon Testing*, 4th edition, November 1985. Copies available from History Division, US Department of Energy, Washington, DC.
17. Margaret Gowing, *Britain and Atomic Energy, 1939–1945* (London: Macmillan, 1964); Margaret Gowing, *Independence and Deterrence: Britain and Atomic Energy. 1945–1952*, Volume I *Policy Making*, Volume II *Policy Execution* (London: Macmillan, 1974). The following are examples of federal institutional histories in the United States: Richard G. Hewlett and Oscar E. Anderson, Jr, *The New World, 1939–1946*, Volume I of A History of the US Atomic Energy Commission (University Park, Pa.: Pennsylvania State University Press. 1962); Richard G. Hewlett and Francis Duncan, *Atomic Shield, 1947–1952*, Volume II of A History of the US Atomic Energy Commission (University Park, Pa.: Pennsylvania State University Press, 1969); Richard G. Hewlett and Francis Duncan, *Nuclear Navy, 1939–1962* University of Chicago Press, 1975); George T. Mazuzan and J. Samuel Walker, *Controlling the Atom: The Beginnings of Nuclear Regulation. 1946–1962* (Berkeley: University of California Press, 1984); Courtney C. Brooks, James M. Grimwood and Lloyd S. Swenson, Jr, *Chariots for Apollo: A History of Manned Lunar Spacecraft* (Washington: Government Printing Office, 1979).
18. Paul J. Scheips, moderator, 'Roundtable: what is a federal historian?', *The Public Historian*, II (1980) pp. 84–100; Jack M. Holl, 'The New

Washington Monument: history in the Federal Government', ibid., VII (1985) pp. 9–20.

19. Richard G. Hewlett, 'Government history: writing from the inside', in Frank B. Evans and Harold T. Pinkett, eds, *Research in the Administration of Public Policy* (Washington, DC: Howard University Press, 1975).

20. George O. Kent, 'Clio the tyrant: historical analogies and the meaning of history', in Vaughn, *The Vital Past*, pp. 302–10; Otis L. Graham, 'Uses and misuses of history: roles in policy making', *The Public Historian*, V (1983) pp. 5–19; Peter N. Stearns, 'History and policy analysis: toward maturity,' ibid., IV (1983) pp. 5–29.

21. Ernest R. May, *'Lessons of the Past': The Use and Misuse of History in America* (New York: Oxford University Press, 1973).

22. Anna K. Nelson, 'History without historians,' in American Historical Association, *AHA Newsletter*, XVI (February 1978).

23. For an extensive list of histories of American corporations see W. David Lewis and Wesley Phillips Newton, 'The writing of corporate history', *The Public Historian*, III (1981) pp. 84–5. This entire issue of *The Public Historian* is devoted to business history.

24. George David Smith and Laurence E. Steadman, 'Present value of corporate history', *Harvard Business Review*, LIX (1981) pp. 164–73.

25. *Public History Education in America: A Guide* (National Council on Public History, 1986).

26. American Historical Association, 'Draft ethics statement, April 1986', copies available from the American Historical Association, Washington, DC.

27. Society for History in the Federal Government, *Principles and Standards for Federal Historical Programs*, reprinted in *The Public Historian*, VIII (1986) pp. 60–3. Martin Reuss, 'Federal Historians: Ethics and Responsibility in the Bureaucracy,' ibid., pp. 13–20.

28. J. Morgan Kousser, 'Are expert witnesses whores? Reflections on objectivity in scholarship and expert witnessing', *The Public Historian*, VI (1984) pp. 5–11.

13 Postscript
Sir Michael Howard

Si monumentum requiris, circumspice. This is the advice which we can give not only to the reader, but to Margaret Gowing herself on the completion of this volume. The Festschrift is a pleasant academic institution enabling pupils and colleagues to express their gratitude to a revered teacher by showing how effectively they can practice the skills in which he or she has excelled. This volume, however, is something more. Every one of the contributions in this book has dealt with that social dimension of scientific activity to which Margaret Gowing drew attention, and whose importance she constantly emphasised, both by teaching and example. It would be untrue to say that, but for her, these contributions could not have been written. Good work was being done and would have been done in the field, even if she had never held the Oxford Chair. But the emphasis she gave to this area of study, the leadership and encouragement she provided for scholars working within it, and her tireless missionary activity in drawing the attention both of historians and of scientists to its importance gave the subject an entirely new significance, in the eyes both of the scholarly world and increasingly of the general public as a whole.

It is worth reiterating the message conveyed both by Margaret Gowing herself and by the contributors to this book. Science is not simply knowledge, but activity, and a social activity. In the seventeenth and eighteenth centuries, there did exist scientists of independent means engaged in pure speculation of a kind which could, like the speculations of other 'philosophers' (and there are still universities where science is called 'Natural Philosophy') be considered in isolation or as part of a social unrelated 'history of ideas'. In dealing with such thinkers, a history of science consisting simply in descriptions of what scientists thought, or how their ideas developed out of one another, had a certain validity. But by the nineteenth century, such figures were exceptional and by the twentieth, they had virtually ceased to exist. Science had become a highly sophisticated activity responsive to social needs. It barely existed outside university and government laboratories, and it required for its pursuit a good deal of money. That money was mainly provided, directly or indirectly, by governments who were increasingly conscious of the importance of scientific knowledge for

239

the wealth and security of the State in an era of intense international competition. In the nineteenth and even more in the twentieth centuries, scientific knowledge was directly related to economic and military power. Germany, achieving belated national unity in a period of economic and industrial 'take off', understood this lesson and applied it diligently. Britain, comfortably enjoying a dominance established in the early industrial era was, disastrously, the last to learn it. We may lament the degree to which the pursuit of scientific knowledge has been fuelled by the search for greater military security, but it has been a fact of life for the past hundred years, and it is with such facts that historians have to be concerned.

The History of Science as a discipline touches and draws strength from at least three related fields of knowledge: the natural and applied sciences themselves; history; and, not least important, philosophy, with which it is most closely bonded in the University of Cambridge. In Oxford, thanks to Margaret Gowing's activity, it has flourished with the active support of the natural scientists, but more especially of the historians. The scientific movement in the seventeenth century is now a well established subject of study in the Oxford History School, while the cultural history of Victorian Britain, and the central part which scientific thought played in its development is increasingly popular both with research students and undergraduates. The Wellcome Unit for the History of Medicine and the Museum of the History of Science provide foci of special expertise. Finally, the traditional links between Oxford and the metropolis have made Oxford the natural centre for the study of relations between science and government. All these opportunities Professor Gowing has exploited to the full, and she leaves behind her a merry blaze of activity in all departments.

Thanks to her work the subject will continue to flourish in all its associated faculties in Oxford, that of History most of all: the list of contributors to this volume gives a fair indication of the talent available to teach it. The time when the History of Science could be regarded as a marginal and expendable subject, of concern only to specialists, is now safely past. Margaret Gowing has changed our awareness; and the change is irreversible.

A List of the Published Work of Margaret Gowing

I. Books and Chapters in Books

(joint author with W.K. Hancock) *British War Economy* (London: HMSO, 1949; 2nd, revised edition, 1975)

(joint author with E.L. Hargreaves) *Civil Industry and Trade* (London: HMSO, 1952)

'Introductory: the growth of Government action and the ups and downs of the family', in Sheila Ferguson and Hilde Fitzgerald, *Studies in the Social Services* (London: HMSO, 1954)

Britain and Atomic Energy, 1939–1945 (London: Macmillan, 1964)

Dossier secret des relations atomiques entre alliés 1939–1948 (Paris: Plon, 1965)

(joint author with A.H.K. Slater) 'Britain in the Second World War', in Robin Higham (ed.), *A Guide to the Sources of Military History* (Berkeley: University of California Press, 1971) pp. 512–41

Independence and Deterrence. Britain and Atomic Energy. 1945–1952 (assisted by Lorna Arnold), vol. I, *Policy Making* (London: Macmillan, 1974)

Independence and Deterrence. Britain and Atomic Energy. 1945–1952 (assisted by Lorna Arnold), vol. II, *Policy Execution* (London: Macmillan, 1974)

'Anglo-French economic collaboration up to the outbreak of the Second World War', in *Les Relations franco-britanniques de 1935 à 1939* (Paris: CNRS, 1975) pp. 179–88

'Anglo-French economic collaboration before the Second World War: oil and coal', in *Les Relations franco-britanniques de 1935 à 1939* (Paris: CNRS, 1975) pp. 263–75

(joint author with Lorna Arnold) *The Atomic Bomb* (London: Butterworth, 1979)

'Britain, America and the bomb', in David Dilks (ed.), *Retreat from Power. Studies in Britain's Foreign Policy of the Twentieth Century*, Vol. II, *After 1939* (London: Macmillan, 1981) pp. 120–37

'Does the timing of scientific discovery matter?', in John Kendrew and Julian Shelley (eds), *Priorities in Research* (*Excerpta Medica*, 1983) pp. 3–33

'The history of science, politics and political economy', in Pietro Corsi and Paul Weindling (eds), *Information Sources in the History of Science and Medicine* (London: Butterworth, 1983) pp. 99–115

'Niels Bohr and nuclear weapons', in A.P. French and P.J. Kennedy (eds), *Niels Bohr. A Centenary Volume* (Cambridge Mass.: Harvard University Press, 1985) pp. 266–77; the same essay appears, in slightly different forms, in A. Boserop, L. Christensen and O. Nathan (eds), *The Challenge of Nuclear Armaments: Essays Dedicated to Niels Bohr and his Appeal for an Open World* (Copenhagen: Rhodos, 1985); and in J. de Boer, E. Dal and O. Ulfbeck (eds), *The Lessons of Quantum Theory* (Amsterdam: Elsevier, 1986)

'Nuclear weapons and the "special relationship"', in Roger Louis and Hedley Bull (eds), *'The Special Relationship': Anglo-American Relations since 1945* (Oxford: Clarendon Press, 1986) 117–28

II. Special Lectures

(Inaugural Lecture) *What's Science to History or History to Science?* (Oxford: Clarendon Press, 1975)

(Wilkins Lecture) 'Science, technology and education: England in 1870', *Notes and Records of the Royal Society of London*, XXXII (1977) pp. 71–90; also in the *Oxford Review of Education*, IV (1978) pp. 3–17

(Bernal Lecture) *Science and Politics* (London: Birkbeck College, 1977)

(Rede Lecture) *Reflections on Atomic Energy History* (Cambridge University Press, 1978); also in the *Bulletin of Atomic Scientists*, XXXV (1979) pp. 51–4

(Annual Lecture to the Institution of Nuclear Engineers) 'Principalities and nuclear power: the origins of reactor systems', *Nuclear Engineer*, XXIII (1982) pp. 70–6)

(Spencer Lecture) 'An old and intimate relationship', in Vernon Bogdanor (ed.), *Science and Politics. The Herbert Spencer Lectures 1982* (Oxford: Clarendon Press, 1984) pp. 52–69; also in A. Boserop, L. Christensen and O. Nathan (eds), *The Challenge of Nuclear Armaments: Essays Dedicated to Niels Bohr and his Appeal for an Open World* (Copenhagen: Rhodos, 1986)

(University of Southampton and Central Electricity Generating Board Lecture) *How Nuclear Power Began* (University of Southampton, 1987)

III. Articles in Learned Journals

'The organisation of manpower in Britain during the Second World War', *Journal of Contemporary History*, VII (1972) pp. 147–67

'La mobilisation économique', *Revue d'histoire de la deuxième guerre mondiale* (1973) pp. 11–22

'The Contemporary Scientific Archives Centre', *Archives*, XI (1973) pp. 73–5

'A refuge for scientists' writings', *Nature*, CCLXXVII (1979) p. 7

'The Contemporary Scientific Archives Centre', *Notes and Records of the Royal Society of London*, XXXIV (1979) pp. 123–31

'Science, space and survival' (speech given at the 25th anniversary, Women of the Year Luncheon, autumn 1980), *Science and Public Policy*, VIII (1981) pp. 155–6

'Modern public records: selection and access. The report of the Wilson Committee', *Social History*, VI (1981) pp. 351–7

'British modern public records: a vital raw material', *Archives and Manuscripts: the Journal of the Australian Society of Archivists*, IX (1981)

'Les savants nucléaires dans la tourmente', *Echos du groupe CEA*, No. 1 (1984) pp. 12–15

IV. Biographical Essays

'Reminiscences in Whitehall', in *Essays Presented to Sir Keith Hancock* (Melbourne: *Historical Studies*, XIII, 1968)

'Dr E. Bretscher CBE. Obiturary', *Nature*, CCXLIV (1973) pp. 319–20

'Richard Morris Titmuss. A memoir', *Proceedings of the British Academy*, LXI (1975) pp. 401–28

'Sir Charles Galton Darwin', *Dictionary of National Biography, 1961–1970* (Oxford: Clarendon Press, 1981) pp. 272–4

'James Chadwick', 'Frederick Lindemann', 'Nevill Mott', 'Mark Oliphant', 'Robert Oppenheimer', 'George Sarton', 'Leo Szilard', 'Edward Teller', 'Henry Tizard', in Alan Bullock and R.B. Woodings (eds), *The Fontana Biographical Companion to Modern Thought* (1983)

'Christopher Hinton. Lord Hinton of Bankside (1901–1983)', *Dictionary of Business Biography*, Vol. III (London: Butterworth, 1985) pp. 268–74

'Sir Nevill Mott. An appreciation', *Philosophical Magazine*, B. LII (1985) pp. 215–16

'George Cyril Allen, 1900–1982', *Proceedings of the British Academy*, LXXI (1985) pp. 473–91

V. Articles in the Daily and Weekly Press

'Atomic energy archives', *New Scientist*, XXV (18 March 1965) pp. 726–8

'Science and the modern historian', *Times Literary Supplement*, 7 May 1970, pp. 515–16

(jointly with Lorna Arnold) 'Health and safety in Britain's nuclear programme', *New Scientist*, LXIV (28 Nov. 1974) pp. 659–61

(jointly with Lorna Arnold) 'The early politics of nuclear safety', *New Scientist*, LXIV (5 Dec. 1974) pp. 741–3

'Lost opportunities in an age of imperialism', *Times Higher Education Supplement*, 26 November 1976, p. 15

'Are historians really necessary?', *Times Higher Education Supplement*, 9 June 1978, p. 11

'Records: tomorrow's history', *Listener*, 17 Jan. 1980, p. 75

'How Britain produced the bomb', *Guardian*, 8 April 1985, p. 9

'The man who caught a glimpse of Armageddon', *Guardian*, 25 July 1985, p. 13

VI. A Select List of Book Reviews

'A.S. Milward, *The German Economy at War*', *Economist*, 15 May 1965, p. 772

'*The Journals of David E. Lilienthal. Vol. I. The TVA Years, 1939–45; Vol. II. The Atomic Energy Years, 1945–50*', *New Statesman*, 31 Dec. 1965, pp. 1035–6

'Hilary Jenkinson, *A Manual of Archive Administration*; and T.R. Schellenberg, *The Management of Archives*', *Journal of Documentation*, XXII (1966) pp. 253–4

'David Irving, *The Virus House*', *New Statesman*, 24 Febr. 1967, pp. 260, 262

'Ronald Clark, *Queen Victoria's Bomb*', *Times* (Saturday Review), 9 Dec. 1967, p. 19

'E. Tal and Y. Ezrahi, *Science Policy and Development: the Case of Israel*', *Nature*, CCXLIII (1973) pp. 550

'G.A.W. Boehm and A. Groner, *Science in the Service of Mankind. The Battelle Story*', *Nature*, CCXLIV (1973) pp. 122

'A.J. Pierre, *Nuclear Politics*', *Nature*, CCXLIV (1973) pp. 425

'Kurt Mendelssohn, *The World of Walter Nernst: the Rise and Fall of German Science*', *Lycidas* (Wolfson College Magazine), No. 1 (1972–3) pp. 26–7

'Peter Mathias (ed.), *Science and Society, 1600–1900*', *History of Science*, XI (1973) pp. 143–5

'J.R. Ravetz. *Scientific Knowledge and its Social Problems*', *British Journal of the History of Science*, VII (1974) pp. 72–5

'P. Forman, J.L. Heilbron and S. Weart, *Physics circa 1900*', *Annals of Science*, XXXIII (1976) pp. 610–11

'Jerry Gaston, *Originality and Competition in Science: a Study of the British*

High Energy Physics Community', *Nature*, CCLIV (1975) pp. 217–18

'Mel Thistle (ed.), *The Mackenzie–McNaughton Wartime Letters'*, *Science*, NS CXCII (1976) pp. 363

'W.J. Reader, *Imperial Chemical Industries: a History. vol. II. 1926–52'*, *English Historical Review*, XCL (1976) pp. 875–6

'G.B. Kistiakovsky, *A Scientist at the White House'*, *Times Literary Supplement*, 8 Nov. 1977, 1348

'W.M. Elsasser (ed.), *Memoirs of a Physicist in the Atomic Age'*, *Contemporary Physics*, XX (1979) p. 368

'Max Born, *My Life: Recollections of a Nobel Laureate'*, *Contemporary Physics*, XX (1979) pp. 485–6

'Otto R. Frisch, *What Little I Remember'*, *Contemporary Physics*, XX (1979) pp. 655–7

'G.M. Caroe, *William Henry Bragg, 1862–1942: Man and Scientist'*, *English Historical Review*, XCV (1980) p. 234

'R.V. Jones. *The Wizard War: British Scientific Intelligence. 1939–1945'*, *Isis*, LXXI (1980) pp. 518–19

'L.M. Libby, *The Uranium People'*, *Contemporary Physics*, XXI (1980) pp. 653–6

'Roger Williams, *The Nuclear Power Decisions'*, *New Scientist*, LXXXVI (19 June 1980) p. 329

'A.K. Smith and C. Weiner (eds), *Robert Oppenheimer: Letters and Recollections*; Peter Goodchild, *J. Robert Oppenheimer: 'Shatterer of Worlds'*; L. Badash, J.O. Hirschfelder and H. Broda (eds), *Reminiscences of Los Alamos'*, *Contemporary Physics*, XXII (1981) pp. 681–6

'C.P. Snow, *The Physicists'*, *New Scientist*, XCI (1 Oct. 1981) pp. 49–50

'S. Cockburn and D. Ellyard, *The Life and Times of Sir Mark Oliphant'*, *New Scientist*, XCIII (4 March 1982) p. 585

'John Simpson, *The Independent Nuclear State: the United States, Britain and the Military Atom'*, *Survival*, Nov.–Dec. 1984, pp. 285–6

'Lawrence Badash. *Kapitza, Rutherford and the Kremlin'*, *International Affairs*, LXII (1985) pp. 120–1

'Nevill Mott, *A Life in Science'*, *New Scientist*, CX (12 June 1986) pp. 52–3

'Crispin Tickell, *Climatic Change and World Affairs'*, *New Scientist*, CXI (24 July 1986) p. 57

'Richard Rhodes, *The Making of the Atomic Bomb'*, *New Scientist*, CXIV (21 May 1987) p. 70

'L.F. Haber, *The Poisonous Cloud: Chemical Warfare in the First World War'*, *English Historical Review* (in press).

VII. Tape-recording

(jointly with David Holloway), *Government and Science in Britain, the United States of America and the USSR* (Devizes: Sussex Publications, 1981) 30 minutes

VIII. Contributions to Parliamentary Papers (see Editor's Preface)

Report of the Committee on Departmental Records (Grigg Report), Cmd 9163 (London: HMSO, 1954)

Modern Public Records: Selection and Access (Wilson Report), Cmnd 8204 (London: HMSO, 1981)

Public records. Minutes of evidence taken before the Education. Science and Arts Committee (House of Commons) 4 May 1983 (London: HMSO, 1983)

IX. Published Interviews with Margaret Gowing

Alan Cane, 'Bringing science into orthodox history', *Times Higher Education Supplement*, 9 March 1973, p.6

Sarah White, 'Nuclear historian', *New Scientist*, LXIV (28 Nov. 1974) pp. 656–9

Ian Smith, 'Atomic energy historian once shunned science', *Oxford Times*, 3 Oct. 1986, p. 13

Index

number of colleges offering
courses 231
problem of clients' needs
232–3, 234, 235
professional standing 223
Public Historian, The 222
skills of public historian 223–5
Society for History in the
Federal Government 221,
227,234
standards and ethics,233–6
see also Academic history in US

Quarterly Review 76, 80, 81
'The British Museum' 75

Radiation
ALARA (as low as reasonably
achievable) 170, 174, 179
ALARP (as low as reasonably
practicable) 170, 174, 179
ALATA (as low as technically
achievable) 179
ALI (annual limits on intakes)
180
components of 169
dangers 169, 171, 172
discovery of X-rays and
radioactivity 171
increased exposure following
development of atomic
bomb 172–3
linear dose-response
relationship 178, 181
measurement 169–70, 175, 182n
'permissible dose' concept 175,
176
problem of neutral scientific
terms 181
reconstitution of international
protection agency, 1950 *see*
International Commission on
Radiological Protection
(ICRP)
scientific questions raised,
1950s 174–5
'threshold' concept 172, 177–8
'tolerance dose' concept 171,
172
Railway Gauge Commission,
1845–6 44, 45

Rainbow, early iron vessel 43
Ramsay, Andrew 27
Ranke, Leopold von 217
Rayleigh (R. J. Strutt), Lord 91,
98
Read, Holliday Co., Huddersfield:
industrial research laboratory,
1890 91
Reagan, Pres. Ronald 168
Reche, Otto 132
Reconstruction (Priorities)
Committee, Second World
War 194, 195,196
Roberthall, Lord 213
Rockefeller Bureau of Social
Hygiene 119, 130
Rockefeller Foundation 119, 120
biochemistry and psychobiology
targetted, inter-war 130–1,
132, 137
comes to support German
eugenics 130–1
development from welfare to
grant administration 122
Division of Medical Education
121
embarrassed by Rockefeller
business methods 121
established, 1913 119
evolution of German
programme, after First
World War 122–8
German Fellowships, 1922–39
129
help for persecuted German
scientists 134, 137
ideal of internationalism in
science 135
impressed by German higher
education 120–1, 122, 136
New York Office 133
Paris Office 122, 126, 127, 133
persuaded to support German
psychiatry 131–2, 133
problem of German nationalism
for 136
problem of Nazi takeover in
Germany, 1933 128, 132,
133–4
progress of 'scientisation' 122
research orientation established,

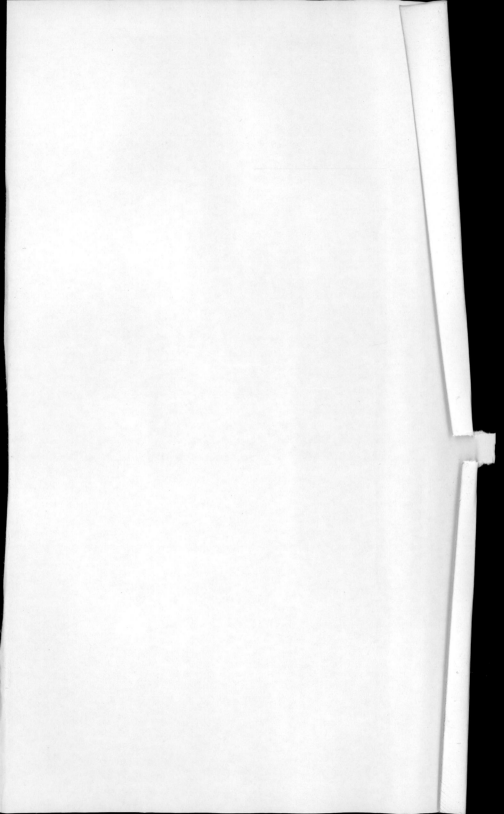